Palgrave Insights into Apocalypse Economics

Series Editor
Richard Westra
Centre for Macau Studies
University of Macau
Macau, China

This series is set to become the lodestone for critical Marxist and related Left scholarship on the raft of apocalyptic tendencies enveloping the global economy and society. Its working premise is that neoliberal policies from the 1980s not only failed to rejuvenate capitalist prosperity lost with the demise of the post-Second World War 'golden age' economy but in fact have generated a widening spectrum of pathologies that threaten humanity itself. At the most fundamental level the series cultivates state of the art critical political economic analysis of the crises, recessionary, deflationary and austerity conditions that have beset the world economy since the global meltdown of 2008–2009. However, though centered on work that critically explores global propensities for devastating financial convulsions, ever-widening inequalities and economic marginalisation due to information technologies, robotised production and low wage outsourcing, it seeks to draw on exacerbating factors such as climate change and global environmental despoliation, corrupted food systems and land-grabbing, rampant militarism, cyber crime and terrorism, all together which defy mainstream economics and conventional political policy solutions.

For critical Marxist and related Left scholars the series offers a non-sectarian outlet for academic work that is hard-hitting, inter/trans-disciplinary and multiperspectival. Its readership draws in academics, researchers, students, progressive governmental and non-governmental actors and the academically-informed public.

More information about this series at
http://www.palgrave.com/gp/series/15867

David Hawkes

The Reign of Anti-logos

Performance in Postmodernity

David Hawkes
Department of English
Arizona State University
Tempe, AZ, USA

ISSN 2523-8108 ISSN 2523-8116 (electronic)
Palgrave Insights into Apocalypse Economics
ISBN 978-3-030-55939-7 ISBN 978-3-030-55940-3 (eBook)
https://doi.org/10.1007/978-3-030-55940-3

This Palgrave Macmillan imprint is published by the registered company Springer Nature
Switzerland AG
The registered company address is: Gewerbestrasse 11, 6330 Cham, Switzerland

To my mother, Ann Hawkes

ACKNOWLEDGMENTS

I've accrued innumerable obligations to many people while writing this book. My colleagues at Arizona State University have been tremendously helpful. As Chairs of the English Department, Mark Lussier and Krista Radcliffe have offered every possible assistance, while productive discussions with colleagues like Keith Miller, Joe Lockard, and Richard Newhauser have advanced my thinking enormously. Students like Heather Ackerman, Gabrielle Chen-Dickens, Jennifer Downer, Mark LaRubio, and Mike Noschka have sparked more of my ideas than I can acknowledge. In addition to my friends at ASU, the intellectual comradeship of people like Hugh Grady, Julia Friedman, and Kathy Romack has been an important influence on my work. Sections of this book have previously appeared, in different forms, in the *Times Literary Supplement,* the *Journal of Interdisciplinary Economics, Literature and Theology, English Literary Renaissance* and *Critical Survey.* As always, I owe special gratitude to my wife Simten and my son Ali for their endless love and support.

CONTENTS

CHAPTER 1

Usury, Sodomy and Idolatry

1.1 Three in One, One in Three

A profound hostility to *logos* permeates every aspect of modern, and especially of postmodern culture. This book argues that this anti-logocentrism depends upon the attribution of efficacious power to performative signs of all kinds, including the linguistic, religious, aesthetic, erotic, and, most prominently today, the financial (the Spanish word for 'cash,' *efectivo*, eloquently conveys modern money's performative function). But the modern era is only the latest in a long historical series of dialectical clashes between *logos* and *eidolon*. The following chapters examine a selection of such conflicts drawn from a wide variety of local contexts, from ancient Ionia to postmodern Yorubaland. They also deal with what may, at first, appear to be an unfeasibly diverse range of issues. In the course of writing the book, however, I have found that the ostensibly infinite expressions of anti-logocentrism tend, in practice, to flow into three main channels. These three manifestations of anti-logocentrism rise and fall together throughout history, although their simultaneous advance is particularly conspicuous in the twenty-first century. In fact, their association is so frequent and so intimate as to suggest that they are, in reality, different forms of appearance taken by a single essence. Before examining specific cases, it will be useful to consider these three prominent forms of rebellion against *logos*, to ask what they may have in common, and to raise the question of their relevance to the postmodern condition.

© The Author(s) 2020
D. Hawkes, *The Reign of Anti-logos*, Palgrave
Insights into Apocalypse Economics,
https://doi.org/10.1007/978-3-030-55940-3_1

Anti-logocentrism has historically manifested itself in 'usury,' 'idolatry,' and non-reproductive sexuality—traditionally known as 'sodomy.' The early modern era often conceived of usury, sodomy, and idolatry as vices practiced by marginalized and stigmatized social groups. Usury was associated with Jews, sodomy with homosexuals, and idolatry with the natives of the colonized world. The tendency to personify such psychological tendencies, to project them onto alien groups of people, bespeaks the ideological error of 'reification.' Reification involves misconceiving something that is actually spiritual or abstract as if it were concrete or material. As a consequence of this error, popular opposition to usury, sodomy and idolatry has frequently been directed against particular groups of human beings, and channeled into such morally repellent dead-ends as anti-Semitism, homophobia, and racism. It is now time to consign such errors permanently to the past, and this book hopes to make a small contribution to that process. The postmodern condition proves that all human beings are equally vulnerable to the machinations of *anti-logos*. Today, critics of *anti-logos* must understand their opponent as an abstract, conceptual force capable of exerting its influence upon anybody.

The term 'usury' has historically referred to a vast range of economic sharp practice, including the mere intention to make illegitimate or excessive profit, and the payment as well as the taking of interest. It was once seen as a well-nigh universal temptation. By the seventeenth century, however, the demands of the early capitalist economy necessitated a redefinition. A convenient fantasy developed that usury was the exclusive preserve of pariahs—that it was a sin practiced only by others.[1] A literalist interpretation of the Deuteronomic prohibition[2] made it seem plausible that Jews permitted themselves to take interest from Christians. At the same time, legal restrictions effectively coerced many of Europe's Jews into money-lending, while simultaneously limiting that profession to them in theory (though certainly not in practice). As a result, the terms 'usurer' and 'Jew' remained virtually synonymous through the century of Trollope, Marx, Dostoevsky, and Wilde and, as we shall see in Chapter 7, well into the century of Hemingway, Pound, and Eliot. During the modern age, then, usury's true nature was concealed by its association with a specific group of people.

Usury's influence on subjectivity has always been profound and today, as Maurizio Lazzarato concludes: 'Debt is the technique most adequate to the production of neoliberalism's *homo economicus*.'[3] Economic man is not necessarily an individual agent, however, and over the course of the nineteenth and twentieth centuries the characteristics once seen as typical of individual usurers were assimilated into the wider, macro-economic structures that Bernard Dempsey called 'institutional, or systemic usury.'[4] Writing in 1943, Dempsey argued that usury should no longer be regarded as an aberration practiced by outcasts, but as the very essence of the modern economy. The ethical implication of Dempsey's theory was that, in the words of D. Stephen Long, 'our modern economic system creates the effect of usury without personal culpability.'[5] The usurious economy remained ethically reprehensible *tout court*, at least according to traditional standards, but this was no longer an issue of personal morality.

The same is increasingly true of concupiscent sexuality, or 'sodomy,' which is no more aberrational than usury in the postmodern context. It is important to remember that 'sodomy' is not exclusive to homosexuality. It was not particularly associated with homosexuality until the Enlightenment. Before the eighteenth century, as we shall see in the following chapters, the term might be used of any sexual act which was not aimed at reproduction, and all such acts were deemed unnatural. In fact, 'sodomy' was often just as likely to denote commercial sex as homosexuality: the King James Bible (1611) gives 'sodomitress' as a translation of 'whore.'[6] If we seek a twenty-first century equivalent of 'sodomy,' the merged prostitution and pornography so prevalent on the internet might be the closest. The vice could involve any erotic focus on the body, regardless of gender, and it could manifest itself in any non-procreative sexual act, including masturbation. The idea that sodomy might be restricted to 'homosexuals' or 'queers' is specific to modernity[7] and, like usury, the concept of sodomy is distorted when conceived as limited to any particular group of people.

As we shall see in the following chapters, sodomy and usury have always been closely related, in theory and in practice. The Aristotelian and Biblical traditions treat them as logically homologous as well as empirically inseparable. Furthermore, sodomy and usury are traditionally classified as sub-species of idolatry, on the grounds that both vices make fetishizes of symbols. Usury conceives of financial symbols as sexual and fertile, while sodomy prioritizes the body—which in the Platonic tradition is conceived as the sign of the soul—above its referent. The association of usury, sodomy, and idolatry has deep roots in Scripture, where St. Paul repeatedly declares that 'covetousness is idolatry.'[8] The Hebrew Bible warns against 'whoring after strange gods,'[9] and in Paul's epistle to the Romans those who 'changed the glory of the uncorruptible God into an image' (1.23) are given over to 'vile affections, for even their women did change the natural use into that which is against nature: And likewise also the men, leaving the natural use of the woman, burned in their lust one toward another' (1.26–27). Paul emphasizes that sodomy is an appropriate consequence of idolatry, describing the men as 'receiving in themselves that recompence of their error which was meet' (1.27). Following the Platonic tradition, he conceives of the body as the sign of the soul, and of sexual concupiscence as an idolatrous fetishism of the sign to the exclusion of the referent.

The sin of sodomy thus traditionally carries a semiotic component and, as Tom Betteridge observes, 'literary critics have viewed sodomy as a protean deconstructive category.'[10] In the twelfth century, Alain de Lille's influential *Complaint of Nature* presented sexual transgression as a violation of *logos* in language. Alain describes sodomy as working through grammar itself, so that a homosexual man 'is both predicate and subject, he becomes likewise of two declensions, he pushes the laws of grammar too far.'[11] The extent, as well as the breadth, of sodomy is evident from Peter Damian's eleventh-century *Book of Gomorrah*, which declares: 'this vice cannot in any way be compared to any others, because its enormity supersedes them all.'[12] Damian lists four types of sexual vice: solo and mutual masturbation, inter-femural, and anal intercourse. The salient factor is thus not homosexuality but sterility, which is unnatural because the natural *telos* of sex is reproduction. Damian emphasizes that all four acts count as 'sodomy' because they are 'against nature... whether one pollutes himself or another in any manner whatsoever... he is undoubtedly to be convicted of having committed the crime of Sodom' (78). As St. Thomas Aquinas later confirmed: 'Whoever... uses copulation for the delight that is in it, not referring the intention to the end which is intended by nature, acts against nature.'[13]

Damian also locates the sin of sodomy within the mind, when he insists that any failure to 'tame manfully the lascivious pimping of lust' (33) is necessarily sodomitical. Like usury and idolatry, the sin of sodomy is psychological before it is physical. The same is true of idolatry, which is yet more inclusive than either usury or sodomy because it encompasses both of those vices. The first two prohibitions of the Decalogue posit idolatry as the foundational sin, from which all other sins flow. Mankind's incessant battle against idolatry is the literal topic of the Old Testament and the figurative topic of the New. It is treated by all monotheisms as the archetypal, paradigmatic heresy. Idolatry or *shirk* is Islam's most heinous sin (closely followed by *riba*, or usury, and *zina*, or sodomy). Monotheistic religion thus concurs with rational philosophy, for idolatry is also the error committed by the prisoners in Plato's cave. We commit idolatry whenever we worship 'the works of men's hands'[14]—as for instance when we take sense-perception, which is constructed from the categories of the human mind, for the unmediated manifestation of *logos*.

Like usury and sodomy, in short, idolatry incessantly (and inevitably) recurs throughout postlapsarian history. The struggle against liturgical idolatry produced centuries-long internecine conflicts throughout Christendom, from seventh-century Byzantium to seventeenth-century Massachusetts. Over this long process, however, the meaning of the term 'idolatry' changed. It ceased to designate a universal, ineradicable tendency of fallen humanity, and became instead a set of rituals performed by 'idolaters.' In the modern era it became useful to identify these idolaters as the subjugated 'natives' of the colonized world, and the Catholic Irish provided a convenient paradigm. Like usury and sodomy, idolatry was reified—transformed from a concept into a thing—and thus successfully disguised as a practice exclusive to specific groups of people. Throughout the modern period, usury, sodomy, and idolatry used that disguise as a way of avoiding criticism. Any critique of those vices could easily be made to look like a bigoted attack on the group of human beings with whom they were associated. My main aim in this book is to divert the ethical critique of usury, sodomy, and idolatry away from particular sectors of humanity, and toward the abstract, conceptual power of *anti-logos*.

For the conflict between *logos* and *anti-logos* should not be imagined as akin to a pitched battle or a football match. It is not a struggle between different groups of human beings. The struggle against *anti-logos* and its manifestations in usury, sodomy, and idolatry can take place only within the individual *psyche*. Only in the *psyche* does money reproduce; only in the *psyche* does an icon become an idol; only in the *psyche* is spiritual *caritas* transformed into carnal *cupiditas*. Above all, representation can become performative—signs can do things—only within the human *psyche*. Indeed, the belief that signs can work outside the *psyche*, that they can alter the condition of the external, objective world, is a fine provisional definition of idolatry.

1.2   THE ETHICS OF HYPER-REALITY

My argument here will be that the postmodern condition is dominated by usury, sodomy, and idolatry. These psychological tendencies find expression in today's prevailing systems of economics, sexuality, and representation. Since their practice is no longer confined even in theory to particular, socially marginalized groups, their essential, underlying unity has grown increasingly visible. Although they manifest themselves in what we have learned to consider different 'spheres' of experience, these forms of anti-logocentrism are united by their systematic refusal of the Western tradition's constitutive ethical polarities. Usury, sodomy, and idolatry all collapse essence into appearance, nature into custom, substance into accident, and subject into object. They are *reductive* patterns of thought and behavior. They abolish logical oppositions, not by logic, but by the violent, irrational reduction of one side of the polarity to the other.

All such reductionism depends on the single, fundamental reduction of sign to referent. The deconstruction of the sign/referent polarity is the definitive error of the postmodern epoch, for it erases the distinction between representation and reality itself. The postmodern condition cannot be called 'surreal,' for that term implies a foundational reality on which to construct a fantastic superstructure. The postmodern condition is rather, as Jean Baudrillard puts it, 'hyper-real.' According to Baudrillard's widely influential diagnosis we now live in the 'era of simulation,' which 'is inaugurated by a liquidation of all referentials—worse: with their artificial resurrection in the systems of signs.'[15] When signs cease to be referential, they become performative.

Usury, sodomy, and idolatry are the palpable effects of the performative sign's rise to power. Each of them results from a failure to understand the world of appearances as the representation of an ontologically, epistemologically and ethically prior realm of ideas. Even well-educated adults now instinctively assume, as an ontological default position, that sense-perception gives unmediated access to reality. We never develop beyond the child's innocent assumption that appearance is identical with reality, that the man with the white beard literally is Santa—or, more to the point, that the man with the goatee and the widow's peak literally is Satan. Our culture is defined by the supposition that symbols—whether financial, linguistic, religious, aesthetic, or erotic—lack any anterior reference.

In today's usurious financial sector, for example, monetary signs reproduce while signifying no use-value, no substantial commodity. They become *autotelic*, ends-in-themselves, and this process is not limited to financial signs. Since the 1960s this development has found a resonant echo in post-structuralist linguistics. Bruno Latour describes the emergence of a parallel auto-teleology in verbal significance:

> This is the major achievement of the sixties and of their 'linguistic turn' or 'semiotic turn.' Instead of being means of communications between human actors and nature, meaning productions became the only important thing to study. Instead of being unproblematic they became opaque. The task was no longer to make them more transparent but to recognize and relish their thick, rich, layered and complex matter. Instead of mere intermediary they had become mediators. From a mean, meaning has been made an end-in-itself.[16]

The medium of representation becomes the object of analysis because it has become problematic and controversial. Representation is no longer 'transparent' but 'opaque.' Signs have become indistinguishable from things, and it has become difficult to see through them. In the twenty-first century, even physical bodies are often replaced as objects of sexual desire by purely visual images. As we shall see in Chapter 5, pornography was identified with rebellion against *logos* as early as Christopher Marlowe's *Doctor Faustus* (1592) when, despite his best efforts at rational self-control, the magician becomes sexually aroused by the mere image of Helen of Troy. To Marlowe the causal link between Faustus' sexual fetishism, his obsessive pursuit of money and his practice of magic was obvious; today such connections are more covert. In any kind of idolatry, however, symbols obscure their own referents, and today's technology gives unprecedented scope for the various kinds of passion once aroused by liturgical icons to invade the realm of sexuality.

As the following chapters will show, Western thought from Aristotle to Francis Bacon condemns usury, sodomy, and idolatry as unethical, unnatural and illogical, because these vices systematically mistake signs for referents. To mistake apparent signs for essential referents has always been recognized as humanity's fatal error. For instance, to mistake a person's appearance for their essence is to consign them to death, for their appearance is their body, and their body dies. To live in a culture dominated by usury, sodomy, and idolatry is to live under the tyranny of the performative sign. As a result of our infantile belief—if 'belief' is the right word for so entirely unreflective a supposition—that appearance is reality, image has displaced essence from every aspect of life. In postmodernity, experience no longer divides as easily as it once did into such discrete categories as 'economic,' 'sexual,' 'aesthetic,' 'ethical,' or 'semiotic.' The same fetishism occurs in each of these 'fields,' because they are all constructed out of the same raw material: representation. All human experience is constructed through signs. When signs become indistinguishable from referents, however, they cease to be signs. They become agents.

All symbols are customary and conventional; they do not exist in nature. The systems of symbols that tyrannize over us today have been constructed by people, and so they can also be deconstructed by people. To take only the most obvious instance: a moment's thought will show that the allegedly omnipotent symbol known as 'money' has no material or physical existence beyond its representations. And yet it rules the world. The world is not ruled by the possessors of money, but by money itself. The decisions and behavior of the people who used to be called the 'bourgeoisie' and are known today as 'the 1%' are determined entirely by money's need to reproduce—a need that money must fulfill even when it damages the interests of its owners. As Karl Marx explains:

> ... what distinguishes this form from all previous ones is that the capitalist does not rule the worker in any kind of personal capacity, but only in so far as he is "capital"; his rule is only that of objectified labour over living labour; the rule of the worker's product over the worker himself.[17]

By this logic, class warfare is obsolete. It has been replaced by a conflict between human beings and the alienated, autonomous, symbolic form of human activity that we call 'money.' Money is powerful because of what postmodernist thinkers call 'performativity': the process by which symbols achieve objective effects and abandon their referential function. A performative symbol ceases to be symbolic. Abandoning reference to luxuriate in *jouissance*, signs lose their meaning. They conceal rather than designate *logos*. The performative sign is, in fact, the dialectical antithesis of *logos*, and the following chapters trace performativity's rise to its current, historically unprecedented power.

Although the degree of performativity's power in postmodernity is unprecedented, ours is by no means the first era to witness representation's attempts at self-assertion. As this book will show, the rise of the performative sign has been a circuitous, sometimes repetitive process. What is new today, however, is the applause with which the cultural prominence of performativity is greeted by progressives, liberals, and, above all, by academic intellectuals. Their conviction that performativity represents emancipation is the postmodern *trahison des clercs*. In the past, by contrast, the independent power of symbols was fiercely criticized by intellectuals, on logical, practical, and, most of all, on ethical grounds. When intellectuals neglect such criticism, plebians often take matters into their own hands. Wherever they appear usury, idolatry, and sodomy produce visceral, sometimes violent reactions. The popular iconoclasm of the Reformation, the eradication of hedge-magic by means of witch-hunts, and spontaneous, popular repudiations of debt were all reactions to the performative power of signs. But such mass movements will be futile, misdirected, and counter-productive unless supported by a critique of performativity. In the absence of such a critique, any practical action is likely to be directed against particular groups of people, as it has often been in the past, and it will therefore remain doomed to impotence. Until we can clearly say what is morally wrong with efficacious representation per se, we are likely to remain under its thrall.

1.3   THE POLITICS OF *ANTI-LOGOS*

In the political climate of the early third millennium, to oppose *anti-logos* is to risk being accused of belonging to the 'right-wing,' or even to the radical 'alt.right.' That is obviously one reason why few professional intellectuals take such a position. Yet the idea that politics is a spectrum running from left to right, and thus susceptible to 'radical' or 'moderate' opinion, dates only from the French Revolution. It was initially invoked to describe the seating arrangements of the National Assembly, where King Louis XVI's most loyal supporters sat on his right-hand side and his most dedicated opponents on his far left. During the modern epoch, the dialectically opposed forces of capital and labor power temporarily coalesced into two groups of people, or social classes, known as the 'bourgeoisie' and the 'proletariat.' For most of the nineteenth and twentieth centuries, support for the economic interests of the proletariat was widely regarded as a 'left-wing' position, while the interests of the bourgeoisie were generally advanced by parties of the 'right-wing.'

But the notion that shades of political opinion can be expressed by means of a spatial metaphor grew less plausible as the third millennium approached. The rise of autonomously performative representation in economics, technology, linguistics, philosophy, sexuality, entertainment, and throughout everyday life deconstructed the ancient binary opposition between *phusis* and *nomos*. To the extent that the *eidola* of sense-perception blocked the access of *nous* to *logos*, personal identity was no longer experienced as a natural condition, inherited at birth and sustained throughout life. Identity came rather to seem cultural, customary, a matter to be defined by appearance rather than by essence, something that one performed rather than something that one was. As this understanding of character took root in the popular mind, the concept of a political spectrum based on objective social class began to recede. In its place grew up an 'identity politics,' whose most basic assumption was that subjectivity is artificially 'constructed' by external, symbolic forces such as linguistic representation, visual signs, and financial status.

Whatever is constructed can be deconstructed. As this began to dawn on the theorists of identity politics over the 1970s and '80s, a previously undreamt—of but apparently wide—open route to power hove into view. The advocates of identity politics are often denounced as 'cultural Marxists.' But no one suggests that their 'long march through the institutions'[18] of cultural, social and academic influence was undertaken in the interest of the proletariat. Instead, first women, then African-Americans, then homosexuals and, most recently, the queer movement in general, have replaced the working class as the vanguard promoted by revolutionary intellectuals. Having seen its economic theories refuted by history, the political left shifted its subversive energies onto the cultural sphere. In the area of civil society, this strategy has brought remarkable success: the integration of women into the workforce, the legalization of contraception and abortion, the introduction of homosexuality into mainstream society, the imposition of legal prohibition and social taboo on all forms of prejudice and discrimination, the destruction of canonical aesthetics, the redefinition of identity by custom rather than nature, the right to change race and gender—in a word, the multifarious collection of cultural developments collectively known as 'postmodernism.'

But can we consider these 'left-wing' developments? The most obviously powerful system of performative representation today is financialized capital, previously known as 'usury.' The practice of usury long predates the idea that politics is a spectrum, and usury's predominance today is the best evidence of that idea's obsolescence. For usury does not fit easily into the left-right spectrum. Nor indeed do idolatry or sodomy. And yet the combined power of usury, sodomy, and idolatry is the definitive characteristic of postmodern culture. As this book will show, the simultaneous rise and reign of these three manifestations of *anti-logos* would not have seemed surprising in the past. Usury, sodomy, and idolatry do not, historically speaking, merely accompany each other, associate or coincide. They are essentially identical. Although such claims do not fit onto the last century's mental map of politics, there is surely now ample empirical evidence of their veracity. Usury, sodomy and idolatry were either illegal or heavily stigmatized well within living memory; today they are dominant in every way. We need a new political map.

It is admittedly true, as conservatives point out, that identity politics can be traced to ideas originally formulated within the political left. It was the Italian Communist leader Antonio Gramsci who first distinguished between the 'war of position' (a struggle for physical control of state institutions like parliament, police, and the armed forces) and the 'war of maneuver,' a battle for cultural influence in such institutions of 'civil society' as the church, the media, the creative arts, and the education system. When Gramsci developed these ideas in the 1920s, the most important ideological struggle was the *Kulturkampf* for the allegiance of the proletariat, which was being waged between the 'left-wing' Communist Party and the 'right-wing' Catholic Church. A century later, the political spectrum seems very different. Perhaps postmodern politics is best conceived as a struggle between those whose allegiance is to *logos* and those who believe in, practice and seek to establish the permanent hegemony of the performative sign.

After the Second World War, the Western world implemented a massive, unprecedented expansion of the higher education system. Nor was this expansion limited to the *banausic* or pragmatic sciences: the humanities, philosophy, art, and literature were, at first, included almost as equals. Entire classes, genders, races, and religions were thus suddenly granted access to a vastly complex intellectual tradition previously accessible only to a tiny, privileged elite. Having for centuries been violently excluded from that tradition's benefits, having indeed for centuries been violently oppressed by that tradition's beneficiaries, subaltern populations reacted to the imposition of the Western canon as the price of admission to post-imperial global culture with a predictable lack of enthusiasm. In fact the subaltern response frequently took the form of a violent attack on *logos* in all its forms. Reason, logic, essence, substance, quality, virtue, spirit, soul, ideas, concepts, truth, even (or especially) God himself could easily seem oppressive when viewed from the perspective of excluded, marginal subjectivity. Within a remarkably short space of time, anti-logocentrism became the radical shibboleth of humanities departments throughout the Western world.

The influence exerted by academic advocates of identity politics on a socially unprepared and ideologically defenseless student body was profound and immense. Conservative opponents of identity politics assume that such extensive influence can only have been achieved by a conscious, conspiratorial 'cultural Marxism,' akin to the Machiavellian schemes plotted a century ago in Gramsci's prison cell. Even fifty years ago, such charges held some credibility. In the UK the extraordinary influence exerted by Raymond Williams' *Culture and Society* (1958) inspired a generation of radicals such as Terry Eagleton and Stuart Hall to infiltrate elite academies, transforming them from within into hotbeds of political ferment, in a more successful deployment of the 'entryist' tactics adopted during the same period by Trotskyite groupuscules within labor unions and social democratic political parties. A decade later, politically active post-colonial scholars like Gayatri Spivak and Edward Said brought the cultural politics espoused by continental thinkers like Michel Foucault and Julia Kristeva into the mainstream of the American academy. On both sides of the Atlantic, the militant students of such teachers fanned out rapidly throughout the liberal professions. By the end of the twentieth century, Gramsci's 'war of maneuver' within the cultural institutions of Anglo-American capitalism had effectively been won.

But who was the victor? Obviously not the proletariat, whose institutional and ideological power had been decisively crushed over the same period. The significance of Gramsci for the Western left was that, by arguing for 'the relative autonomy of the superstructure' and for the vital importance of the cultural 'war of maneuver,' he made it possible to extend the vanguard function that Marxism ascribes to the proletariat to any 'marginalized' social group. When the proletariat abdicated its revolutionary responsibility, therefore, its vanguard role could readily be passed on to women, racial minorities, or minorities constructed around sexual preference. After the Second World War, interpreters and translators of Gramsci like Cornell West and Joseph Buttigieg began to apply his originally Communist tactics to 'marginal' or 'subaltern' groups other than the proletariat, especially to racial and sexual minorities. For such commentators, Gramsci's importance lay in the fact that he could be used to rationalize the politics of 'the subaltern' for its own sake. 'Marginality' thus became *autotelic*, an end-in-itself.

As Buttigieg remarks, 'Gramsci was primarily concerned with the phenomenon of marginality,' and 'Gramsci provides us with the most thorough study that has yet been formulated on the question of subalternity.'[19] *Kulturkampf* can be conducted by 'marginal' cultures just as well as by the proletariat. Certainly Buttigieg's philosophical and biological heir, the Democrat Presidential candidate Pete Buttigieg, could not be less interested in establishing the dictatorship of the proletariat. To the contrary, Buttigieg Jr., is deeply committed to consolidating the rule of financial capital. He is just as committed to furthering the assimilation of homosexuality into mainstream culture. The obvious question raised by his candidacy is the nature of the connection between these commitments.

The following chapters argue that the convergence between usury, sodomy, and idolatry depends on the idea that representation is not referential but performative: that signs do not describe an external, pre-linguistic world but construct it—or rather perform it—for us. The rise of performative representation implies that custom rather than reason rules our lives, that culture rather than nature is the foundation of our experience, and that we are therefore free to deconstruct and reconstruct both the self and society at will. This is what previous eras called 'license' as opposed to 'liberty,' and ours is the most licentious society since the decadence of imperial Rome. However, we must avoid the temptation to blame society's ills on any particular section of society. The performative sign of postmodernity has achieved a degree of autonomous power, and an independent agency, that elevates it far above the need for any merely human accomplice.

NOTES

1. See Benjamin Nelson, *The Idea of Usury: From Tribal Brotherhood to Universal Otherhood* (Princeton UP, 1951).
2. Deuteronomy 23.20: 'Unto a stranger thou mayest lend upon usury; but unto thy brother thou shalt not lend upon usury....'
3. Maurizio Lazzarato, *Governing by Debt*, trans. Joshua David Jordan (Semiotext(e), 2015), 70.
4. Bernard W. Dempsey, *Interest and Usury* (Washington, DC, 1943), 220.
5. D. Stephen Long, 'Bernard Dempsey's Theological Economics: Usury, Profit, and Human Fulfillment,' *Theological Studies* 57 (1996), 690–706, 700.
6. Alan Bray, *Homosexuality in Renaissance England* (Columbia UP, 1982), 14.

7. As Michel Foucault famously declared: 'The sodomite had been a temporary aberration; the homosexual was now a species.' *The History of Sexuality: Volume I*, trans. Robert Hurley (New York: Vintage Books, 1990), 43.
8. Colossians 3.5–6; Ephesians 5.3–5.
9. Judges 2.17; Deuteronomy 31.16.
10. Tom Betteridge, *Sodomy in Early Modern Europe* (Manchester UP, 2002), 2.
11. Alain de Lille, *Complaint of Nature*, trans. Douglas M. Moffat (New York: Henry Holt and Co., 1908), 22.
12. St. Peter Damien, *The Book of Gomorrah* (Ite Ad Thomam Books and Media, 2015), 3.
13. St. Thomas Aquinas, *Commentary on the Four Books of the Sentences* 4.33.1.3, cit. John P. Noonan, *Contraception: A History of Its Treatment by the Catholic Theologians and Canonists* (Belknap Press, 1986), 293.
14. Psalms 115.4: 'Their idols are silver and gold, the works of mens' hands,' Psalms 135.15: 'The idols of the heathen are silver and gold, the work of men's hands,' Isaiah 2.8: 'they worship the work of their own hands,' Isaiah 37.19: 'they were no gods, but the work of men's hands, wood and stone.'
15. Jean Baudrillard, *Simulacra and Simulation*, trans. Sheila Faria Glaser (U of Michigan P, 1994), 2–3.
16. Bruno Latour, 'On Actor Network Theory: A Few Clarifications,' *Soziale Welt* 47.4 (1996), 369–381, 373.
17. Karl Marx, *Economic Manuscripts of 1861–63 Part 3: Relative Surplus Value*, trans. Ben Fowkes: https://marxists.catbull.com/archive/marx/works/1861/economic/ch38.htm. Retrieved April 1, 2020.
18. This phrase is usually attributed to the German student leader, Rudi Dutschke.
19. Joseph Buttigieg, 'The Open Marxism of Antonio Gramsci,' review of *Antonio Gramsci: Architect of a New Politics* by Dante Germano, *The Review of Politics* 54.1 (Winter 1992), 177–180, 180. See E. Michael Jones, *Logos Rising* (Fidelity Press, 2020).

CHAPTER 2

Performativity in Postmodernity

2.1   EXCHANGE VALUE AND THE QUEER

Like compound interest itself, the expansion of money's autonomous power has been exponential. Financial value has been growing more powerful, and more independent of any external referent, with increasing velocity, since the relaxations of the usury laws in the sixteenth century. Naturally enough, our ability to identify the delusions induced by autonomous signs has diminished along with the growth of their power. Although the dialectic between *logos* and *eidolon* is ancient, the extent of the latter's dominance in modernity is unprecedented. It was made possible above all by the European discovery of America, which precipitated a sudden, massive inflow of precious metals into Europe. This rapidly monetized the economy, replacing feudal relations with the cash nexus, instituting wage labor as the dominant mode of productive activity, and unleashing the accumulated power of human labor-power projected into its own alienated, financial form. This chapter prepares the ground for the rest of the book, by tracing the decline of *logos* in postmodern thought to the economic predominance of symbolic exchange-value.

The primal form of exchange value is the mental image of the pig which is imposed upon the physical body of the cow in the simplest act of barter. As people, cows, and pigs multiply, and as barter consequently grows more complicated, that image evolves into the general equivalent form of money. Money is a sign representing the source of any object's

© The Author(s) 2020   15
D. Hawkes, *The Reign of Anti-logos*, Palgrave
Insights into Apocalypse Economics,
https://doi.org/10.1007/978-3-030-55940-3_2

use-value, which is human labor power. By its very nature, then, money represents a *fetish*, a potent 'work of men's hands.' As William Pietz reminds us: 'The pan-European word whose English version is "fetish" derives linguistically from the Latin *facticius* or *factitius*, an adjective formed from the past participle of the verb "to make."'[1] As the abstract symbol of human labor power, money provides a common denominator to facilitate increasingly complex exchange transactions. The history of money shows a steady evolution into ever more abstract forms. Just as exchange value is a symbolic abstraction from use-value, so paper money is a symbolic abstraction from precious metal. A further abstraction took place with President Nixon's abandonment of the gold standard in 1971, since which money no longer even purports to refer to anything beyond the system of financial representation.

Yet this was merely the harbinger of the thoroughgoing deregulation of the 1990s, which removed the final obstacles to money's independent reproduction. Over the last two or three decades, the progressive abstraction of financial symbols has entered a new stage. Not only does the economy dominate society; not only does the financial sector dominate the economy; the financial sector itself is now dominated by the innovative symbolic instruments collectively known as 'derivatives.' As we shall see in Chapter 8, the concept of the 'financial derivative' takes the process of symbolic abstraction to a whole new level. The term refers to an immense variety of financial products—swaps, options, futures—that occupy a qualitatively different, more rarified level of abstraction than twentieth-century money. Financial derivatives are a meta-money, the money of money: a medium in which to express the already abstract, purely conceptual (we might rather say 'imaginary') fluctuations of currencies, stocks, shares and bonds. The dominance of derivatives in the financial system is as profound a departure from the previous media of exchange as was the introduction of paper money in the seventeenth century. It involves a correspondingly dramatic alteration in the status of representation, and thus it induces comparably profound changes in the operations of *polis* and *psyche* alike.

The value of a financial derivative arises out of the exchange of different forms of money, in the same way that financial value itself arises out of the exchange of different objects. To put it differently: the value of a financial derivative is based on the exchange of exchange values, just as exchange value itself is based on the exchange of use-values. Usury has traditionally been criticized for 'reification'—making the medium of exchange into an object of exchange. Today that process has intensified, and the baroque financial instruments spawned by usury are themselves reified and traded as commodities. The market in derivatives involves a heightened form of symbolic abstraction, in which financial value is as far removed from use-value as verbal signs are distant from reality in post-structuralist linguistics. By the late twentieth century, financial value—the power that rules our world—was widely recognized as nothing more than a performative sign. In *Given Time: I. Counterfeit Money* (1992), Jacques Derrida details the semiotic implications of money's 'dematerialization':

> ... for example, in so-called modern literature, that is, contemporaneous with capital—city, *polis*, metropolis—of a state and with a state of capital, the transformation of money forms (metallic, fiduciary—the bank note—or scriptural—the bank check), a certain rarification of payments in cash, the recourse to credit cards, the coded signature, and so forth, in short, a certain dematerialization of money, and therefore of all the scenes that depend on it.[2]

Derrida describes a process of symbolic abstraction operating simultaneously in finance and literature. His followers frequently extend such parallels to other cultural phenomena. The performative view of representation is readily applicable to issues of personal identity, gender and sexuality. While the period of production-based capitalism produced a widespread 'homohysteria' in which the active repudiation of 'queer' sexuality was an important factor in defining masculinity, the quantum leap forward taken by financial capital in the early third millennium has been matched by comparably dramatic advances in the cultural and legal status of both 'queer' sexualities and non-binary conceptions of gender. Usury and what previous eras knew as 'sodomy' advance together in postmodernity, as they have throughout history, and both of them depend on idolatry: the attribution of performative agency to symbols.

The term 'queer performativity' was coined by Eve Kosofsky Sedgwick, who was also among the first to argue that 'gender can best be discussed as a form of performativity.'[3] In an essay co-written with Andrew Parker, Sedgwick declared that the concept of performativity was 'from its inception already infected with queerness.'[4] Judith Butler also notes that '"queering" persists as a defining moment in performativity,'[5] but the birth of the 'queer' is more often located in the late nineteenth century. Thus in *Sexual Dissidence* (1991) Jonathan Dollimore conveys the effect of 'queering' on personal identity through an analysis of Oscar Wilde's attempt to seduce Andre Gide. The puritanical Gide is in no doubt that indulgence in sodomy entails rebellion against the interior *logos*, the coherent subject, or what the nineteenth century still called the 'soul.' He protests: 'Wilde is religiously contriving to kill what remains of my soul, because he says that in order to know an essence, one must eliminate it: he wants me to miss my soul.'[6]

The idea that to prioritize *libido* over reproduction, the natural end of sexuality, is to overthrow the natural order within the *psyche*, and thus to threaten its coherence, has been commonplace since Plato. As Dollimore puts it, 'deviant desire... actually decenters or disperses the self' (7). The moral ambivalence with which Dollimore describes 'deviant' desire's dissolution of the self is unusual among postmodernists, who generally view the idea of a coherent, non-material subject as intrinsically oppressive and actively celebrate its demise. Desire is 'deviant' when it is *autotelic*. Since the natural *telos* of *libido* is reproduction, *autotelic* desire was traditionally denounced as 'concupiscence' or 'sodomy.' Dollimore fully acknowledges its disruptive effect on the unitary subject: 'for me sexual desire confuses, undermines or at least alters my sense of self' (54). In his autobiographical *Desire: A Memoir* (2017) he reflects on autotelic desire's reversal of the Platonic ethical hierarchy within the *psyche*: 'We didn't give much thought to anything outside our passions; for as long as they gripped us, we lived in the present in a way which was as spontaneous as it was ignorant.'[7] Thus Dollimore evokes the wrenching re-orientation toward passion and appetite that defined the psychological experience of his 'Boomer' generation.

The ethics of the postwar Western world repudiated the Platonic model, in which reason (*nous*) occupies the highest place within the *psyche*, because it is unique to, and therefore definitive of, human beings. We share passion and appetite with other animals, and therefore a psychological orientation that prioritizes such urges is traditionally viewed as bestial. By the late twentieth century, however, the influence of Freudian psychoanalysis had fostered a new ethical emphasis on the *libido*. The appetitive element of the soul, which Plato had subordinated to *nous*, rapidly grew respectable, while feminist and queer theorists increasingly favored desire over reason on political as well as ethical grounds. In short, the promotion of *libido* above *nous* became a progressive or 'left-wing' cause. This state of affairs would have astonished previous ages, which assumed that the psychological prioritization of *libido* was a fundamentally servile condition—and also a technique that could be used to reduce people to servility. In ancient Rome, slaves were legally and ideologically sub-human. They were officially categorized as *rei* (things) because they were objects of commodity exchange. Throughout antiquity, the Middle Ages and early modernity the servile mentality was regarded as carnal or fleshly: in a word, as 'objectified.' For most of civilized history, the kind of materialist subjectivity endorsed by postmodernist philosophy would have been understood as a servile psychology.

A performative approach to subjectivity is necessarily materialist. In postmodernist thought, moreover, even so fundamental an element of subjectivity as gender is understood as performative. A performative approach to gender defines it, not as something that one is, but as something that one does—or rather, as something that one performs. In the words of Butler: 'There is no gender identity behind the expressions of gender; that identity is performatively constituted by the very "expressions" that are said to be its results.'[8] In Butler's widely influential work, the performative approach to gender deconstructs the patriarchal, 'phallogocentric' myth that sexuality is constituted by the 'prediscursive' binary opposition of male and female. Patriarchal ideology suggests that it is natural, and therefore ethical, for people to behave in a manner determined by their biological sex. For Butler, in contrast, this causality is reversed, so that identity is determined by behavior rather than by biology. In fact, the binary conception of biological sex is itself a cultural consequence of gender's performance. Actions and attitudes that once seemed rooted in biology are revealed to be customary, constructed modes of behavior that produce binary sexuality in the act of performing it.

Butler and her followers thus use performativity to deconstruct the ancient opposition between nature (*phusis*) and custom (*nomos*). The confusion of *phusis* and *nomos* is acknowledged as a constant danger in ancient philosophy. Aristotle calls custom the 'second nature' precisely because of the ease with which it can be mistaken for nature itself. In the *Magna Moralia* he declares 'the reason why custom is held to be so strong is that it turns things into nature.'[9] According to Butler, however, the very idea of 'natural' sexuality is itself a product of custom: 'this production of sex as the prediscursive ought to be understood as the effect of the apparatus of cultural construction designated by gender.'[10] Nature is unmasked as custom in disguise. In fact, the polarity between custom and nature is construed as ipso facto politically reactionary, in contrast to the allegedly liberating politics of performativity. Those who argue that performativity is politically progressive tend to neglect its manifestations in the sphere of finance. Yet to 'queer' gender by rendering it performative is to risk connecting, or even identifying, the cultural prominence of queer sexuality with the economic dominance of financial representation. The hegemony of the performative sign abandons the traditional *telos* of economics, just as it ignores the traditional *telos* of sexuality. Indeed, the simultaneous rise of representation in both areas forces us to question whether economics and sexuality are discrete aspects of experience at all.

2.2   The Decline of Reference

The traditional Western world-view is often called 'logocentric.' First coined in this context by Derrida, the term refers to the tendency of Western thought to refer the surface phenomena of experience to an ulterior source of significance or *logos*. Logocentric thought constructs binary oppositions between appearance and essence, between representation and reality, and between body and soul. *Logos* is both the transcendent guarantor of such distinctions and the facilitator of their dialectical synthesis. *Logos* enables the existence of meaning and intention in an apparently random and insignificant world. *Logos* makes it possible to differentiate between sign and thing. It forces us to divide appearance from reality, by enabling us to understand that the world we perceive with our senses derives from, and refers to an anterior world of concepts or abstractions, which Plato calls *eidos*, Aquinas calls *res non apparens* and Kant calls *noumena*. As the power that allows us to have any kind of recognizably human experience, *logos* creates the world for us. It is the Second Person of the Christian Trinity: the original Greek term translated into Latin as *verba* and then into English as 'Word' in John 1.1. Socrates' *ratio*, Aristotle's *nous*, Augustine's *mens*, Descartes' Reason, Kant's *ding-an-sich*, Hegel's *Geist*, arguably even Marx's 'labor-power' are all philosophical expressions of *logos*.

In the twentieth century, the concept of *logos* came under concerted attack by the cultural forces collectively known first as 'modernism' and then as 'postmodernism.' The common factor uniting the impact of these cultural movements across various sections of experience was their concentration on appearance to the exclusion of essence: their focus on representation rather than reality, which soon became intense enough to erase the distinction. Prior to the twentieth century idolatry, usury, and sodomy were generally conceived as one, essentially identical vice because they all make this same hermeneutic error. They all violate the privilege of *logos*, by deconstructing the 'metaphors of depth' that structure rationalist philosophy and monotheistic theology. The postmodern era has therefore been described as bearing witness to the death of *logos*, or at least of logocentrism. By the end of the twentieth century, many thinkers were declaring logocentrism untenable in politics and culture, as well as in philosophy, psychology, and literary criticism.

Terms like 'modernism' and 'postmodernism' suggest a teleological narrative, but it would be wrong to see this as the culmination of a progressive, evolutionary process. The autonomous power of representation is certainly not unique to our age. The process that Derrida calls 'rarification,' whereby financial and linguistic values take increasingly abstract, symbolic forms, was already familiar in sixth-century Lydia, when coined money first came into public use. The value of coins is originally derived from reference to bullion. As Matthew Bishop remarks: 'people often forget that one of the earliest derivatives was money, which for many centuries derived its value from the gold into which it could be converted.'[11] Giovanni Arrighi and other recent historians persuasively present financialization as one among many recurrent processes of symbolic abstraction, involving a transition from production to exchange, followed by a transition from the exchange of tangible commodities to the exchange of the medium of exchange itself.

In the humanities, the early twentieth century's turn to symbolics abstraction is known as 'modernism.' The modernist moment in linguistics arrived with the advent of structuralism, which was heralded by Ferdinand de Saussure's *Course in General Linguistics* (1916). In a revolutionary departure from logocentric assumptions, Saussure relocated the ideal concept within the verbal sign. He divided words into the 'signifier' (the verbal icon, either the written letters C-O-W or the sound of their pronunciation) and the 'signified' (the concept designated by the word, the idea produced in the mind on hearing or reading the letters C-O-W). In turn, this internally-divided 'sign' designated the 'referent,' which was the milk-giving mammal in the extralinguistic world of nature. The concept of a cow was now contained within the word 'cow.' As 'post-structuralist' thinkers were quick to point out, this undermined any philosophical claim to conceptual truth. The Platonic realm of ideas was now imprisoned within the sphere of images. Rather than located outside language, in *logos*, conceptual truth was 'constructed' by and through the medium of representation.

Yet verbal meaning still remained referential in structuralism. Not only did Saussure distinguish between the signifier and the signified within the sign; the sign as a whole still denoted an extralinguistic referent. By the 1960s, however, post-structuralists like Derrida were deconstructing the polarity between signifier and signified, demonstrating the mutually definitive character of these categories, even arguing that concepts were themselves semiotic in nature, and that ideas could not be distinguished from their expression. Derrida viewed linguistic meaning as the product of *differance*: an endless chain of signifiers, each one differing from the next, but none of them deriving their meaning from a signified, still less from any extralinguistic sphere of 'reality.' The relativist skepticism that characterizes postmodern thought rests on the assumption that the human mind can perceive nothing but the symbolic, alienated form of its own works. Like the prisoners in Plato's cave, we perceive only images. Unlike Plato, however, Derrida suggests that this perception is perfectly accurate. Like one of Plato's prisoners, he denies the existence of any outside to the cave.

Thomas Hobbes had reached similar conclusions in the seventeenth century. Although he scornfully relegated ideas and concepts to the unreal 'Kingdom of Faeries,' Hobbes saw no reason to believe that the *eidola* we receive through sense-impressions are any more real. Not only does sense perception fail to designate anything non-apparent, it does not even provide a reliable view of appearances. Hobbes' philosophy is often interpreted as a response to the initial emergence of financial value as an independent power,[12] and it is true that, in early modern empiricism as in postmodernism, appearance quite literally turns into reality. As Hobbes well knew, what we perceive with our senses are images, and in his day the equation of images with reality was known as 'idolatry' and his philosophy suggests that human beings are idolators by nature. Images are the only reality we can know. And when images are believed to be real, they are naturally credited with the capacity to achieve real effects in the real world.

The vast majority of the world's wealth now takes the form of performative financial images. Such attribution of autonomous efficacy to images has historically had a very bad ethical reputation, but it has always retained a few defenders. In the sphere of linguistics, J. L. Austin's *How to Do Things with Words* (1962) is generally acknowledged as the inspiration behind today's ethically positive evaluation of performativity. Austin famously distinguishes between 'constative' statements, which describe an extralinguistic reality and can therefore be evaluated as either true or false (for example 'the fox is brown'), and 'performative' statements, which refer to nothing beyond themselves, but rather perform the action they describe (for example 'I name this ship the Queen Elizabeth' or 'Open Sesame!'). Performative statements are neither true nor false; they can only be evaluated as successful or unsuccessful. In *The Postmodern Condition* (1979), Jean-Francois Lyotard calls attention to the authoritarian nature of the performative. He compares a figural statement like 'the university is sick,' which is subject to rational, logical debate, with a 'performative' statement like 'the university is open' when pronounced by the Dean at convocation:

> The distinctive feature of this second, 'performative,' utterance is that its effect upon the referent coincides with its enunciation. The university is open because it has been declared open in the above-mentioned circumstances. That this is so is not subject to discussion or verification on the part of the addressee, who is immediately placed within the new context created by the utterance.[13]

As we will see in the next chapter, the equation of tyranny with irrationality is ancient. Socrates condemned the Sophists as tyrannical because they deployed irrational techniques of persuasion. He also criticized them because they worked for money, which distorted the content of their teaching. They were able to commodify their rhetoric only because they understood it as performative: it only sold because it worked. Indeed, sophistry implicitly aspires to the condition of magic. A Sophist's greatest conceivable success would be to concoct a verbal formula, 'charm' or 'spell' that was actually coercive. Euripides, Gorgias and Plato all used Helen of Troy as a trope to debate the ethics and the extent of rhetoric's power. Did Helen abscond of her own volition, or was she in some sense forced, raped by rhetoric? In other words, were Paris' words performative?[14] Over two millennia later, postmodernists continue the same debate.

Lyotard follows Plato by presenting performativity as an authoritarian agent of *anti-logos*, whose rule is de facto rather than *de jure*, whose claim to power is pragmatic rather than rational, and whose reign he calls 'the postmodern condition.' This condition took germinal form in Austin's conclusion that constative, referential, or descriptive statements are 'parasitic' on performative statements. Austin called the idea that language is essentially or typically referential 'the descriptive fallacy.' Departing from this fallacy, he declared that, while all constative utterances are also performative, not all performatives are constative: 'When we issue any utterance at all, are we not "doing something?"'[15] All statements have performative effects, even those that claim to be descriptive. A constative statement like 'the man is old' will have tangible effects on the way them man is treated socially, culturally and medically. Such statements are both constative and performative. However, a statement like 'I now declare you man and wife' is *only* performative. It is neither true nor false; it can only be evaluated as either successful or unsuccessful, depending on who says it in which circumstances. According to Austin, then, the performative turns out to be logically prior to the constative.

Like Saussure's relocation of the concept within the sign, Austin's prioritizing of performative above referential representation posed a threat to the most fundamental assumptions of Western metaphysics. It challenged the idea that meaning is the product of a conscious subject, it denied that verbal signs derive their meaning from reference to a prelinguistic reality and—in the interpretations of Austin's most extreme exegetes—it cast doubt on the very existence of objective truth itself. J. R. Searle reached similar conclusions in *Speech Acts: An Essay in the Philosophy of Language* (1969), which placed performative or 'illocutionary' statements at the center of Anglo-American 'speech act theory.' Continental treatments of performative representation tended to emphasize the wider, political implications of such ideas. Derrida's influential deconstruction of Austin's work, and his dispute with Searle in *Limited, Inc.*, angered the Anglophones by pushing their ideas to such radical conclusions. However, these Continental and Anglophone thinkers share much in common: they both accept that no words are merely descriptive, and that all utterances have some objective effect. Such claims in turn provided the foundation for an entire politics of performativity that has had a considerable impact throughout the Western world. Theorists of performance like Judith Butler and Donna Haraway have become public intellectuals, enjoying a wide reputation beyond the academy.

This rise to cultural prominence of performative representation forces us to question the ancient conception of hermeneutics as communication between two individual and independent minds, as summarized

by St. Augustine: 'There is no reason for us to signify something...
except to express and transmit to another's mind what is in the mind
of the person who gives the sign.'[16] This idea that signification necessarily involves communication between prelinguistic subjects was central
to ancient and medieval morality. When signs were seen to be efficacious
in themselves, without regard to any origin in the mind of a sender or to
any destination in the mind of a receiver, the ancient and medieval worlds
considered them magical and demonic in nature. Although Austin chose
not to emphasize, and may not have fully appreciated, the radical implications of his theory, these were fully exposed by Derrida in 'Signature
Event Context' (1968). Derrida argued that it was the invention of 'writing' that brought into being the notion of an 'author'—a conscious
logos which functions as the source and guarantor of textual significance.
He describes three unconscious assumptions inherent in this logocentric
model of representation:

> If men write it is: (1) because they have to communicate; (2) because what
> they have to communicate is their 'thought,' their 'ideas,' their represen-
> tations. Thought, as representation, precedes and governs communication,
> which transports the 'idea,' the Signified content; (3) because men are
> already in a state that allows them to communicate their thought to them-
> selves and to each other when, in a continuous manner, they invent the
> particular means of communication, writing.[17]

Derrida uses the term 'writing' (*ecriture*) to designate any non-referential,
self-generating system of meaning. In what he regards as the obsolete, Enlightenment realist model of representation, it was assumed that
'writing will never have the slightest effect on either the structure or
the contents of the meaning (the ideas) that it is supposed to transmit' (4). Linguistic mediation was supposed to offer transparent access
to reality, just as the financial sign of paper money was supposed to refer
directly to its worth in physical gold. But first modernism and then postmodernism altered the realist understanding of representation, according
instead a determining influence to the medium, and attributing determining power to the signs rather than to their author or referent. Derrida
argues that subjectivity itself is mediated through various representational
discourses, or forms of 'writing,' of which the financial and the linguistic
are homologous examples. On this basis, Derrida's post-structuralist

followers have constructed a politicized ethics of performativity, whose radical implications are announced by Butler:

> If gender attributes … are not expressive but performative, then these attributes effectively constitute the identity they are said to express or reveal … gender cannot be understood as a role which either expresses or disguises an interior 'self'…. As performance which is performative, gender is an 'act'… which constructs the social fiction of its own psychological interiority.[18]

Butler views the interior self or subject as a 'fiction' which is constructed in the act of material performance. Thoughts do not precede their expression; rather, the thinking subject is constructed in the act of expression. We do not speak language; language speaks us. Verbal significance is not produced by the conscious intention of the speaker, but by the autonomous force of linguistic *differance*.

Following the same logic that prioritizes the word over the idea, Derrida argues that writing is logically prior to speech. This is because writing originally represented speech and is therefore 'the sign of a sign.' Once again, Derrida assumes that signs are prior to and constitutive of their referents. The central characteristic of 'writing' is 'iterability,' the capacity to transmit meaning when repeated in the author's absence, and thus to dispense with the subject as a source of significance. Iterability depends on language possessing an autonomously performative force that does not originate in a prelinguistic *logos* or authorial subject. Butler shows how Derrida's logic can apply beyond the sphere of linguistics, when she defines iterability as performative discourse in general: 'that reiterative power of discourse to produce the phenomena that it regulates and constrains.'[19]

According to Derrida's 'logic of the supplement,' the 'other' is the constitutive factor of any identity. The other is necessary to the existence of the self, because the self is defined by its exclusion of the other. The logic of the supplement announces this dependence of the self on the other, suggesting for example that masculinity is defined by the exclusion of femininity, or that 'straight' sexuality is constituted by the 'othering' of the 'queer.' As Annamarie Jagose puts it, the discourse of normative sexuality 'claims heterosexuality as its origin, when it is more properly its effect.'[20] The political potential of deconstruction lies in its ability to subvert such mutually constitutive binary oppositions, and the polarity between sign and referent looms largest in the radicals' sights. From a post-structuralist perspective, in fact, the fundamental error of all Western metaphysics is to understand reality as prior to representation. As Derrida explains in *Of Grammatology* (1968), the logic of the supplement challenges that hierarchy, thus removing the logical necessity of *logos*. Things fall apart, the center cannot hold:

> The surrogate does not substitute itself for anything which has somehow preexisted it. From then on it was probably necessary to begin to think that there was no center, that the center could not be thought of in the form of a being-present, that the center had no natural locus, that it was not a fixed locus, but a function, a sort of non-locus in which an infinite number of sign-substitutions came into play. This moment was that in which language invaded the universal problematic: that in which, in the absence of a center or origin, everything became discourse—provided we can agree on this word—that is to say, when everything became a system where the central signified, the original or transcendental signified, is never absolutely present outside a system of differences. The absence of the transcendental signified extends the domain and interplay of signification ad infinitum.[21]

Hark what discord follows. Today, many philosophers hail the autonomous power of representation as politically and personally liberating. Western universities are packed with ardent advocates of performativity, which they deploy in revolt against the allegedly oppressive constrictions of essentialist identity. A walk across any college campus in the Anglophone world confirms the galvanizing impact of performative theories of gender and identity on politically conscious youth. Yet the connection between the rise of performative gender and the rise of performative finance goes largely unremarked. Usury has been permitted to plague the young generation to a degree unprecedented for centuries, but its effects on sexuality remain covert, or at least unspoken. The connection between usury and sodomy—as well as the conception of them both as sub-species of idolatry—was axiomatic in Western thought for millennia. This connection is the proverbial elephant in the drawing room of postmodern philosophy. Once we understand that performative theories of personal identity are conceptually implicated in, as well as historically simultaneous with, the logic of derivative-based financial capitalism, the entire field of identity politics, and its relations to the politics of the 'economy,' will have to be substantially re-evaluated.

2.3   The Death of the Soul
I: The Materialist Subject

The performative power of financial symbols is causally as well as conceptually connected to the performative power of linguistic symbols. As
Dierdre McCloskey pointed out in *The Rhetoric of Economics* (1985),
what we now take to be an objective sphere of experience called 'the
economy' is to a large extent artificially constructed out of rhetorical
tropes. These often include personification, for instance, as when markets
are said to be 'nervous,' or when subjective experiences like 'credit' and
'confidence' are expressed in alienated, symbolic form. A burgeoning
movement in aesthetics has emerged to explore this inter-penetration of
subject and object, and a growing body of popular art and literature now
incorporates the psychological impact of usury, credit and debt among
its major themes. In *Dead Pledges* (2017), Annie McClanahan describes
the aftermath of 2008s financial crash in the terms familiar from media
reports:

> Dozens of major international financial institutions failed or were bailed
> out; almost unimaginably large amounts of money were infused into
> collapsing markets by both federal governments and the International
> Monetary Fund (IMF)/World Bank; a looming sovereign-debt crisis in
> Europe was exacerbated by the contagion in financial markets, eventu-
> ally leading to a seemingly permanent state of imposed austerity; and a
> downturn in global economic activity overall, including productive invest-
> ment and state investment, caused a global recession whose consequences
> (both in and outside the United States) included massive unemployment,
> food crises, and increased rates of eviction, bankruptcy, homelessness, and
> suicide....[22]

McClanahan is addressing two different orders of reality here. One is
literal: eviction, homelessness, hunger, and suicide are objective, observ-
able phenomena. The other is figural. Nothing was literally 'bailed out'
or 'infused,' nothing was literally 'collapsing,' nothing literally 'loomed,'
there was no literal 'contagion.' All these things certainly happened,
but they happened at the figural level. They were symbolic events that,
because of the symbolic nature of the postmodern economy, were simultaneously objective. Representation, that is to say, had become reality:
symbols had become performative. In fact, the very nature of postmodernity can be grasped by considering the causal relation between the

two orders of reality McClanahan describes. In postmodern economic discourse, the literal, real world does not give rise to its own figural representation. On the contrary, figural representations cause real events, they construct the real world. Purely metaphorical tropes like 'collapse' and 'contagion' cause all-too literal events like eviction and homelessness. In postmodernity, representation determines reality. The tail wags the dog.

Arguably the most important consequence of performative representation's power is the demise of the interior self, or 'subject.' Once again, this involves the triumph of appearance over essence. When we say that we have no soul, no self, no unified, autonomous subjectivity, we identify ourselves with our appearance, our body. This materialism corresponds to and coincides with the elevation of financial and linguistic signs over their referents. Yet another instance of the power accorded to images is the cultural dominance of sexual concupiscence, or sodomy, which is an erotic focus on the body—the sign of the soul—to the exclusion of the soul itself. To regard a person as a body is an instance of reification: reduction to a thing. Reified sexuality is common among reified people. Any wage worker—and we are almost all wage workers now—is accustomed to self-objectification, to translating his or her life into alien, symbolic, financial form on an hourly basis. This objectification of the subject is also a subjectification of the object, and money becomes an active agent to the same extent that human beings are regarded as objects. Mark Kear has recently described the paradoxical relationship between a human subject and his or her credit score:

> Credit building was, contradictorily, a set of alien practices aimed at aligning self-perceptions with financial representations. It was about learning to personify the object of the credit score–the central legal technology of arbitration in US consumer credit markets. The credit score willed what the subject would not will on their own. Subject and object were acting in tandem as a sort of socio-financial hybrid.[23]

To allow money to reproduce is to treat it as a living thing: as a part of nature, or *phusis*, rather than as a merely customary convention, or *nomos*. Once it becomes an active agent, money naturally acquires its own subjective interests, appetites, and desires, which often conflict with the interests, appetites, and desires of the human beings whose activity it represents. The financialized economy is a gigantic mechanism for the systematic and simultaneous transformation of subjects into objects, and of objects into subjects. Although Butler concedes that philosophy still 'sometimes appears to assume the existence of a choosing and constituting agent prior to language (who poses as the sole source of its constituting acts),' she proposes abandoning such antiquated illusions in favor of a 'more radical' approach 'that takes the social agent as an object rather than the subject of constitutive acts.'[24] Objectification, reification, reduction to a thing are for Butler 'radical' modes of thought, and this is a position endorsed by many prominent postmodernists. In 1991 its political implications were spelled out fluently by Donna Haraway in *A Cyborg Manifesto*:

> By the late twentieth century, our time, a mythic time, we are all chimeras, theorized and fabricated hybrids of machine and organism—in short, cyborgs. The cyborg is our ontology; it gives us our politics. The cyborg is a condensed image of both imagination and material reality, the two joined centers structuring any possibility of historical transformation. In the traditions of 'Western' science and politics—the tradition of racist, male-dominant capitalism; the tradition of progress; the tradition of the appropriation of nature as resource for the productions of culture; the tradition of reproduction of the self from the reflections of the other—the relation between organism and machine has been a border war.[25]

Haraway's cyborg originates in the materialism of Hobbes, as developed by the eighteenth-century French philosophes. The most basic premise of capitalist economics is that people will, in the state of nature and *ceteris paribus*, reliably pursue their own self-interest. The Marquis de Sade's *Juliette* (1797) reveals the implications of this logic by extending it to sexuality:

> ... is it not certain that every man has been infused with the idea of acquiring wealth? That being so, the means he employs to become rich are just as natural as they are lawful. Similarly, are not all men given to seeking the greatest amount of delight in their pleasure-taking? Well, if sodomy is the unfailing means to this acknowledged end, sodomy is no infamy.[26]

In its Hobbesian form, such thinking derives from the Calvinist notion that fallen humanity is ineradicably and totally depraved. It seemed logical to infer that, rather than attempt to eradicate depravity, it should be channelled and limited to the 'economic sphere.' In *Economic Thought and*

Ideology in Seventeenth-Century England (1978), Joyce Oldham Appleby describes how the 'market' was initially defined as a tolerance zone for covetousness and, given the Biblical equations of the two vices, thus also for idolatry. In 1680, as money was beginning its long march to power, John Bunyan composed a meticulous study of its effects on the soul, *The Life and Death of Mr. Badman*. The title character is an archetypal reprobate, just as Christian, the hero of Bunyan's *The Pilgrim's Progress* (1678), is an archetype of the elect. But Mr. Badman is also an allegorical personification of *homo economicus*—the abstract, self-interested participant in the marketplace, who was just making his theoretical debut in early political economy. Badman deals in every kind of financial trickery, as he boasts of dedicating his life to the end of 'making the Shekel great.'[27] He is also addicted to whoring, a staunch supporter of what Bunyan regarded as the idolatrous Anglican state church, and a ruthless persecutor of nonconformist iconoclasts. But the most conspicuous effect of Badman's badness is his lack of anything resembling a coherent subjectivity. He possesses no stable essence that might remain consistent amid the flux of events. The artificial self that he acquires as a result of his market dealings is plural, disparate, fluid—in a word, postmodern:

> ... to pursue his ends the better, he began now to study to please all men... he could now be as they, say as they... when he perceived that by so doing, he might either make them his Customers or Creditors for his Commodities.... He would often-times please himself with the thoughts of what he could do in this matter, saying within himself; I can be religious, and irreligious, I can be any thing, or nothing; I can swear, and speak against swearing; I can lye, and speak against lying; I can drink, wench, be unclean, and defraud, and not be troubled for it: Now I enjoy my Self, and am Master of mine own wayes, and not they of me. (517)

When Badman speaks 'within himself,' it is only to brag that his self is unreal. He conceives of his self as a thing that he can manipulate to his own advantage. There is considerably pathos in his puerile proclamation: 'Now I enjoy my Self.' To 'enjoy' something, in seventeenth-century English, was to own it, to possesses it. When Badman declares that he 'enjoys' his self, he claims ownership over his own essence. In this, of course, he is sadly deluded. The book's humor lies in the precision with which, unknown to him, Badman's behavior is predestined by his allegorical significance as an archetypal bad man, which is in turn a literary analogue of his predestined reprobation according to Calvinist theology. The reader is encouraged to laugh at the other characters' ignorance concerning the predestined nature of Badman's behavior. When he predictably turns informer, for example, the naïve figure Attentive refuses to believe it: 'But do you think Mr. Badman would have been so base?' (515). The reader, in contrast, is aware that the allegorical form determines Badman's behavior with the same inexorable precision as, in Calvin's theology, divine providence determines the behavior of the reprobate.

The irony is that Badman experiences the loss of his self—the death of his soul—as a liberation. He feels free, because he knows he is free to change his appearance, and he identifies his appearance with his self. He does not experience himself as possessing any stable essence beneath his appearance. But Bunyan's didactic allegory shows that Badman's supposedly free thoughts and actions are determined by the demands of the marketplace, just as inflexibly as they are determined by his allegorical role, and just as inexorably as they are predestined by his reprobation. As the incarnation of *homo economicus*, his every action is dictated by his ceaseless pursuit of profit, and Bunyan communicates this by the comic precision with which Badman's behavior corresponds to his allegorical title. Far from being 'master of mine owne wayes,' Badman's profit-seeking 'ways' have completely mastered him. He lacks the kind of autonomous subjectivity that derives from allegiance to *nous* rather than to *sarx*, from attention to *virtu* rather than to *fortuna* and from adoration of *logos* rather than *eidolon*. He has, in other words, no soul.

The identification of appearance with essence leads inevitably to the death of the soul, for the soul is not apparent. The re-emergence of popular materialism in modernity returns us to the prehistory of philosophy, for the first theoretical reflections of pre-Socratic 'naturalists' like Thales and Anaximander, were instinctively materialist. When we look around us it *appears* as though everything is material, and the earliest theoretical impulse is to find some essence, a unifying principle to this matter, whether it be water, air or fire. However, later Greek thinkers soon concluded that Ionic monism was logically untenable. In the very act of identifying one thing, such as matter, the existence of something other than that thing becomes conceptually unavoidable. The identification of matter brings non-matter into being, and so monist materialism is self-refuting. Its appeal to sense-perception makes it a tenacious point of view, however, and monist materialism continually recurs throughout philosophical history.

During the seventeenth century, in fact, an extreme, eliminative form of skeptical materialism began a rise to predominance that continues to this day. The ideas of Hobbes gained great popularity in Restoration England, and Hobbes' logic was extended in eighteenth-century French Enlightenment works such as de la Maetrrie's *L'Homme Machine* (1747), which espoused a fully fledged materialist theory of subjectivity. Over the last two centuries, the basic assumptions of philosophical materialism have spread widely among people of all educational levels. Fyodor Dostoevsky satirizes this process with great acuity in his prophetic novel *Devils* (1871). Dostoevsky contemptuously puts facile, materialist dogma into the mouth of a teenage girl maddened by lust for the charismatic Stavrogin. Her materialism leads her instinctively into aggressive provocation against every form of patriarchal *logos*:

> 'We know, for instance, that the superstition about God came from thunder and lightning.' The girl-student rushed into the fray again, staring at Stavrogin with her eyes almost jumping out of her head. 'It's well-known that primitive man, scared by thunder and lightning, made a god of the unseen enemy, feeling their weakness before it. But how did the superstition of the family arise? How did the family itself arise?'[28]

Such defiance of logocentric patriarchy comes easily to many people today. Indeed, reductive materialism seems as natural to postmodernity as Christianity was to the fourteenth century. It is the default position arrived at by purely spontaneous, uncritical thought in the early twenty-first century. In a striking historical irony, however, this instinctive, automatic appeal of materialism has achieved consummation at the very moment when, scientifically speaking, matter itself has ceased to be material. With the ability to study sub-atomic particles comes the realization that 'matter' is nothing but energy. The world of experience thus comes to seem more like a continuum of 'stuff' than a binary opposition between matter and ideas, and many scientists now prefer to call themselves 'physicalists' rather than 'materialists.' Yet physicalism is perfectly compatible with the substance of the reductive materialist case, which is ontological monism. Physicalists believe that there is only one kind of thing in the universe. They reject the dualist, dialectical case that the existence of any one thing is logically predicated on the existence of its other. The rule of representation, or 'hyperreality' is similarly monist, rejecting as it does the predication of the sign upon the referent.

Clearly, neither physicalism nor materialism will countenance the idea of the soul. Nor will they tolerate such possible surrogates as the unified subject or the coherent self. The idea that we possess any essential identity lurking behind our physical appearances, or that we consist of any formal unity that is more than the sum of its parts, is anathema to physicalism and materialism alike. The postmodern attack on the human subject as illusory and oppressive can be dated from a notorious passage in Friedrich Nietzsche's *On the Genealogy of Morals* (1887): 'there is no "being" behind the deed, its effect and what becomes of it; "the doer" is invented as an afterthought, – the doing is everything.'[29] For Nietzsche, performance is all. There is no element of a human being prior to expression in action, just as for post-structuralist linguistics there is no thought prior to its expression in language. There is no point in seeking a text's significance in the mind of its author. In 'The Death of the Author' (1967), Roland Barthes points out that:

> The author is a modern figure, a product of our society insofar as, emerging from the Middle Ages with English empiricism, French rationalism and the personal faith of the Reformation, it discovered the prestige of the individual, of, as it is more nobly put, the 'human person.'[30]

Following the Symbolist poet Stephane Mallarme, Barthes locates the source of verbal significance in the words themselves: 'it is language which speaks, not the author.' Furthermore, Barthes claims, subjectivity itself is irreducibly textual: 'Did he [i.e. the author] wish to express himself, he ought at least to know that the inner "thing" he thinks to "translate" is itself only a ready-formed dictionary, its words only explainable through other words, and so on indefinitely' (46). Writing is no longer to be regarded as 'representation,' either of external reality or of the thoughts within the author's mind, but as a 'performative' discourse. The verb 'to write' becomes intransitive.[31] Writing generates itself, just like money.

2.4   THE DEATH OF THE SOUL II: SADIAN SOCIETY

In both the economic and the linguistic spheres, the late twentieth century witnessed a decisive shift from referential to relational value. Neither financial value nor linguistic significance derived any longer from reference to a prediscursive reality, but rather from the relations among the signs that convey them. Since both money and language are universal media of representation, moreover, any change in their relation to external reality will rapidly spread throughout culture and society. In linguistics, Derrida's adjustment of Saussure's theory led to the widespread belief that all meaning, indeed identity itself, is relational. The idea of a referent, an essence, or even a self that could exist in the absence of the sign, appearance or body that represents it is obsolescent. In analogous fashion, economic neoliberalism conceives of value as arising from the exchange of exchange value, rather than from the exchange of useful products, and still less from production itself. It is out of the relations between financial signs that financial value is produced, no longer from their reference to substantial commodities. In postmodern economics as in semiotics, the signified has the same ontological status as the signifier. The rise of autonomous representation and its correlative, the death of referentiality, are processes that span the disciplines and unite the disparate realms of human experience.

The consequences of representation's autonomy are profound. The 'performative turn' in the *psyche* undermines the logocentric assumptions behind rationalist philosophy and monotheist religion alike. The human soul cannot survive the death of referentiality. The rise to power of independent signs is equally destructive of art and culture as traditionally understood. This destruction was first manifested as artistic modernism, which systematically reversed the traditional rules of canonical aesthetics. Modernist art and literature ostentatiously displayed its own destructive—or destroyed—nature, presenting itself as the tragic expression of the Lost Generation's postwar trauma. As we shall see in Chapter 7, Ezra Pound's modernist poetics was consciously constructed as a parallel to contemporary financial developments, and especially as a response to the shift in the concept of value enforced by the rampant inflation of the early 1920s. Pound's *Cantos* (1922), like other archetypal modernist works such as T. S. Eliot's 'The Waste Land' (1922), Sigmund Freud's *Civilization and its Discontents* (1930) or Theodor Adorno's *Minima Moralia* (1951) depict the modern self as damaged, pathological, and profoundly miserable.

Over the last four or five decades, by contrast, the multiple, discursive self of postmodernism has frequently been presented in an appealing light, as playful, progressive, and liberating.[32] In *Sade, Fourier, Loyola* (1971) for example, Roland Barthes celebrates the three titular authors as prophets of postmodernity. He notes that they are 'committed, through historical position, to an ideology of representation and sign.'[33] Although they were born into the era of realism, when signs were conceived as representing an anterior reality, they boldly defied this 'ideology,' so that 'what our logothetes produce is already text' (ibid.). Their works produced significance out of 'a row of signifiers' rather than by what their words purported to represent. Barthes reads Sade's *The 120 Days of Sodom* (1785) as the ultimate in 'writerly' literature, because it scorns the referential notion that 'the word is nothing but a window looking out onto the real' (37). In its heroic revolt against realism the Sadian text concentrates on connotation rather than denotation, on the pleasure of the text as an end-in-itself rather than a medium through which reality is depicted:

> Being a writer and not a realistic author, Sade always chooses the discourse over the referent; he always sides with *semiosis* rather than *mimesis*: what he 'represents' is constantly being deformed by the meaning, and it is on the level of the meaning, not of the referent, that we should read him. (36–37)

Barthes emphasizes the identity between the ecstatic *jouissance* of Sade's writing and the erotic pleasures of the sodomy it depicts—or rather, as Barthes would say, produces. For the sexual scenes enacted in *The 120 Days of Sodom* are theatrical spectacles, often meticulously directed and rehearsed, and designed for visual gratification as much as for any other mode of sensuality. As Barthes points out, non-referential verbal semantics, fetishized visual images, and nonteleological sexuality—sophistry, idolatry, and sodomy—all produce the same kind of pleasure, the essence of which is their common rebellion against *logos*. 'All immoralities are connected,' as Sade himself put it.[34]

In *The Sadian Woman* (1971) Angela Carter calls attention to the performative nature of pornography in general, noting that 'in its directly frontal assault upon the senses of the reader, its straightforward engagement of him at a non-intellectual level' pornography employs 'the methodology of propaganda.'[35] Carter emphasizes the violence inherent in the reification that pornography imposes on human beings in the act of representing them. In contrast Barthes, like Foucault, finds Sade's systematic subversion of sexual *logos* both ethically and erotically attractive. The rebellion of *eros* against *nous* (or in Freudian terms the liberation of *libido* from *superego*), and the celebration of such psychological revolutions as politically progressive, are among the many ways in which, as Georg Lukacs observed, modern materialism constitutes an 'inverted Platonism.'[36] Freud and his followers concede the veracity of Plato's tripartite division of the *psyche* into reason, passion, and appetite but, in direct contrast to Plato, they claim that the ethical rights of appetite and passion are as at least equal, and in some cases superior, to the traditional prerogatives of reason.

Having established the Sadian homology between sodomy and idolatry, Barthes proceeds to discuss the function of usury in Sade's dystopias. Discussing *Juliette*, Barthes observes that 'Sadian money has two different functions. First it appears to play a practical role, it allows for the purchase and upkeep of the harems: pure means....'[37] This is money used as a means to the end of realizing use-value. Yet Barthes goes on to note a different sense, in which 'money is far more than a means: it is an honor, it clearly designates the evildoers and criminals who are permitted to accumulate it' (23). This is money as an end-in-itself, valued not for what it can buy but for what it can do. Thus when the heroine

> ... shuts herself away from time to time to count her gold, with a jubilation that drives her to ecstasy, she is not contemplating the sum of her possible pleasures, but the sum of her accomplished crimes, the common poverty, positively refracted in this gold which, being there, cannot be elsewhere; money therefore in no way designates what it can *acquire* (not a *value*) but what it can withhold (a sign of separation). (24)

Juliette fetishizes money in an explicitly sexual sense, not for what it can buy but for what it can do, not for what it represents but for what it effects—or rather for its single, central effect of facilitating her tyranny over her victims. Her sister Justine is initiated into vice by Harpin, 'a famous Parisian usurer' (24). For Sade's libertines, usury is a financial perversion from which they derive a satisfaction indistinguishable from their sexual sadism:

> With me greed went far: to the point, indeed, of usury. Once finding myself with eight hundred thousand francs worth of objects in pledge, objects which would not, had I auctioned them off, have fetched a fourth of that sum, I declared bankruptcy, and the gesture sufficed to ruin twenty humble families who had deposited into my keeping all they had of value in exchange for a pitiful fugitive subsistence, no more than enough to

enable them to pursue the desperate toiling whence they earned practically nothing. (25)

In the surreal societies of Sade's fantasies, then, we find a paradigmatic coalescence of usury, sodomy, and idolatry, united by their common commitment to performative representation. The sadistic perpetrators are disarmingly frank concerning the tyrannical nature of that commitment. In the relatively innocent era of the early 1970s, located on the cusp between modernism and postmodernism, the semiotic and sexual energies whose liberation had been heralded by prophets like Sade and Nietzsche could still appear potentially emancipatory to Barthes and Carter. Fifty years later, they may look rather different.

To summarize: the collapse of the distinction between appearance and essence is the basic characteristic of postmodernity. In ontology it gives rise to reductive materialism: matter is all that appears, therefore matter is all that exists. If applied to human beings, it announces the death of the soul. Only bodies appear, and so only bodies exist. Hence the current popularity of evolutionary psychology, sociobiology, and militant atheism, all conveniently personified in the figure of Richard Dawkins.[38] Such ultra-materialist modes of thought clearly strike a chord in the popular mind, which indicates that they fit perfectly into the currently dominant system of economic exchange. In linguistics and economics alike, the collapse of essence into appearance abolishes the polarity between signifier and signified, thus rendering both systems non-referential. The current economic crisis results from the further autonomy of representation within the financial system itself, as financial instruments become self-referential through the chain of derivatives. With regard to human identity, the loss of essence gives rise to the manifold forms of the 'post-human': artificial intelligence, genetic engineering, cyborgs, prostheses, cosmetic surgery, smart drugs, sex changes, even materialist and linguistic determinism themselves, which combine to confirm the widespread assumption that appearance and essence are indistinguishable, if not identical.

NOTES

1. William Pietz, 'The Problem of the Fetish II: The Origin of the Fetish,' *RES: Anthropology and Aesthetics* 13 (Spring 1987), 23–45, 24.

2. Jacques Derrida, *Given Time I: Counterfeit Money*, trans. Peggy Kamuf (U of Chicago P, 1992), 110.
3. Eve Kosofsky Sedgwick, 'Queer Performativity: Henry James' "The Art of the Novel",' *GLQ* 1 (1993), 1–16, 1.
4. Andrew Parker and Eve Kosofsky Sedgwick, (eds.), *Performativity and Performance* (New York, 2005), 5.
5. Judith Butler, *Bodies That Matter: On the Discursive Limits of Sex* (New York, 2011), 228.
6. Cit. Jonathan Dollimore, *Sexual Dissidence: Augustine to Wilde, Freud to Foucault* (Oxford UP, 1991), 4.
7. Jonathan Dollimore, *Desire: A Memoir* (London: Bloomsbury, 2017), 10.
8. Judith Butler, *Gender Trouble*, Preface to 1999 edition. xvi.
9. Aristotle, *Magna Moralia* (1203b30-1) in *The Complete Works of Aristotle: The Revised Oxford Translation*, ed. Jonathan Barnes (Oxford UP, 1984). Subsequent references are to this edition.
10. Judith Butler, *Bodies That Matter: On the Discursive Limits of Sex* (Routledge, 1993), 7.
11. Matthew Bishop, 'A Brief History of Derivatives,' *The Economist* 338.7952 (1996), 6–9, 1.
12. See especially C.B. MacPherson, *The Political Theory of Possessive Individualism: Hobbes to Locke* (Clarendon P, 1962).
13. Jean-Francois Lyotard, *The Postmodern Condition: A Report on Knowledge*, trans. Geoff Bennington and Brian Massumi (U of Minnesota P, 1984), 9.
14. See Matthew Gumpert, *Grafting Helen: The Abduction of the Classical Past* (U of Wisconsin P, 2001).
15. J.L. Austin, *How to Do Things with Words* (Clarendon P, 1962), 92.
16. St. Augustine, *Of Christian Teaching* book II, cit. Brannon Hancock, *The Scandal of Sacramentality: The Eucharist in Literary and Theological Perspectives* (James Clarke and Co.), 2014, 30.
17. Jacques Derrida, 'Signature Event Context', trans. Samuel Weber and Jeffrey Mehlman in *Limited, Inc.* (Johns Hopkins UP, 1977), 4.
18. Judith Butler, 'Performative Acts and Gender Constitution: An Essay in Phenomenology and Feminist Theory,' *Theatre Journal* 40.4 (December 1988), 519–531, 519.
19. Judith Butler, *Bodies That Matter: On the Discursive Limits of "Sex"* (New York: Routledge, 1993), 2.
20. Annamarie Jagose, *Queer Theory: An Introduction* (Melbourne UP, 1996), 3.
21. Jacques Derrida, *Writing and Difference*, trans. Alan Bass (U of Chicago P, 1978), 280.
22. Annie McClanahan, *Dead Pledges: Debt, Crisis and Twenty-First Century Culture* (Stanford UP, 2017), 5.

23. Mark Kear, 'Playing the Credit Score Game: Algorithms, "Positive" Data and the Personification of Financial Objects,' *Economy and Society* 46.3–4 (2017).

24. Butler, 1988, 519.

25. Donna Haraway, 'A Cyborg Manifesto: Science, Technology, and Socialist-Feminism in the Late Twentieth Century," in *Simians, Cyborgs and Women: The Reinvention of Nature* (New York: Routledge, 1991),149–181, 149.

26. Marquis de Sade, *Juliette*, trans. Austryn Wainhouse (New York: Grove Press), 1968.

27. John Bunyan, *The Life and Death of Mr. Badman* in *The Complete Works of John Bunyan* (Philadelphia, 1877), 511.

28. Fyodor Dostoevsky, *The Possessed (or Devils)*, trans. Constance Garnett (Wordsworth Editions Limited, 2015), 415.

29. Friedrich Nietzsche, *On the Geneaology of Morals*, trans. Carol Diethe (Cambridge UP, 2006), 26.

30. Roland Barthes, 'The Death of the Author,' in *Image, Music, Text*, trans. Stephen Heath (London: Fontana, 1977), 142–143.

31. See Roland Barthes, 'To Write: An Intransitive Verb?' in *The Structuralist Controversy: The Languages of Criticism and the Science of Man*, ed. Richard Macksey and Eugenio Donato (Johns Hopkins UP, 1971).

32. See Andreas Huyssen, *After the Great Divide: Modernism, Mass Culture, Postmodernism* (Indiana UP, 1987).

33. Roland Barthes, *Sade, Fourier, Loyola*, trans. Richard Miller (U of California P, 1976), 6.

34. Cit. Barthes, *Sade, Fourier, Loyola*, 7.

35. Angela Carter, *The Sadeian Woman: An Exercise in Cultural History* (Virago, 1979).

36. Georg Lukacs, letter to Karl Popper (December 1910), cit. Mary Gluck (ed.), *Georg Lukacs and His Generation 1900–1918* (Harvard UP, 1985), 165.

37. Marquis de Sade, *Juliette*, trans. Austryn Wainhouse (Grove Press, 1968), 23.

38. See David Hawkes, 'Literalism, Slavery and the New Atheism,' *Cross Currents* 66.3 (September 2016), 321–336.

CHAPTER 3

The Commodification of Rhetoric in Classical Athens

3.1 Solon Meets Thespis

Plutarch's 'Life of Solon' describes an early dispute between *logos* and *eidolon*. When he first sees an actor openly pretending to be another person, the proverbially wise Solon is outraged. The spectacle of a man who is systematically not what he seems shocks and disturbs him. Solon recognizes the actor as a threat to the distinction between essence and appearance. As Plutarch describes the encounter:

> Thespis, at this time, beginning to act tragedies, and the thing, because it was new, taking very much with the multitude, though it was not yet me a matter of competition, Solon, being by nature fond of hearing and learning something new, and now, in his old age, living idly, and enjoying himself, indeed, with music and with wine, went to see Thespis himself, as the ancient custom was, act: and after the play was done, he addressed him, and asked him if he was not ashamed to tell so many lies before such a number of people; and Thespis replying that it was no harm to say or do so in play, Solon vehemently struck his staff against the ground: 'Ah,' said he, 'if we honour and commend such play as this, we shall find it some day in our business.'[1]

The new genre known as 'tragedy' demands that, for the drama's duration, the audience identify the actor with the character he represents. The theater not only abrogates the vital distinction between sign and referent,

© The Author(s) 2020
D. Hawkes, *The Reign of Anti-logos*, Palgrave
Insights into Apocalypse Economics,
https://doi.org/10.1007/978-3-030-55940-3_3

it insists that the audience do likewise. Solon was therefore convinced that the theatrical replacement of reality by representation would not confine itself to the stage for long. Wisdom naturally distrusts 'hypocrisy.' The latter term has acquired strongly negative ethical associations, but originally it referred merely to acting on stage. Its etymology reveals the intimate connection between performance and deception:

> ... from Attic Greek *hypokrisis* 'acting on the stage; pretense,' metaphorically, 'hypocrisy,' from *hypokrinesthai* 'play a part, pretend,' also 'answer,' from *hypo-* "under' (see hypo-) + middle voice of *krinein* 'to sift, decide' (from PIE root *krei-) 'to sieve,' thus 'discriminate, distinguish'). The sense evolution in Attic Greek is from 'separate gradually' to 'answer' to 'answer a fellow actor on stage' to 'play a part.'[2]

The sense of the word 'hypocrisy' thus evolves as the individual actor emerges from the tragic chorus. For the first time in Western history, human beings contemplated their own images represented in objective form. The classical Athenians were no iconoclasts, and Solon presumably had no puritanical objection to visual imagery per se. What he fears is the spread of hypocrisy beyond the stage, into the serious affairs of 'business.' He does not wish to see the polarity between image and reality challenged in the economic or political sphere. He fears that the audience's habit of taking the actor for the character may carry over into everyday life. Solon is afraid that images may displace reality and acquire the kind of independent agency enjoyed by the actor on stage. His antitheatricalism expands into a thoroughgoing ethics of representation. In the theater, Solon discovers a secular version of what the Hebrews called 'idolatry.'

The polytheistic Hellenic world was not much concerned with idolatry in the religious sense, but it did develop an ethics of representation in economic exchange: the 'business' of Solon's prophetic warning. The invention of coined money in seventh-century Lydia, and its rapid spread throughout the eastern Mediterranean and Asia Minor, concentrated the Greeks' attention on the consequences of attributing efficacious power to symbols. Lydia was the land of mythic kings like Midas, Gyges and Croesus, whose legends expressed the effects of money on the mind. Marc Shell's influential studies have shown how the story of Gyges connects the indiscriminate power of coinage with the arbitrary power of political tyranny,[3] and how the Midas myth is a seminal meditation on the distinction between use-value and exchange value.[4] According to Herodotus, the inhabitants of ancient Lydia were distinguished by three exotic and inter-related characteristics: 'they prostitute their female children; and they were the first of men, so far as we know, who struck and used coin of gold or silver; and also they were the first retail-traders.'[5] The Lydians understood exchange value of every kind—indeed, as Glyn Davies puts it, 'the Lydians have given the Midas touch to economic history.'[6]

It was initially through mythology that the Greeks began to reflect on their use of financial symbols. The magical potency that the legends of Midas, Gyges and Croesus attribute to money confirms Richard Seaford's observation that '[m]oney was often imagined as having a superhuman will of its own' in ancient Lydia, and soon also in adjacent Ionia.[7] The use of coinage allowed the Ionic cities of Asia Minor to perceive that financial value is primarily symbolic, as opposed to physically inherent in precious metal.[8] They were able to see that the value of a coin does not derive mainly from its material, but from the mark engraved on it, and this mark, as Seaford notes, is 'a mere sign' (6). Seaford explains how, after the invention of coinage 'any other value the metal may have had (whether beauty, status, social relations, or immortality) seems to have been marginalized by the practical effectiveness of the coins as signs of monetary value' (6). In other words, the Greeks were the first to recognize and exploit the kind of value that Seaford calls 'fiduciarity': 'the excess of the fixed conventional value of pieces of money over their intrinsic value' (7). Thus financial value first revealed its symbolic nature, which it proceeded to exploit to powerful, performative effect, much like an actor on the stage.

The classical Athenians were the first thinkers in the Western tradition to comment critically on money's fiduciary status, and in doing so they gave birth to Western drama and philosophy. In the comedies of Aristophanes and the dialogues of Plato, the idea that financial value can be distinguished from its material incarnation produces a critical reaction that challenges the autonomous power of signs in the name of *logos*. Today, of course, most financial value has no material form at all. This almost total dominance of the fiduciary may be unprecedented in modern times, but people have been aware of money's symbolic aspect since the time of Midas. In the past, when the power of symbols was still limited and thus perceptible, people were able to see the ethical problems raised by performative representation more clearly than today, when signs seem omnipotent, and the morality of their rule is rarely questioned. That is why it is salutary to study the reflections of past societies on the ethics of representation. The thinkers of earlier eras operated in historical contexts where the moral implications of using signs to practical ends were more obvious than they are to us. We can learn how to deal with the phenomena of the present from the literature of the past.

3.2   Money Personified: Aristophanes' *Plutus*

Throughout history, literary depictions of money use the device of *prosopopoeia*, or personification, to comment on the subjective agency acquired by objective financial value. This technique fades out of regular use only when money's autonomy is so firmly established as no longer to seem worthy of remark. As Frederic Jameson has recently observed: 'it is the disappearance of personification that signals the emergence of modernity.'[9] John Bunyan's use of personification to parody *homo economicus* in the form of 'Mr. Badman' is one example, and in the eighteenth century the allegorical figure of 'Lady Credit' was familiar to readers of Addison and Defoe. Yet this tradition reaches as far back as Hesiod's *Theogony* (c.700), where Plutus (Wealth) is called 'a kindly god who goes everywhere over land and the sea's wide back, and him who finds him and into whose hands he comes he makes rich, bestowing great wealth upon him.'[10] Hesiod predates coinage, however, and his capacity to imagine money's autonomous agency is consequently limited. Greek writers did not fully explore the independence of a symbol from its referent until the classical age, when Aristophanes' *Plutus* (388) portrayed the power of autonomous representation in its financial form. In contrast to Hesiod's more abstract conception of Plutus, Aristophanes gives the money-god carefully individualized character traits, and the play shows Plutus gradually learning about his own nature.

When he first appears, Plutus is blind. At this stage he espouses a logocentric theology, assuming that Zeus is omnipotent. He is amazed to learn that he himself possesses a more fundamental form of power, without which the worship of Zeus would immediately cease. With this revelation, money is revealed as the source of all value. Much to Plutus' surprise, the play's main human protagonist Chremylus assures him that: 'Whatever is dazzling, beautiful or charming in the eyes of mankind, comes from you.'[11] But Plutus does not stand for wealth in general, so much as for a particular kind of wealth. He represents what the Greeks called 'chrematistics,' the pursuit of money for its own sake, as an end-in-itself, rather than as a means of acquiring useful goods. Robert Tordoff has shown how the economic situation of fourth-century Athens shaped Aristophanes' vision in *Plutus*. The city debased its coinage in 406, issuing silver-plated bronze coins that circulated at a value far above their specie content. This was obviously symbolic, fiduciary value, and its sudden power caused considerable alarm. Tordoff explains the social implications:

> Coins could bring any and every man on to a level playing field in economic transactions, regardless of his qualities or worth in any other matrix of value: the 'fiduciarity' of the coin obviates the need for trust in personal, embedded relationships, and this could be seen by mass and elite alike as socially corrupting at the very same time that it also facilitated exchange.[12]

Alan Baily argues that the introduction of coinage to the *polis* created a 'crisis of reciprocity,' displacing gift-exchange while bringing 'the realm of individualistic, utilitarian exchange—formerly marginalized—into the heart of the city.'[13] From the perspective of the hereditary aristocracy, the blind, irrational force of money seemed connected to (or even identical with) the arbitrary political power of 'tyranny.' As Marc Shell notes, 'Gyges… was the archetypal tyrant as he was the archetypal minter' (22). Aristophanes' earlier work *Frogs* (405) contains a lengthy discussion of the financial debasement and its social consequences. In this play, Gresham's law is in effect, and bad money has driven out good. The introduction of inherently worthless, symbolic money has driven the old, intrinsically valuable gold and silver coins out of circulation. Aristophanes compares this debasement of the coinage to Athens' recent bestowal of citizenship on mercenaries and former slaves which, he claims, has debased society in a comparable fashion:

> It's often struck us that the city deals with its fine upstanding citizens just as with the old coinage and the new gold. Though both of these are unalloyed, indeed considered the finest of all coins, the only ones minted true and tested everywhere among the Greeks and barbarians alike, we make no use of them; instead we use these crummy coppers, struck yesterday or the day before with a stamp of the lowest quality. Just so with our citizens: the ones we acknowledge to be well-born, well-behaved, just, fine, and outstanding men, men brought up in wrestling schools, choruses, and the arts, we treat them shabbily, while for all purposes we choose the coppers, the latest arrivals, whom formerly the city wouldn't readily have used even as scapegoats.[14]

This is more than an analogy. The abstract nature of financial representation really does eliminate personal qualities from consideration in economic affairs, rendering all people formally equal for the purposes of exchange. Aristophanes signals his snobbish disdain for this process in *Plutus*. The play reveals the disreputable associations into which the god's blindness has misled him, forcing the audience to confront the ethically repugnant influence of money on human behavior. Among other examples, Chremylus laments the mercenary attitude of Corinthian prostitutes: 'If a poor man offers them proposals, they do not listen; but if it be a rich one, instantly they turn their arses to him.' The slave Cario is quick to provide a homosexual inflection that will remain associated with finance for the next two and a half millennia: 'It's the same with the lads; they care not for love, to them money means everything.' Chremylus defends the 'male whores,' claiming that 'some of them are honest, and it's not money they ask of their patrons,' but he is forced to concede that even the honest ones require such payment as '[a] fine horse, a pack of hounds.' Cario sneers: 'Yes, they would blush to ask for money and cleverly disguise their shame.' The joke, of course, is that they effectively *are* asking for money when they ask for things that money can buy. A moral stigma evidently still clings to the symbolic mediator of money, so that the boys draw the line at asking for cash.

Although the human characters agree that all their endeavors are aimed at winning his favor, Plutus is unsure how to use his independent agency: 'This power that you say I have,' he skeptically asks, 'how can I become master of it?' Chremylus attempts to teach the befuddled deity about his potency and its accompanying moral responsibility: 'it is through you that everything is done; you must realize that you are the sole cause both of good and evil.' Being blind however, Plutus is unable to select his associates on merit. His installation as the universal *telos* of human life introduces a disjunction between virtue and value, for unworthy people often become wealthy, while the worthy frequently languish in poverty. Apparently nostalgic for an earlier, moral economy, Aristophanes explores what might happen if Plutus were to regain his sight, and with it his ability to choose his friends using rational criteria. According to David Konstan and Matthew Dillon, sight represents Plutus' performative power:

> The word for power here, *dynamis* (200), is pivotal: it looks back to the signs of Plutus' potency in the world, the fact that he alone is responsible, as Chremylus says, for all things good and bad; to which Plutus

responds, 'Am I, one person, capable (*dynatos*) of doing all this?' (186). Looking forward, however, *dynamis* must refer to the power of sight; the way that Plutus will become master of his own potency is to regain his vision. His sight, then, is his power. To put it another way, Plutus' blindness is an emblem of his powerlessness, and his healing is synonymous with the realization of his puissance in the world.[15]

The Greeks associated sight with power: deposed tyrants were usually blinded, since this supposedly made them incapable of ruling. Thus Aristophanes assumes that, as Konstan and Dillon put it: 'The god's vision is the condition for his efficacy' (192). But Tordoff complicates this by introducing the Athenians' distinction between 'visible wealth' (*phanera ousia*) and 'invisible wealth' (*aphanes ousia*). Visible wealth had use-value and consisted of useful commodities like land, slaves and livestock; while 'invisible wealth' had exchange value and consisted of chrematistic, financial wealth. Aristophanes alludes to this distinction in *Assemblywomen* (392), when a citizen asks: 'what about any of us who don't own land, but invisible wealth in silver and gold darics?' Tordoff argues that Plutus' blindness identifies him specifically with the subversive social influence of 'invisible wealth.' The play shows how the rise of fiduciary value causes the collapse of social distinctions based on birth, and their replacement by purely financial considerations.

So perhaps Aristophanes identifies Plutus' sight, not with his power per se, but rather with his *consciousness* of that power. As Plutus explains, he was quite capable of making moral distinctions before he lost his sight: 'when I was a boy I vowed that I'd only visit the houses of just, wise, and decent people, so Zeus made me blind, to keep me from recognizing any of them.' In such moments, it seems that the blinding of Plutus represents the replacement of inherent use-value by symbolic exchange-value. In previous stages of its development, wealth was inseparable from family and personal character. Land was inherited; barter was conducted in person; the value of a gift was inseparable from the character of the giver. With the rise of fiduciary value, however, all people are rendered equivalent in economic exchange,[16] the significance of personal character is erased and, in this sense, wealth becomes indiscriminate or 'blind.' In the comedies of Aristophanes, the emergence of invisible wealth facilitates its transfer to the kind of people who were not wealthy in terms of tangible possessions such as land. In *Plutus*, the prominence of invisible wealth also obscures the origin of value in labor. Chremylus and Cario inform Plutus that he—money—is the *telos* of all labor:

> *Chremylus*: It is in you that every art, all human inventions, have had their
>   origin; it is through you that one man sits cutting leather in his shop.
> *Cario*: That another fashions iron or wood.
> *Chremylus*: That yet another chases the gold he has received from you.
> *Cario*: That one is a fuller.
> *Chremylus*: That the other washes wool.
> *Cario*: That this one is a tanner.
> *Chremylus*: And that other sells onions.

According to this logic, the carpenter's main aim is not to make tables and
chairs but to make money. To perceive Plutus as the *telos* of labor is to
elevate symbolic exchange-value above practical use-value as the ultimate
end of human activity. Cario reveals the fundamental error of this logic
when he promises the chorus that they will all become 'Midases' (287). In
supposing that money is the purpose of labor he assumes, like Midas, that
to possess exchange value is to be wealthy. He mistakes exchange value
for the essence of wealth, rather than its symbol. Taking the sign for the
referent, he assumes that whoever has money is therefore rich: he does not
understand that the only real wealth is use-value. Having attained Plutus'
friendship, therefore, he wastes the god's power in pointless ostentation,
adorning useful objects with expensive decoration: 'all the platters are of
brass; our rotten old wooden trenchers for the fish have to-day become
dishes of silver; even the thunder-mug is of ivory' (813–815).

Like the old Lydian myths of Midas, Gyges and Croesus, *Plutus* is
a moralistic warning against identifying wealth with money. It reminds
the audience that exchange value is appearance, not essence, and that
money is only a symbol, while use-value is real. Aristophanes cautions
against fetishizing this symbol and permitting it to act on its own unfet-
tered agency. This lesson is not limited to exchange value but applies to
fetishized symbols of every kind—the iconoclastic implications of *Plutus*
are emphasized by the title of a 1659 translation by 'H.H.B.': *The World's
Idol*. In his commentary on this edition, the translator explains that
money becomes an 'Idol' when it acquires subjective agency and objective
potency. It is a fetishized product of human labor, which is accorded an
illusory power over its creators. Money, claims H.H.B., now rules those
who sought to rule by it:

> … the sport of all is, that all this which the Great ones first invented to
> govern by, is now by long succession wrought into such a subtilty, that

it is grown to govern them that thought to govern by it; and sometimes too, not only by necessity, but through real opinion of the thing itself: so natural is it for men, first to make lies, and afterwards come to believe them themselves; the which *Mountain*[17] excellently compares to Boys, that dress up one of their companions, and black his face, to represent the Devil, to make themselves sport; and when they have done, run away for fear of him, and forget that it was the Idol of their own hands. (41)

Idolatry is the attribution of agency to 'the works of men's hands.' The human characters in Aristophanes' *Plutus* make precisely that error, when they conceive of money as the *telos* of labor rather than its symbol. When money's symbolic status is forgotten, it becomes performative. It constitutes itself as an autonomous subject and moves beyond mortal control, turning into an independent agent, alien and opposed to the interests of humanity. The autonomous agency of symbols is antithetical to the concept of *logos*, which posits an essential significance, a fundamental reference, and an ultimate meaning that symbols may designate but can never constitute. Thus Plutus loses his awe of Zeus as soon as he regains his sight. In fact the entire Olympian pantheon immediately becomes obsolete. Hermes is reduced to seeking servile employment alongside Cario, complaining: 'Since Plutus has recovered his sight, there is nothing for us other gods, neither incense, nor laurels, nor cakes, nor victims, nor anything in the world.' Deprived of his income, even the Priest of Zeus deserts his allegiance. The performative power of Plutus is shown to be incompatible with the creative force of *logos*.

Aristophanes understands that the attribution of subjective agency to symbols entails the objectification of human subjects. In the play's opening speech, Cario notes the deleterious effect of Plutus' power on the condition of a slave: 'the *daimon* [i.e. Plutus[18]] does not allow him to dispose of his own body, it belongs to his master who has bought it.' Later he expands: 'I myself was bought for a few coins; if I'm a slave, it's only because I was not rich.' Cario is reified by the same process that bestows subjective agency on Plutus. He objects to money's performative power because he understands its correlation with his own objectification. Once Plutus is regarded as the universal *telos* of mankind, the fundamental binary oppositions between subject and object, essence and appearance, form and matter, and sign and referent all collapse. To restore order, a rational standard must be imposed on Plutus' behavior, and Aristophanes makes this possible by restoring the god's sight in the Asclepeion.

However this immediately conjures up Plutus' dialectical opposite in the shape of personified Poverty (Penia). She explains that Chremylus and Cario are mistaken as to the nature of wealth. The labor of the smith, the fuller and the tanner may be motivated by desire for Plutus, but that does not mean he is its proper purpose or natural *telos*. True wealth consists in use-value, the product of human labor, which is stimulated not by wealth but by its absence: poverty. As Penia tells Chremylus: 'I am the sole cause of all your blessings.' She explains that money is not autonomously efficacious, in spite of appearances. The presence of Plutus alone will bring no benefit, for the true source of value is human industry:

> Let Plutus recover his sight and divide his favours out equally to all, and none will ply either trade or art any longer; all toil would be done away with. Who would wish to hammer iron, build ships, sew, turn, cut up leather, bake bricks, bleach linen, tan hides, or break up the soil of the earth with the plough and garner the gifts of Demeter, if he could live in idleness and free from all this work?

Yet Chremylus proves unable to accept that labor, not money, is the source of value. He does not understand that signs depend on referents, and could not exist without them. Failing to see that Plutus is the product of labor, not its cause, he blithely denies any difficulty: 'What nonsense all this is! All these trades which you just mention will be plied by our slaves.' Since slaves receive no wages, the availability of slave labor has blinded Chremylus, as well as Plutus himself, to the true origin of value, leading them to conceive of money as an animate being with its own independent will and intent. In response, Penia notes that even slave-traders will not work without pay:

> But if your system is applied, there won't be a single slave-dealer left. What rich man would risk his life to devote himself to this traffic? You will have to toil, to dig and submit yourself to all kinds of hard labour; so that your life would be more wretched even than it is now.

Even if they have as much money as Midas, they must still work to eat. Chremylus does not grasp this fact, because he conceives of labor as incarnate in those who perform it: slaves like Cario. The alienation of labor from those who perform it depends upon the attribution of autonomous efficacy to labor's symbolic form. This alone makes it possible to separate the meaning, the significance—the 'value'—of labor from its performance, by projecting the efficacy of subjective activity onto a symbol that can be expropriated by people other than those who carry it out. Slave labor is inseparable from the person of the slave, but proletarian labor is represented in financial form, which is fungible and can therefore be transferred from one person to another. Labor can only be alienated from the laborer by giving it a symbolic form: by turning it into Plutus.

3.3   USURY AND SOPHISTRY IN ARISTOPHANES' *CLOUDS*

Exchange value imposes the same abstract equivalence on labor itself as it does on the products of labor. In the *Nicomachean Ethics*, Aristotle recognizes that 'all products that are exchanged must in some ways be comparable' and that 'it is this that has led to the introduction of money, which serves as a sort of mean (or medium of exchange), since it is a measure of everything, and so a measure of the excess and deficiency of value.'[19] Aristotle understands that exchange value is a sign that functions as a common denominator in which any kind of value can be expressed. However, he never identifies that sign's referent as labor power. It has often been suggested that any society based on slavery must fail to recognize that exchange value represents labor power. In such societies, the paucity of wage-labor (which, unlike slavery, translates labor into financial form) means that labor cannot be conceptually distinguished from its performance. In a society based on slavery, people are exchanged rather than abstract labor-power. In consequence, labor does not appear as a *rei*, a definite object of exchange. In *Capital*, Karl Marx observes that Aristotle understood how commodity exchange requires the imposition of symbolic equivalence on objects that are essentially different, and also that this calls for a common denominator in which the value of any object can be expressed. Aristotle failed, however, to recognize that common denominator as abstract human labor:

> There was... an important fact which prevented Aristotle from seeing that, to attribute value to commodities, is merely a mode of expressing all labour as equal human labour, and consequently as labour of equal quality. Greek society was founded upon slavery, and had, therefore, for its natural basis, the inequality of men and of their labour powers. The secret of the expression of value, namely, that all kinds of labour are equal and equivalent,

because, and so far as they are human labour in general, cannot be deciphered, until the notion of human equality has already acquired the fixity of a popular prejudice. This, however, is possible only in a society in which the great mass of the produce of labour takes the form of commodities, in which, consequently, the dominant relation between man and man, is that of owners of commodities. The brilliancy of Aristotle's genius is shown by this alone, that he discovered, in the expression of the value of commodities, a relation of equality. The peculiar conditions of the society in which he lived, alone prevented him from discovering what, 'in truth,' was at the bottom of this equality.[20]

Marx claims that the fundamental role of slave labor in classical Athens made it impossible to conceive of labor power in the abstract, as a symbol that can be separated from its performance. The slave is alienated entirely, his whole being is the property of his owner. In contrast, a wage worker's activity is alienated piecemeal, by the hour, and in the guise of financial value it confronts him in palpably symbolic form. The slave qua slave has no independent interest, no legal identity, apart from his master. In contrast, the interests of those who sell their own labor are openly opposed to those who buy it, so that a society based on wage labor automatically generates class conflict. Slave revolts were not uncommon in antiquity, but they were conceived as conflicts between entire societies and alien, anti-social forces. The form taken by class conflict in modern society, when labor is embodied in the proletariat and capital in the bourgeoisie, was insignificant in Aristotle's world. As K. J. Dover explains:

So few citizens were regularly employed by other citizens that it was hard for an individual to feel that his own labor was directly enriching someone else; hence polarization of capital and labour could not play any significant part in the political life of the citizen-body.[21]

Yet it is not clear why Aristotle's blind spot, common though it was, should necessarily have been universal in classical Athens. It is arguable that, by showing how the company of Plutus does not bring wealth in the absence of work, Aristophanes arrived at the labor theory of value that eluded the Philosopher. Several of his other plays also remark critically on the autonomous power of money. In *Frogs*, Dionysus is dismayed enough by Charon's fare to protest that money retains the same power in Hades as in life: 'Fie! The power two obols have, the whole world through!' The close association between Pluto, god of the underworld and Plutus, god of wealth, lasted throughout antiquity. Half a millennium after Aristophanes, in Lucian of Samosata's second-century A.D. dialogue *Timon the Misanthrope*, Plutus admits: 'it is not Zeus who sends me, but Hades, who has his own ways of conferring wealth and making presents. Hades and Plutus are not unconnected, you see.' Lucian's Plutus describes the systematic deceit by which he contrives to make himself acceptable to humanity:

> ... not to be an absolute fright when they see me, I put on a charming mask, all gilt and jewels, and dress myself up. They take the mask for my face, fall in love with its beauty, and are dying to possess it. If anyone were to strip and show me to them naked, they would doubtless reproach themselves for their blindness in being captivated by such an ugly misshapen creature.[22]

Lucian's Plutus defines himself by the discrepancy between his appearance and his essence: we might even say that he personifies that discrepancy. Even Hermes acknowledges his protean qualities: 'What a smooth, slippery, unstable, evasive fellow you are, Plutus! there is no getting a firm hold of you; you wriggle through one's fingers somehow, like an eel or a snake.' This is high praise coming from Hermes, and it recalls the manner in which the power of Aristophanes' Plutus reduces Hermes to servitude. The newly sighted, and therefore omnipotent, Plutus removes the need for Zeus and the patriarchal Olympian pantheon. His influence is fundamentally anti-logocentric. Although the exact relation of the character to the playwright is debatable, Plato's *Symposium* shows Aristophanes espousing a non-binary view of gender that chimes harmoniously with the anti-logocentrism espoused by Plutus. Plato's Aristophanes claims that gender was not always constructed according to a mutually definitive polarity between male and female.

> The sexes were not two as they are now, but originally three in number; there was man, woman, and the union of the two, having a name corresponding to this double nature, which had once a real existence, but is now lost, and the word 'Androgynous' is only preserved as a term of reproach. (189e)[23]

According to the myth that Aristophanes proceeds to relate, all three genders were originally 'circlemen' (as modern critics style them[24]):

spherical beings who were doubles of modern humans, with four arms and legs, two faces, and so on. Binary gender was originally a punishment inflicted by Zeus on the tri-gender society of circlemen because, in their formidably unified condition, they were powerful enough to threaten Olympian authority. The patriarchal deity's division of humanity also accounts for the binary division of sexual taste into hetero- and homosexual:

> Men who are a section of that double nature which was once called Androgynous are lovers of women; adulterers are generally of this breed, and also adulterous women who lust after men: the women who are a section of the woman do not care for men, but have female attachments; the female companions are of this sort. But they who are a section of the male follow the male, and while they are young, being slices of the original man, they hang about men and embrace them, and they are themselves the best of boys and youths, because they have the most manly nature. (191d–192a)

Binary sexuality and binary gender are, according to Plato's Aristophanes, the results of a primal fall from grace, a punishment inflicted by a patriarchal *logos*. Aristophanes the playwright shows a similar fascination with anti-logocentric patterns of thought and behavior. Years before *Plutus* he explored the subversive nature of money in *Clouds*. This play is perhaps the earliest investigation of usury's impact on the *psyche* in the Western canon. It opens with the *senex iratus* Strepsiades lamenting his debts: 'My creditors have distrained on my goods, and here are others again, who demand security for their interest.'[25] In desperation he turns to Socrates, who is found among 'the sophists.' Strepsiades implores Socrates to teach his son rhetoric, so that he can persuade the court to forgive his father's debts. This immediately arouses suspicion, for Aristophanes is generally dubious about the practical deployment of rhetoric.[26] In his *Acharnians* a venerable old solider complains of being harassed in the law courts by 'the scorn of stripling orators' who 'overwhelm[s] us with [their] ready rhetoric.'[27] The play's chorus mocks the Athenians for their susceptibility to rhetorical flattery:

> ... when delegates from other cities wanted to deceive you, they had but to style you, 'the people crowned with violets,' and at the word 'violets' you at once sat erect on the tips of your bums. Or if, to tickle your vanity, someone spoke of 'rich and sleek Athens,' in return for that 'sleekness'

he would get all, because he spoke of you as he would have of anchovies in oil. In cautioning you against such wiles, the poet has done you great service as well as in forcing you to understand what is really the democratic principle. (628)

The 'democratic principle' evidently does not involve the cynical manipulation of rhetoric to political ends. We have already seen how coined money was associated with political tyranny in classical Athens; here the power of rhetoric is presented in the same light. The use of rhetoric in politics is a form of flattery that, since it seeks to persuade by irrational means, threatens to undermine rational rule in favor of arbitrary rule (although Aristophanes fears the tyranny of the *demos* more than the individual ruler). In *Clouds*, Strepsiades assumes that the sophists' commodified rhetoric is completely malleable, both practically and ethically, and thus available to serve his amoral pursuit of economic self-interest. In a prefiguration of Simon Magus' approach to St. Peter in the Biblical Book of Acts, Strepsiades attempts to purchase Socrates' rhetorical efficacy. He tells his son:

It seems they have two courses of reasoning, the true and the false, and that, thanks to the false, the worst law-suits can be gained. If then you learn this science, which is false, I shall not have to pay an obolus of all the debts I have contracted on your account.

To Strepsiades, sophistry implies relativism. He presumes that the purpose of sophistical rhetoric is to circumvent *logos* and to trump truth.[28] He declares his self-interest to Socrates with disarming frankness: 'I want to learn how to speak. I have borrowed money, and my merciless creditors do not leave me a moment's peace; all my goods are at stake.' He even offers to guarantee his fee by swearing to the gods. As a 'sophist,' however, Socrates is unimpressed by such an appeal and retorts 'the gods are not a coin current with us.' Strepsiades takes this literally, and assumes that Socrates will accept some other 'coin' as his ultimate authority: 'But what do you swear by then? By the iron money of Byzantium?' His whole purpose is to purchase the defeat of reason in pursuit of his own economic self-interest, so he has already demonstrated his contempt for *logos*. He even considers buying supernatural assistance:

> *Strepsiades*: Tell me, if I purchased a Thessalian witch, I could make the
> moon descend during the night and shut it, like a mirror, into a round
> box and there keep it carefully....
> *Socrates*: How would you gain by that?
> *Strepsiades*: How? why, if the moon did not rise, I would have no interest
> to pay.
> *Socrates*: Why so?
> *Strepsiades*: Because money is lent by the month.

The notion that money can increase with time, breeding like a natural creature, is as absurd as trying to catch the moon. Strepsiades' criticism of usury focuses relentlessly on its confusion of *phusis* with *nomos*. 'What kind of animal is interest?' he asks a usurer, before dismissing him: 'poor fool, the sea, that receives the rivers, never grows, and yet you would have your money grow?' Nevertheless, he insists that his son must learn rhetoric, in order to fight against the usurers with their own weapons. Turning to rhetoric in order to avoid paying usury, he deploys one species of quasi-magical sign against another. Enraptured at the prospect of the youth's verbal dexterity, he bursts into song:

> Woe to the usurers, woe to their capital and their interest and their
> compound interest! You shall play me no more bad turns. My son is being
> taught there, his tongue is being sharpened into a double-edged weapon;
> he is my defender, the saviour of my house, the ruin of my foes!

Strepsiades uses verbal signs as a weapon against financial signs. He denies neither the legality of his debts nor the efficacy of money. On the contrary, he struggles against usury on its own terms. His first encounter with one of his creditors goes well because, just as the sophists refuse to swear by the gods, so the usurer's belief in the autonomous power of financial signs prevents any appeal to *logos*. The debt proves unenforceable, since Strepsiades recognizes no authority outside systems of representation:

> *Pasias*: Will you dare to swear by the gods that you owe me nothing?
> *Strepsiades*: By which gods?
> *Pasias*: By Zeus, Hermes and Posidon!
> *Strepsiades*: Why, I would give three obols for the pleasure of swearing by
> them.
> *Pasias*: Impudent knave!

Strepsiades mocks the idea of appealing to transcendent authority when he compares the gods to money. As in the earlier encounter with Socrates, he holds nothing sacred because he recognizes the existence of nothing beyond the sphere of representation. He makes rhetoric do battle with usury, because he knows the two powers are of the same nature. They are both systems of performative signs, and they both provide means to circumvent *logos*. The comedies of Aristophanes chronicle the impact of this emergent symbolic power on classical Athenian society, and this was also the pre-eminent concern of the first Athenian philosophers. The debates between Socrates and the sophists, as recounted in Plato's dialogues, contain a protracted dispute between performative and referential models of representation, in which Socrates aligns himself firmly with the latter. In modified but by no means unrecognizable form, the dispute between Socrates and the sophists continues to this day.

3.4   PHILOSOPHY CONTRA SOPHISTRY

Like Hellenic drama and Hebraic monotheism, Western philosophy originates as a meditation on the ethical ramifications of the performative sign. The invention of coined money introduced the concept of a universal referent into the Greek mind. Coinage assumes *logos*. It is predicated on the existence of a metaphysical, abstract source of value, from which the material coins derive and to which they refer. The first, instinctive impulse of philosophy among the Ionian naturalists was to bestow some material form on this universal abstraction. Thus Thales claimed the whole world was water, while Anaximenes said it was air. The next stage was to concentrate on the principle of abstraction itself. In Anaximander the universal substance is abstracted into the 'first principle' or *arche*, and in Anaxagoras this is identified with 'reason' or *nous*.

Coined money raised the conceptual need for a universal referent, producing the philosophical impulse toward *logos*. As depicted in Aristophanes' *Plutus*, the rising influence of money undermined the gods of Olympus, just as rational philosophy challenged polytheism. As Seaford puts it: 'the anthropomorphic deities are replaced... by the metaphysical projection of the impersonal, unitary, abstract, transcendent, seemingly self-sufficient power of money' (14). Such critics as Seaford, Shell, Alfred Sohn-Rethel and Jean-Joseph Goux have pointed to the connections between coinage and Platonic philosophy. The relation between the Platonic One and the many is comparable to (but subtly different from) the relation between a coin of large denomination and the smaller coins into which it may be divided. The Platonic dialectic suggests, as Shell puts it: 'that most men unwittingly divide the conceptual and political world in which they live by a kind of division that is formally identical with money changing.'[29]

This is not to suggest that Plato endorsed the autonomous power of symbols. The rhetorical self-assertion of the theatrical performer is subjected to severe criticism in several dialogues. In the *Ion*, for instance, the eponymous rhapsode's 'ecstasy' draws him out of his true identity and into a purely imaginary realm. Like Solon addressing Thespis, Socrates asks Ion whether this 'ecstasy' prevents him from distinguishing image from reality: 'does your soul in an ecstasy suppose herself to be among the scenes you are describing?' (535b–535c). If this question applied only to Ion's private experience there would be little cause for concern, but Socrates again echoes Solon with his further caution that 'you rhapsodes produce the same effects on most of the spectators' (535d). The power of autonomous symbols is dangerously infectious, but Ion ignores Socrates' admonition, and his rationale for doing so establishes a link between financial value and theatrical representation that still perdures today. Because Ion must sell his performance to survive, he views his art as a commodity, and so he prioritizes its exchange value above its use-value. He happily agrees that he manipulates the audience's response, but unlike Socrates he sees this as a good thing, because his motive is economic self-interest: 'if I set them crying, I shall laugh myself because of the money I take, but if they laugh, I myself shall cry because of the money I lose' (535e).

All commodification imposes an image (exchange-value) on a substantial reality (use-value), and Plato's critique of autonomous representation includes its commercial as well as its theatrical aspects. The *Republic* explains that money's natural *telos* is to serve as a mediator for different use-values, rather than as an end-in-itself: it is 'a symbol for the purpose of exchange' (371b). Plato's idealism assumes that essence underlies appearance, and that signs necessarily designate referents. Signs are not part of nature (*phusis*) but belong to the sphere of custom (*nomos*), which Aristotle calls the 'second nature.' As Sohn-Rethel observes: '[s]econd nature finds its external expression in money....'[30] Coins are certainly made from natural materials. But their *value*, although not material, is in the Platonic sense even more real, because it is not a prey to the vicissitudes of matter. The realm inhabited by financial value is conceived as above material change and decay. But once abstract value starts to grow and reproduce, as if it were a physical, natural creature, this fundamental polarity between matter and ideas is subverted.

We have seen how Aristophanes conveyed the need to impose an ethical limitation on money's random affiliations by restoring sight to Plutus. A parallel movement took place in philosophy, when Plato used logic to curb the pragmatism of sophistical rhetoric. Plato elaborated an ethical critique of the treatment of verbal signs as efficacious, which he deprecated as 'sophistry.' Sophistry is thus philosophy's original opponent. It consists in commodification: the sophists manipulate rhetoric to performative effect in return for money. They are forced into their opinion that words can do things, because they must be able to guarantee some tangible benefit in return for their customers' investment. This reification of rhetoric leads the sophists to treat words as things, not as signs, and to employ them as tools for the purposes of pragmatic persuasion, using connotation rather than denotation, and relying on performance rather than logic.

In his canonical study of the sophists, G. B. Kerford attributes Plato's contempt for commodification to the same anti-democratic impulse as Aristophanes' snobbish attitude toward the debased Athenian currency: 'What is wrong is that the sophists sell wisdom *to all comers* without discrimination—by charging fees they have deprived themselves of the right to pick and choose among their pupils.'[31] Like Aristophanes' Plutus, the sophists are 'blind' when it comes to personal character. They will teach anyone who pays. Socrates compares them to prostitutes for the same reason.[32] The real problem, however, is not the quality of the sophists' students but the content of their teaching. They taught a performative, pragmatic approach to language, and for Socrates the moral peril involved in the sale of rhetoric is closely connected to the ethical problems implicit in such an approach. The sophists' practice of charging fees for their instruction seemed appropriate to the message they conveyed. They instructed their pupils in the means of circumventing *logos* by the manipulation of verbal signs, so it was only to be expected that their motive for teaching should be the desire for financial recompence.

Unlike Aristophanes, Plato does not class Socrates among the sophists. On the contrary, Socrates' philosophy develops as a reaction against the sophists' commodification of rhetoric. This is perhaps most obvious in his encounter with Protagoras, who W. K. C. Guthrie calls the 'earliest and greatest of the Sophists.'[33] Plato's *Protagoras* opens in the early hours of an Athenian morning, as the excited Hippocrates awakens Socrates with the news that the famous sophist Protagoras has arrived in town. The sage attempts to calm the youth by gently asking whether, since he charges fees for his instruction 'the sophist is really a sort of merchant or dealer in provisions on which a soul is nourished?' (313c). Socrates points out that the *telos* of Protagoras' teaching is not truth but money. He is not, therefore, really a philosopher at all. He is essentially a merchant and, by definition, merchants are not sources of knowledge: philosophers are. In fact the sophists were like day-laborers, whose rank was barely distinguishable from slavery. As a pragmatic art—one whose *telos* lay outside itself—sophistry was for Plato a *banausic*, or servile occupation. In contrast, philosophy as the disinterested pursuit of truth was an end-in-itself, and therefore reserved for virtuous, free men who acknowledge no external constraint on their thought or behavior.

Socrates never tires of linking the sophists to the *agora*. In the *Hippias Minor* he sarcastically recalls hearing the eponymous thinker 'recounting your great and enviable wisdom in the market-place at the tables of the moneychangers' (368b). In the *Hippias Major* he responds to the sophist's boasts of financial success with the full force of his irony:

> ... the earlier sophists of the school of Anaxagoras must have been very ignorant to judge from what is said, according to your view; for they say that what happened to Anaxagoras was the opposite of what happens to you; for though much money was left him, he neglected it and lost it all so senseless was his wisdom. And they tell similar tales about others among the ancients. So this seems to me fine testimony that you adduce for the wisdom of the men of today as compared with the earlier men, and many people agree with me that the wise man must be wise for himself especially; and the test of this is, who makes the most money. (283a–283b)

Socrates' irony is merciless on this subject. He strains every mental muscle to show that the sophists' commodification of their teaching has corrupted their thought. Hippias' mercenary attitude leads him to identify gold as the essence of beauty, on the grounds that 'even what before appears ugly will appear beautiful when adorned with gold' (290a). The mistaking of apparent for actual gold is Aristotle's first example of a fallacy in *Sophistical Refutations*, which notes that of objects 'some are really silver and others gold, while others are not and merely seem to be such to our sense' (1.1). In Plato, Hippias' identification of money as the good is co-terminus with his identification of gold as the beautiful, and behind both errors there lurks the more general identification of 'adornment' with essence, appearance with reality. In 'The Sophist' the Eleatic Stranger bluntly describes the sophists as 'merchants in the goods of the soul,' who buy up the knowledge of virtue wholesale and sell it retail:

> ... so this trader in virtue again turns out to be our friend the Sophist, whose art may now be traced from the art of acquisition through exchange, trade, merchandise, to a merchandise of the soul which is concerned with speech and the knowledge of virtue. (224d)

Plato invariably construes commodification as corruption. He is convinced that the sophists' logic must be impaired, because in order to market it they are forced to take the vagaries of public opinion into account, rather than dedicate themselves to the disinterested pursuit of truth. Their commitment to performative rhetoric is the direct result of commodification, for the customer will naturally expect tangible benefits in return for his money, and this consolidates Plato's criticism of autonomous representation in general. In 'The Sophist' the eponymous thinkers are said to practice the 'image-making art.' This 'art' is described as an especially predatory species of commerce:

> ...a branch of the appropriative, acquisitive family, which hunts animals, living, land-tame animals; which hunts man, privately, for hire, taking money in exchange, having the semblance of education; and this is termed Sophistry, and is a hunt after young men of wealth and rank. (223b)

Since the main purpose of his art is to make money, the Sophist is a merchant, not a philosopher. For him wisdom is merely the 'merchandise of the soul' in which he trades, and that fact ineluctably determines the content of that wisdom. Commodification forces the sophists to prioritize image over reality. As the Eleatic Stranger demands: 'Of this merchandise of the soul, may not one part be fairly termed the art of display?' (224b). Any retailer must make his goods as attractive as possible, and the Sophist sells the ability to put symbols to practical effect in the pursuit of economic self-interest. This distorts his ontology as well as his ethics. When questioned, we are told, the Sophist will deny the distinction between reality and images altogether:

... if we say to him that he professes an art of making appearances, he will grapple with us and retort our argument upon ourselves; and when we call him an image-maker he will say, 'Pray what do you mean at all by an image?' (239c–239d)

The Sophist does not recognize images. An image requires a referent, and the Sophist denies the very distinction between image and referent. Like *The Sophist*, the *Protagoras* also likens sophistry to trade, working on the assumption that commodification inevitably entails falsehood. For Socrates as for Jesus, it is impossible to serve both God and Mammon:

... we must take care, my friend, that the Sophist does not deceive us when he praises what he sells, like the dealers wholesale or retail who sell the food of the body; for they praise indiscriminately all their goods, without knowing what are really beneficial or hurtful: neither do their customers know, with the exception of any trainer or physician who may happen to buy of them. In like manner those who carry about the wares of knowledge, and make the round of the cities, and sell or retail them to any customer who is in want of them, praise them all alike; though I should not wonder, O my friend, if many of them were really ignorant of their effect upon the soul; and their customers equally ignorant, unless he who buys of them happens to be a physician of the soul. (313c–313e)

The Stranger finally identifies the Sophist as 'a magician and imitator of true being' to be 'placed in the class of magicians and mimics' (235a). Aristotle follows Plato closely in the *Sophistical Refutations*, where he too defines sophistry as the imposition of false images on reality in the service of commodification: 'The sophistic art appears to be wisdom, without being it, and the sophist is one who makes money from what appears to be, but is not, wisdom' (165a21). Such charges are corroborated by Isocrates' *Against the Sophists* (393): 'They have no concern for the truth but think that their art consists of attracting as many students as possible by the smallness of their fees and the grandness of their instruction, and of being able to earn something from them' (9).

The very existence of professional rhetoricians presupposes a performative view of language, in which the salient consideration is what words can do rather than their correspondence to truth. According to Socrates the true philosopher does not lower himself to dispute with the Sophist, but pursues him as he would a criminal, in order to expose his fraudulence before the tribunal of reason. The philosopher intends, 'if the Sophist does not run away from us, to seize him according to orders and deliver him over to reason, who is the lord of the hunt, and proclaim the capture of him' (235b). Plato goes to great lengths to establish that the 'images' peddled by the Sophist are not some alternative to reality, nor even a relativist challenge to the distinction between image and reality. They are not, in other words, what the postmodernist philosophers of our own day call 'hyper-real.' They are simply unreal:

> *Theaetetus*: How, Stranger, can I describe an image except as something fashioned in the likeness of the true?
> *Stranger*: And do you mean this something to be some other true thing, or what do you mean?
> *Theaetetus*: Certainly not another true thing, but only a resemblance.
> *Stranger*: And you mean by true that which really is?
> *Theaetetus*: Yes.
> *Stranger*: And the not true is that which is the opposite of the true?
> *Theaetetus*: Exactly.
> *Stranger*: A resemblance, then, is not really real, if, as you say, not true?
> *Theaetetus*: Nay, but it is in a certain sense.
> *Stranger*: You mean to say, not in a true sense?
> *Theaetetus*: Yes; it is in reality only an image.
> *Stranger*: Then what we call an image is in reality really unreal.
> *Theaetetus*: In what a strange complication of being and not-being we are involved!
> *Stranger*: Strange! I should think so. See how, by his reciprocation of opposites, the many-headed Sophist has compelled us, quite against our will, to admit the existence of not-being. (240a–240c)

Plato conceives of sophistry as unnatural magic, or what Christianity would term Satanic sorcery. The sophists make Nothingness into Being, and Being into Nothingness. They manipulate verbal images to make the real seem unreal, and to make the unreal appear real. Plato conceives of the sophists' undermining of *logos* as both irrational and unethical, but he emphasizes the former. Monotheistic theology would reverse that emphasis, establishing a moralistic opposition to sophistry that lasted until the twentieth century. As we have seen, the polytheistic, Hellenic tradition did not lack a philosophical ethics of representation, but its approach to images was first expressed in mythology, and it focused sharply on the beguiling figure of Helen of Troy.

3.5   BLAMING HELEN

Plato's portrayal of sophistry is certainly biased, but the surviving works of known sophists lend credibility to his depiction of their thought. For example, Gorgias's *Encomium of Helen* uses Helen of Troy to represent the magical, coercive power of signs.[34] Gorgias absolves Helen of blame for the Trojan War, on the grounds that, although not physically abducted, she was nonetheless compelled to elope with Paris by the force of his seductive rhetoric:

> ... persuasion by speech is equivalent to abduction by force, as she was compelled to agree to what was said, and consent to what was done. It was therefore the persuader, not Helen, who did wrong and should be blamed.[35]

Noting that 'a speech can sway and persuade a crowd, by the skill of its composition, not by the truth of its statements,' Gorgias depicts rhetoric as a species of sorcery, which achieves its coercive effects by the manipulation of verbal signs. Like a drug, rhetoric by-passes reason and usurps the will, thus negating criminal responsibility.[36] Its influence on the behavior of the audience is involuntary. Rhetoric alienates volition, forcing the addressee to act as the rhetor desires:

> The power of speech over the constitution of the soul can be compared with the effect of drugs on the state of the body: just as drugs by driving out different humors from the body can put an end either to the disease or to life, so with speech: different words can induce grief, pleasure or fear; or again, by means of a harmful kind of persuasion, words can drug and bewitch the soul. (133)

Socrates makes the same point in the *Republic*, declaring that '[r]hetoric is the art of 'leading the soul by means of speech' (261a8). His difference from Gorgias, and from the sophists generally, does not lie in acknowledging language's performative power, but in his ethical evaluation of it. In Plato's *Gorgias*, the title character boosts the efficacy of rhetoric in the terms of a salesman:

> What is there greater than the word which persuades the judges in the courts, or the senators in the council, or the citizens in the assembly, or at any other political meeting? If you have the power of uttering this word,

you will have the physician your slave, and the trainer your slave, and the money-maker of whom you talk will be found to gather treasures, not for himself, but for you who are able to speak and to persuade the multitude. (452e)

For Socrates, the power of the rhetorician is tyrannical, illegitimate and unnatural, no matter how effective it may be in practice. He insultingly compares rhetoric to 'cookery,' the art of making food taste good regardless of its nutritional value. If sensual pleasure were the sole criterion of quality, if 'the soul did not discern and discriminate between cookery and medicine, but the body was made the judge of them' (465c), then cookery would certainly be judged superior to nutrition. The same applies to the choice between rhetoric and logic for, as Socrates explains, 'rhetoric... is, in relation to the soul, what cookery is to the body' (465d). For Socrates, rhetoric is finally a kind of sensuality, and he claims that reason offers the only possible protection against its seductive appeal.

Plato's dialogues portray the influence of money as homologous to the effects of rhetoric. However, there is an important difference between the relation Plato posits between rhetoric and money and the connection he sees between rhetoric and cookery—and also a difference from the comparison Gorgias makes between rhetoric and drugs. The latter two are relations of analogy: drugs and cookery are to the body what rhetoric is to the soul. On that much Plato and Gorgias agree. Plato goes further than Gorgias, however, in suggesting that money and language are not analogous but homologous: they are different manifestations of the same essential thing. They are both autonomous systems of signs, and for Plato the main practical and ethical danger inherent in such systems is that the signs may be mistaken for their referents. Such an error would eschew reason in favor of representation, subordinate logic to rhetoric, and elevate the body above the soul. It would render representation performative, and the effacement of reason by performative representation leads straight to political tyranny.

The Republic compares tyranny to love and to drunkenness, on the grounds that all three are irrational challenges to reason's natural mastery in the *psyche*. Plato's ethics of representation receives its fullest exposition in book ten. Having demonstrated that the phenomena of sense-perception are representations of ideal concepts, Socrates points out that an artist painting a picture of a bed is therefore making a representation of a representation. As in the Hebrew Decalogue, man-made images stand at the farthest possible distance from *logos*. The painter is 'a creator of appearances,' and 'what he creates is untrue.' Yet the bed-maker does not make 'the essence of the bed' either, for that essence is an idea:

> *Socrates*: Which is the art of painting designed to be –an imitation of things as they are, or as they appear –of appearance or of reality?
> *Glaucon*: Of appearance.
> *Socrates*: Then the imitator, I said, is a long way off the truth, and can do all things because he lightly touches on a small part of them, and that part an image. (598b)

The 'imitator' possesses a quasi-magical power, he can 'do all things,' because he is exclusively concerned with images and thus free from obligation to *logos*. He possesses 'poetic license.' Like Solon, Plato fears the spread of performative signs beyond the aesthetic sphere. Whether he criticizes sophistry, rhetoric, or poetry, his strictures apply to efficacious representation in general. The performative sign is antipathetic toward the soul, because it eludes the faculty of reason, which is the soul's highest element. The *Republic* leaves no doubt about the intimate connection between the role played by signifying systems and the health of the soul. Socrates declares that the poet 'sets up in each individual soul a vicious constitution by fashioning phantoms far removed from reality' (605c). The gods of Olympus are both fictitious and irrational. Plato rejects them in favor of *logos*, and therefore he banishes 'poets' from his utopia. But poetry is not most dangerous kind of performative representation for Plato. That role is reserved for money.

In Platonic philosophy, the soul is the essence of which the body is the appearance. In that sense, the body represents the soul, and to advance the interests of the body over those of the soul is to prioritize representation over reality. In the *Republic*, the orientation of the soul toward fleshly desires is equated with avarice, which is the lust for the means by which those desires can be indulged. Money is the mediator through which the lower faculties of the soul are satisfied, and the ethical disorientation of the soul is therefore equated with the pursuit of money (St. Paul follows Plato on this issue at 1 Timothy 6:10). In the *Phaedo* money is the means by which the desires of the body are satisfied, and thus also the means by which we are distracted from our proper end:

> ... the body is a source of endless trouble to us by reason of the mere requirement of food; and also is liable to diseases which overtake and

impede us in the search after truth: and by filling us so full of loves, and lusts, and fears, and fancies, and idols, and every sort of folly, prevents our ever having, as people say, so much as a thought. For whence come wars, and fightings, and factions? Whence but from the body and the lusts of the body? For wars are occasioned by the love of money, and money has to be acquired for the sake and in the service of the body; and in consequence of all these things the time which ought to be given to philosophy is lost. (66b–66d)

The *Republic* defines the proper end of the soul as 'virtue,' and the pursuit of money as virtue's opposite: 'when riches and virtue are placed together in the scales of the balance, the one always rises as the other falls' (550e). Socrates expands on this theory in his explanation of the tripartite soul. He identifies the rational element as the highest, and he divides the lower elements into two. He mentions the principle of 'passion,' and also a yet lower principle that 'is denoted by the general term appetitive, from the extraordinary strength and vehemence of the desires of eating and drinking and the other sensual appetites which are the main elements of it; also money-loving, because such desires are generally satisfied by the help of money' (580e). In fact, Socrates effectively says that this appetitive part of the soul *is* the desire for money: 'If we were to say that the loves and pleasures of this third part were concerned with gain, we should then be able to fall back on a single notion; and might truly and intelligibly describe this part of the soul as loving gain or money' (581a). The self-alienation of the soul, the activity whereby it violates its own nature, is effectively equated with the drive to accumulate financial value.

In sum, Plato conceives of sophistry as the *commercialization* of philosophy. The characteristics he ascribes to the sophists remain the definitive characteristics of false consciousness in postmodernity. Sophistry's original sin is its elevation of exchange value above use-value. Its *telos*, the prime purpose of its existence, is the making of money rather than the pursuit of wisdom. That single, primal inversion produces the systematic transvaluation of values, the collapse of axiomatic polarities that defines the postmodern condition. According to Plato, sophistry imposes appearance upon essence, accident upon substance, symbol upon reality, image upon truth, letter upon spirit, body upon soul, idol upon deity, custom upon nature, slavery upon liberty, force upon freedom, magic upon manufacture, appetite upon reason, sign upon referent, signifier upon signified, matter upon form, object upon subject, rhetoric upon logic, and sense-perception upon conceptualization. In place of these mutually definitive binary oppositions, which depend for their existence on their reference to an ultimate, ulterior *logos*, sophistry introduces into philosophy the pragmatic power of the performative sign. It has yet to relinquish its position.

NOTES

1. Plutarch, 'Life of Solon,' from *Plutarch's Lives*, trans. Bernadotte Perrin (Loeb Classics, 1914), 489. See the discussion of this incident in Jonas Barish, *The Antitheatrical Prejudice* (U of California P, 1981).
2. https://www.etymonline.com/word/hypocrisy, retrieved April 1, 2020.
3. Marc Shell, 'The Ring of Gyges,' *Mississippi Review* 17.1/2 (1989), 21–84.
4. Marc Shell, 'Portia's Portrait: Representation as Exchange,' *Common Knowledge* 7.1 (Spring 1998), 94–144.
5. Herodotus, *History of the Greeks and the Persians*, vol. I, trans. G.C. Macaulay (Callender Press, 2013), 94.
6. Glyn Davies, *A History of Money*, 4th edition revised by Duncan Connors (U of Wales P, 2016).
7. Richard Seaford, *Money and the Early Greek Mind: Homer, Philosophy, Tragedy* (Cambridge UP, 2004), 4.
8. Duncan Connors' Introduction to Davies (2016) points out that the cowrie shells used as currency in ancient India and China also lacked any intrinsic value.
9. Frederic Jameson, *Allegory and Ideology* (New York: Verso, 2019), 48.
10. Hesiod, *Theogony* (969–974), trans. Hugh G. Evelyn-White, in *The Homeric Hymns and Homerica* (London: William Heinemann, 1920), 151.
11. Aristophanes, *Plutus* (Internet Classics Archive), retrieved April 1, 2020: http://classics.mit.edu/Aristophanes/plutus.html. Subsequent references are to this edition.
12. Robert L. Tordoff, 'Coins, Money and Exchange in Aristophanes' "Wealth",' *Transactions of the American Philological Association (1974–2014)* 142.2 (Autumn 2012), 257–293, 264. Ephraim David cites the influx of financial subsidies from Persia during the Peloponnesian and Corinthian Wars as another factor in the financialization of the Greek mind in 'The Influx of Money into Sparta,' *Scripta Classica Israelica* 5 (1979/80), 30–45.
13. Alan Baily, '*Ousia Aphanes*: Justice and the Market in Plato's *Republic*, I and II,' *Expositions* 7.2 (2013), 1–27.

14. Aristophanes, *Frogs* (Internet Classics Archive), retrieved April 1, 2020: http://classics.mit.edu/Aristophanes/frogs.html. Subsequent references are to this edition.
15. David Konstan and Matthew Dillon, 'The Ideology of Aristophanes' Wealth,' *The American Journal of Philology* 102.4 (Winter 1981), 371–394, 390.
16. As Walter Sombart reminds us, this is true *a forteriori* in usury: 'In money-lending all conception of quality vanishes and only the quantitative aspect remains.' *The Jews and Modern Capitalism* (Transaction Books, 1982), 189.
17. Presumably 'Montaigne.'
18. See Konstan and Dillon, 372.
19. Aristotle, *Nicomachean Ethics*, trans. J.A.K. Thomson, rev. H. Tredenick (London, 1976), 184.
20. Karl Marx, *Capital: A Critique of Political Economy*, vol. I, trans. Samuel Moore and Edward Aveling (Champaign, IL, 2018), 40.
21. J.K. Dover, *Greek Popular Morality in the Time of Plato and Aristotle* (U of California P, 1974), 38. See also M.I. Finley, 'Was Greek Civilization Based on Slave Labour?' *Historia* 8 (1959), 145–164.
22. Lucian of Samosata, *Timon the Misanthrope*, trans. H.W. Fowler and F.G. Fowler in *Complete Works of Lucian* (Oxford: Clarendon P, 1905), 41.
23. Retrieved from the Internet Classics Archive April 1, 2020: http://classics.mit.edu/Plato/symposium.html. Subsequent references to Plato are to this Archive, which uses the translation by Benjamin Jowett.
24. See Anthony Hooper, 'The Greatest Hope of All: Aristophanes on Human Nature in Plato's *Symposium*,' *Classical Quarterly* 63.2 (2013), 567–579, 567.
25. Aristophanes, *Clouds* (Internet Classics Archive), retrieved April 1, 2020: http://classics.mit.edu/Aristophanes/clouds.html. Subsequent references are to this edition.
26. See Charles T. Murphy, 'Aristophanes and the Art of Rhetoric,' *Harvard Studies in Classical Philology* 49 (1938), 69–113.
27. Aristophanes, *Archanians*, 676. Retrieved April 1, 2020: http://www.perseus.tufts.edu/hopper/text?doc=Perseus%3Atext%3A1999.01.0240%3Acard%3D628. Subsequent references are to this edition.
28. For a salutary challenge to the orthodox view of the sophists as moral relativists see Richard Bett, 'The Sophists and Relativism,' *Phronesis* 34.2 (1989), 139–169.
29. Marc Shell, *Money, Language and Thought* (Johns Hopkins UP, 1982), 131.
30. Alfred Sohn-Rethal, *Intellectual and Manual Labor: A Critique of Epistemology* trans. Martin Sohn-Rethal (Humanities Press, 1978), 60.
31. G.B. Kerferd, *The Sophistic Movement* (Cambridge UP, 1981), 25.

32. See James Fredel, 'Why Shouldn't the Sophists Charge Fees?' *Rhetoric Society Quarterly* 38.2 (Spring 2008), 148–170, 152.
33. W.K.C. Guthrie, *The Sophists* (Cambridge UP, 1971), 4. See David L. Blank, 'Socrates Versus Sophists on Payment for Teaching,' *Classical Antiquity* 4.1 (April 1985), 1–49.
34. See Matthew Gumpert, *Grafting Helen: The Abduction of the Classical Past* (U of Wisconsin P, 2001).
35. Georgias of Leontini *Encomium of Helen*, in *Ancilla to the Pre-Socratic Philosophers*, ed. Kathleen Foreman (Harvard UP, 1948). 132.
36. On the Renaissance theater's interest in drugs as a way of bypassing reason, see Tanya Pollard, *Drugs and Theater in Early Modern England* (Oxford UP, 2005). Pollard argues that rhetorical discourse was often accused of distorting the rational faculties in a manner akin to narcotics, and that the theater itself was often figured as a kind of intoxicant.

CHAPTER 4

Witchcraft and Representation in Early Modern England

4.1 The Logocentric Conception of Magic

A specter haunts Ben Jonson's microcosmic portrayal of the embryonic English marketplace in *Bartholomew Fair* (1614). Its name is Rabbi Zeal-of-the-land Busy, and he stalks through the fair, denouncing its harboring of commercial exchange, sexual license, and liturgical idolatry. He makes no distinction between these forms of fetishism, and Jonson provides him with a surprisingly coherent case against the autonomy of representation in general. He denounces one stall-holder in terms that would fit them all:

> Peace, with thy Apocryphall wares, thou prophane Publican: thy Bells, thy Dragons, and thy Tobie's Dogges. Thy Hobby-horse is an Idoll, a very Idoll, a feirce and rancke Idoll: And thou, the Nabuchadnezzar, the proud Nabuchadnezzar of the Faire, that set'st it up, for children to fall downe to, and worship. (3.6.48–52)

Within a generation of *Bartholomew Fair*'s composition, Busy's ideological heirs would seize state power in the English Revolution, and the character's comic status should not blind us to the impressive heritage of his ideas. A combination of rationalist philosophy and monotheistic theology forged the iconoclastic tradition on which Busy draws in his thoroughgoing critique of performative representation. This chapter will show how conflict over the ethics of the efficacious sign was manifested,

© The Author(s) 2020
D. Hawkes, *The Reign of Anti-logos*, Palgrave
Insights into Apocalypse Economics,
https://doi.org/10.1007/978-3-030-55940-3_4

in early modern England, in a protracted struggle over the moral and legal status of magic.

Plato's ethical critique of the efficacious sign, which we discussed in previous chapters, was deepened and extended by Aristotle. Their combined influence established a tradition of moral semantics that perdured throughout the Christian era. Aristotle adumbrates his semiotic theory in *On Interpretation*: 'Spoken words are the symbols of mental experience and written words are the symbols of spoken words' (16a2–16a4). Aristotle's first point here is that language does not construct but represents our subjectivity. The original 'mental experience' is prelinguistic. Aristotle assumes the existence of a purely ideal *psyche*, whose intentions and experiences are expressed in (but not constituted by) language. He then makes a further distinction between speech and writing, claiming that the latter symbolizes the former, and that it is therefore at a further remove from the prelinguistic subject.

For Aristotle, language is to subjective experience as writing is to speech. Language refers to subjective experience, and writing refers to speech. In both cases, the referent is regarded as prior to, and thus more authentic than the sign. Today, the binary opposition between sign and referent has become the main target of postmodernism's deconstructive energies, for the belief that internal mental experience is language's origin, and as such more real than the signs that represent it, is the fundamental a priori of Western metaphysics. Its implications are ethical and political as well as ontological. All systems of representation contain elements of performativity. But the bolder claim that language is essentially, fundamentally performative—that our experience is not only mediated through but entirely determined by the media of representation—is a direct challenge to the power and authority of *logos*. The rise to power of the performative sign heralds the reign of *anti-logos*.

The practical power of signs involves a challenge to 'binary' thinking in general. Postmodernists often argue that logical oppositions depend upon the subordination of one element of the polarity to the other, and that there is therefore something oppressive about dialectical logic per se. It is often viewed as politically progressive to deconstruct binaries, simply because they are binaries. This political and philosophical hostility to binary logic can be traced back to Saussure's re-discovery of language's constitutive powers in the early twentieth century. As we saw earlier, Saussure's structuralism re-located the concept within the sign. The opposition between word and idea was thus deconstructed, and in the 1960s and '70s post-structuralists such as Derrida extended Saussure's assimilation of ideas to words into a generalized semiotic determinism that collapsed representation into reality. Once the distinction between representation and reality has been erased, other polarities soon follow. The binary opposition between nature (*phusis*) and custom (*nomos*) is fundamental to Greek philosophy, and the implications of subverting it are especially profound. Once *phusis* is indistinguishable from *nomos*, for instance, gender will be regarded as a customary practice rather than a natural condition. Sex will no longer necessarily be associated with reproduction: reproduction will be largely confined to the 'economy.' Natural reproduction, that is to say, will be replaced by unnatural reproduction.

The early Christian Church Fathers were in no doubt about the ethical dangers of the performative sign. Tertullian's second-century tracts *On Idolatry* and *On Spectacles* diagnose a fetishistic fixation on the phenomena of sense-perception as the greatest obstacle to the knowledge of *logos*. To fetishize sense-perception is to take appearance for reality, and to idolize signs at the expense of their referents. St. Augustine gives a similar caution in *Of Christian Doctrine*'s discussion of signs: 'I lay down this direction, not to attend to what they are in themselves, but to the fact that they are signs, that is, to what they signify.'[1] Augustine warns here against the reification of representation, against taking signs for things. He insists that signs are not things but representations of things. Since all human experience is mediated through signs, however, it is very easy—it is indeed natural to the postlapsarian *psyche*—to make the error of mistaking signs for things. It takes a considerable effort of continuous reflection to *interpret* sense-perception, to maintain the awareness that appearances are not reality—to live in the knowledge that sense-perception depends upon anterior, a priori conditions of possibility, which are located in a prelinguistic subject more authentic, more real, and more permanent than the symbolic forms by which it communicates its ideas.

Not all signs originate in human consciousness, however. Augustine goes on to distinguish between signs on the basis of *phusis* and *nomos*. He differentiates 'natural' signs (such as smoke indicating fire or lactation indicating that a birth has taken place) from 'conventional' signs. The significance of 'natural' signs is inherent in their nature. The significance of 'conventional' signs, by contrast, is customary. The meaning of words, pictures—indeed the very concept of 'meaning' itself—only exists for human beings. 'In itself,' as Kant would put it, the world signifies nothing. It is a tale told by an idiot. For logocentric thought on the other hand—that is to say, in monotheist religion and rationalist philosophy–the human experience is imbued with significance by *logos*.

Like Aristotle, Augustine sees 'conventional' signs as emanating from a pre-verbal subject that purposefully translates its intentions into symbolic form. Unlike Aristotle, however, Augustine also assumes a comparable subject *to* whom conventional signs are addressed. In order to qualify as 'conventional,' then, a sign must both be addressed *from* somebody and *to* somebody. Augustine works hard to maintain a link between verbal representation and conscious subjective intention. He seems aware of the potential threat posed by independent performativity, and he goes out of his way to deny the autonomy of conventional signs. He does this in two ways: conventional signs both originate and terminate in the mind:

> Conventional signs... are those which living beings mutually exchange for the purpose of showing, as well as they can, the feelings of their minds, or their perceptions, or their thoughts. Nor is there any reason for giving a sign except the desire of drawing forth and conveying into another's mind what the giver of the sign has in his own mind. (28)

Augustine follows closely in Aristotle's logical footsteps. He posits language as communication between two prelinguistic, self-conscious subjects. He distinguishes between spoken and written signs and, he conceives of writing as the sign of speech. Both Aristotle and Augustine see writing as the sign of a sign. But Augustine also introduces an additional, temporal dimension to the distinction. Writing is different from speech because it can be repeated in the future, in the absence of either the speaker or the original recipient. Writing was invented 'because words pass away as soon as they strike upon the air, and last no longer than their sound, men have by means of letters formed signs of words' (29). Writing, to use the deconstructionist term, is 'iterable,' and its meaning therefore cannot be limited to the intention of either the author or the audience. To the logocentric thinkers of the Aristotelian and Christian traditions, this made writing seem threateningly disruptive, but for that very reason writing (*ecriture*) appears attractively liberating to postmodernists. The traditional positions that writing expresses a prelinguistic intention, that writing is the sign of speech, and that language represents the mental experience of a prelinguistic *psyche*, are theoretical anathema to anti-logocentric postmodernism.

As we shall see in the next chapter, medieval disputes about the ethics of representation tended to focus on the Sacraments. As early as the thirteenth century, radical polemicists declared that Sacramental signs could achieve nothing on their own, nor could they be rendered efficacious by the actions of the priest. They depend for their efficacy on an intelligent recipient. Any attempt to use signs to practical effect must involve an appeal to an agent, and in the case of the Sacraments, that agent was God. The nature of Sacramental representation became literally a burning issue in early modern Europe. Protestants and Catholics alike found it imperative to limit the sphere of efficacious signs to canonical liturgy, and any other attempt to put signs to effective use was denounced as 'magic.' Prosecutors began to ask which agent was being invoked by the '[l]ines, circles, signs, letters, and characters'[2] deployed by magicians. With whom was the magician communicating, or attempting to communicate, when he performed his rites and gestures? Augustine's logic led inexorably to the conclusion that ritual magic *ipso facto* constituted an appeal to demonic powers. Any effort to do things with signs constituted an implicit 'pact' with the devil, regardless of the magician's conscious intent. Aquinas attacks ceremonial sorcerers on these grounds in the *Summa contra gentiles*:

> … in the practice of their art they make use of certain significative words in order to produce certain definite effects. Now, words, in so far as they signify something, have no power except as derived from some intellect; either of the speaker, or of the person to whom they are spoken. From the intellect of the speaker, as when an intellect is of such great power that it can cause things by its mere thought, the voice serving to convey, as it were, this thought to the things that are to be produced. From the intellect of the person to whom the words are addressed, as when the hearer is induced to do some particular thing, through his intellect receiving the signification of those words. Now, it cannot be said that these significative words uttered by magicians derive efficacy from the intellect of the speaker.... man's intellect is invariably of such a disposition that its knowledge is caused by things, rather than that it is able by its mere thought to cause things.... It follows that these effects are accomplished by an intellect to whom the discourse of the person uttering these words is addressed.[3]

Who, asks Aquinas, actually performs the effects that seem to result from the magician's words and gestures? It cannot be the signs themselves, for signs possess no independently performative power. It cannot be the magician, for human beings cannot achieve objective effects by their words alone. Only God can do this, but God cannot be invoked with non-canonical spells, images or rituals. By a process of elimination, then, the agent who performs the magical effects can only be a spiritual power which operates independently of God—that is to say an evil, demonic spirit. This was the logic that sentenced thousands of men, women and children to death during the great European Witch Hunt of the sixteenth and seventeenth centuries.

It was not necessary to secure a conviction that the witch's magic should actually work. In 1645 a typical anonymous tract denounced the witch's intent 'to hurt or destroy any person in his or her body, although the same be not effected and done.'[4] A different tract from the same year draws the logical conclusion: 'people should inquire of no other spirit but of their God only. By which also it is evident, that all spirits that doe suffer themselves to be inquired at, are evill spirits, and therefore Devills.'[5] Whatever the magicians might claim to believe, all magic constitutes an implicit appeal to Satan or his subsidiary demons. For our purposes, the salient point is that the proof of Satan's involvement lay in the witch's use of allegedly efficacious signs—although few experts believed that they were truly efficacious. Aquinas did not even believe that the magicians sincerely credit the efficacy of their own signs. They may pretend to believe in them, he asserts, but only in an attempt to conceal the demonic nature of their arts:

> ... matter cannot, by definite figures, be disposed to receive a certain natural effect. Therefore magicians do not employ figures as dispositions. It remains, then, that they employ them only as signs, for there is no third solution. But we make signs only to other intelligent beings. Therefore the magic arts derive their efficacy from another intelligent being, to whom the magician's words are addressed. This is also proved by the very name of character which they apply to these figures: for a character is a sign. Whereby we are given to understand that they employ these figures merely as signs shown to some intellectual nature. (38)

Only the Creator is capable of altering creation by his Word alone. The divine *logos* is indeed performative, as witnessed by the Sacraments. Whereas *logos* creates substantial effects, however, magic cannot really do anything at all. Monotheism relegates magical efficacy to accidents, to appearances—and finally to mere illusion. With Satan's aid and God's permission, however, magic can alter *appearances* effectively enough to deceive the foolish or unwary, and therein lies its danger.

The influence of this logic is evident in medieval semantics. Jacopo Passavanti's, *The Mirror of True Penitence* (c.1350) observes that 'The devil cannot change one thing substantially into another, transforming the nature of things, or creating something out of nothing, which is proper only to God, although he can make things appear to change.'[6] Since it is prelinguistic and anterior to representation, the human *psyche* itself is inviolable by Satan, who works only through signs and appearances. As the witch-hunters asserted with prosecutorial zeal, Satan can enter the soul only when consciously invited to do so. In sharp contrast to *logos*, which inhabits *psyche* in the form of *nous*, Satan cannot communicate directly with the prelinguistic subject. All communication with him must pass through external media of representation. As Passavanti puts it: 'the devil cannot know the thoughts and will of the human heart except in such a way as can be perceived by act or sign, or by something else that manifests itself externally' (107). In his *Demonologie* (1597) King James VI of Scotland declares that Satan can only know people's secrets 'so being they bee once spoken, for the thought none knows but GOD.'[7] The interior *psyche* was a privileged realm, inaccessible to Satan, whose intelligence—although formidably superhuman—was limited to the sphere of externally perceptible signs. It was precisely that fact that made the perceptible growth in the power and influence of signs seem threatening, and in urgent need of violent repression. To the people of early modern England, the rise of the performative sign was co-terminus with a growth in the power of Satan.

4.2   The Criminalization of Magic

It was this line of reasoning that produced the 'witch hunts' of the sixteenth and seventeenth centuries. The practitioners of ritual magic might claim, and might even believe, that their spells and incantations were capable of altering reality through their own, autonomous power. But to thinkers in the Aristotelian tradition this was logically impossible, and in the Christian tradition it soon came to seem demonic. Reginald Scot's *Discoverie of Witchcraft* (1584) is typical of Protestant witch tracts in its portrayal of ritual magic as basically similar to Catholicism, since both kinds of superstition assume the efficacy of representation. Scot locates his work within a historical trajectory towards the gradual elimination of superstition. He pleads that unless his readers can suspend their prejudices:

I should no more prevaile herein, than if a hundred yeares since I should have intreated your predecessors to beleeve, that Robin goodfellowe, that great and ancient bulbegger, had beene but a cousening merchant, and no divell indeed. If I should go to a papist, and saie; I praie you beleeve my writings, wherein I will proove all popish charmes, conjurations, exorcismes, benedictions and cursses, not onelie to be ridiculous, and of none effect, but also to be impious and contrarie to Gods word: I should as hardlie therein win favour at their hands, as herein obteine credit at yours.[8]

Pagan superstition is thus classed as the same species of error as 'popery.' The equation of magic and popery was commonplace: King James likens the 'murmurings and mutterings of the conjurers' to 'a Papist priest, dispatching a hunting Masse' and compares the notion that Satan can take material form to 'the little transubstantiate god in the Papistes Masse' (40). Scot applauds the Protestant Reformation's attack on superstition, but worries that the recent rise of magic will reverse this progress:

... Robin goodfellowe ceaseth now to be much feared, and poperie is sufficientlie discovered. Nevertheles, witches charms, and conjurors cousenages are yet thought effectuall. Yea the Gentiles have espied the fraud of their cousening oracles, and our cold prophets and inchanters make us fooles still, to the shame of us all, but speciallie of papists, who conjure everie thing, and thereby bring to passe nothing. They saie to their candles; I conjure you to endure for ever: and yet they last not a pater noster while the longer. They conjure water to be wholesome both for bodie and soule: but the bodie (we see) is never the better for it, nor the soule anie whit reformed by it. And therefore I mervell, that when they see their owne conjurations confuted and brought to naught, or at the least void of effect, that they (of all other) will yet give such credit, countenance, and authoritie to the vaine cousenages of witches and conjurors; as though their charmes and conjurations could produce more apparent, certeine, and better effects than their owne. (74)

The 'charmes and conjurartions' used by witches are no more efficacious that the idols of popery, and people whose observance has moved beyond popery should scorn to believe in magic: 'trulie it is manifold idolatrie, to aske that of a creature, which none can give but the Creator. The papist hath some colour of scripture to mainteine his idoll of bread, but no Jesuiticall distinction can cover the witchmongers idolatrie in this behalf' (42). However, the iconoclastic case against performative representation cannot account, on its own, for the prolonged outbreak of witch-hunting in early modern Europe. Some historians connect the popular fear of magic to the rapid monetization of the European economy, which mysteriously ceded control over events to abstract, impalpable, yet strangely powerful symbolic forces. The introduction of a universal financial mediator circumvented ancient economic taboos, leveling kinship relations, and abolishing traditional hierarchies based on blood, age, and wisdom. Monetization permitted previously marginalized groups to acquire wealth and influence by non-traditional, means that were not easily assimilated into established moral schema.

Many effects of monetization were traumatic. They induced a popular reaction against the power of performative representation that frequently expressed itself in an emotional, even violent manner. Iconoclasts and iconodules battled each other with pen and sword for more than a millennium of Christian history. From our postmodern perspective, however, their worldviews appear basically similar at a number of levels. Most obviously, both sides in this ferocious struggle agreed that liturgical images were extremely powerful, potentially dangerous forces, the proper deployment of which was a matter of the highest possible priority, not just for religious discipline but for any secular government. The enemies of images believed in their power more firmly than their worshippers. In seventeenth-century England the iconoclast 'puritans' were more convinced of the objective influence exerted by icons than the Anglican iconodules. In their rage against liturgical icons, mobs often broke into churches to physically attack their enemies of wood and stone. In one London church a man shot arrows at an image of St. Margaret, 'challenging it to defend itself and punish him if it were able.'[9]

At the same time as Reformation iconoclasm spread throughout Europe, and also as usury was being incrementally legitimized, witch-hunters began to persecute people they suspected of practicing ritual magic. Although they occupied what the twenty-first century regards as different areas of experience, the campaigns against idolatry, usury and witchcraft were all directed against the burgeoning power of the performative sign. The people of early modern England associated witchcraft with every kind of social marginality. A few rich and powerful men were executed as 'sorcerers' in Scotland and on the continent, but in England the typical 'hedge-witch' was poor, elderly, and female. Their defenders pointed out that the witches' magic was obviously not efficacious. If it were, they would surely use it to improve their wretched condition. Such arguments were usually unavailing because, in the scholastic tradition, prosecutors argued that witchcraft was a linguistic transgression:

what we might call a 'word crime.' Marion Gibson accurately describes it as 'a crime that consisted almost entirely of the use of words (threats, devil-pacts, curses, spells).'[10]

It was sometimes alleged that to deny the efficacy of witchcraft was to deny its existence. King James' *Demonologie* proclaims that 'one called SCOT an Englishman, is not ashamed in publike print to deny, that ther can be such a thing as Witch-craft: and so mainteines the old error of the Sadducees, in denying of spirits' (1). It is true that Scot's *Discoverie* is often skeptical about the efficacy of witchcraft, but that is beside the point. He is quite certain that witches exist. What troubles Scot are the means by which their magic is supposed to work. He denounces:

> the coosening witch, who will not sticke to take upon hir, by wordes to heale the lame (which was proper onelie to Christ; and to them whom he assisted with his divine power) yea, with hir familiar & charmes she will take upon hir to cure the blind: though in the tenth Joh. 10, 21. of S. *Johns* Gospell it be written, that the divell cannot open the eies of the blind. And they attaine such credit as I have heard (to my greefe) some of the ministerie affirme, that they have had in their parish at one instant, xvii. or xviii. witches: meaning such as could worke miracles supernaturallie. (3)

Here Scot admits that witches can sometimes heal the sick. The problem is that they do so using performative signs: 'wordes' and 'charmes.' James' *Demonologie* also distinguishes witches from legitimate 'Mediciners,' because they work by means of representation rather than by physical intervention. James condemns 'such kinde of Charmes as commonlie dafte wiues vses… by wordes, without applying anie thing, meete to the part offended, as Mediciners doe' 44). The King distinguishes 'dafte wiuues' from serious 'Mediciners' on the grounds that the former relied on solely verbal means to effect their cures. This was magic, and the crime of magic consisted in the mere attempt to make it work, for such an attempt revealed the witch's core assumption that 'wordes' and 'charmes' could be manipulated to performative ends. That belief in itself consti-tuted an objective 'pact' with *anti-logos*. On this James and Scot agree. The illusion that signs are performative is induced by Satan. As James writes:

> … it is no power inherent in the circles, or in the holiness of the names of God blasphemouslie vsed: nor in whatsoeuer rites or ceremonies at that time vsed, that either can raise any infernall spirit, or yet limitat him

perforce within or without these circles. For it is he onelie, the father of all lyes, who hauing first of all prescribed that forme of doing, feining himselfe to be commanded & restreined thereby.... (12)

The devil will pretend to be compelled by the magician's signs, but only in order to entrap him, and the magician's belief in the efficacy of his signs proved that he had been so entrapped. James and Scot concur that the belief that magical signs can achieve objective effects constitutes a pact with the devil. Nor was it any excuse to claim, as 'white' witches did, that their magic was for medicinal purposes. That only aggravated the offence for, as William Perkins explained in 1608, it could make witchcraft seem appealing. Perkins admits that there are 'good' witches as well as 'bad,' but he explains:

> Now howsoever both these be evil, yet of the two the more horrible and detestable monster is the good witch; for look in what place soever there be bad witches that hurt only, there also the Devil hath his good ones, which are better known than the bad, being commonly called wisemen or wisewomen.... For let a man's child, friend or cattle be taken with some sore sickness or strangely tormented with some rare and unknown disease, the first thing he doth is to bethink himself and inquire after some wiseman or wisewoman....The witch, then being certified of the disease, prescribeth either charms of words to be used over him or other such counterfeit means wherein there is no virtue, being nothing else but the Devil's sacraments to cause him to do the cure if it come by witchcraft. Well, the means are received, applied, and used; the sick party accordingly recovereth; and the conclusion of all is the usual acclamation: Oh happy is the day that ever I met with such a man or woman to help me![11]

Yet Perkins insists that the foolish celebrants have paid a terrible price for their friend's recovery. They are now convinced of the performative power of 'charms of words.' They have seen with their own eyes that the witch's 'conterfeit means wherein there is no virtue' apparently can work miracles—they have taken signs for wonders—and this has quite literally destroyed their souls. The risk to the uneducated is made apparent in Edward Poeton's *The Winnowing of White Witchcraft* (c.1630), in which two learned counselors attempt to convince a simple country squire that traditional healers are in league with the devil. The squire's stolid intransigence ('Mee thinks still, that zuch vokes as doo no harme, shud not bee witches')[12] suggests that this was a difficult matter, which would not have been undertaken unless its importance seemed clear.

The concern of the educated was that, if secular authority is foolish enough to allow them licence, 'white' witches will use their healing powers to spread their subtle destruction of human souls. As John Gaule reminded his readers in 1646: 'the accounted Good Witch, is indeed the worse and more wicked of the two. For as Satan, being a Fiend of darknes, is then worst when hee transformes himselfe into an Angel of Light: so likewise are his Ministers.'[13] Thus the essence of the case against magic was that performative representation has its source in *anti-logos*. 'Skeptics' like Reginald Scot and Johannes Hartlieb dismissed the witches' claims to possess superhuman powers, attributing such delusions to Satan's invasion of the *psyche*. Scot begins his *Discoverie of Withcraft* by insisting that he disputes only the efficacy of 'images':

> ... truelie I denie not that there are witches or images: but I detest the idolatrous opinions conceived of them; referring that to Gods worke and ordinance, which they impute to the power and malice of witches; and attributing that honour to God, which they ascribe to idols. (1)

The fact that many people believed in the power of images revealed Satan's ability to deceive by 'conjuring,' or manifest defiance of the laws of nature. Few doubted that *anti-logos* was active in the world, or that it worked through the medium of autonomous representation, which Perkins calls 'the Devil's sacraments.' Johannes Hartlieb's *Book of All Forbidden Arts* describes popular credulity as a:

> ... great foolishness, when people think that witches with magical potions make a horse which enters their houses, and if they wish they sit upon him and ride many miles in a very short time.... This horse is in reality the devil.[14]

The devil, that is to say, was the true source of the hallucinations, which could only be experienced by one who had made a pact with him. That pact might be sub-conscious and implicit, as in Shakespeare's *Macbeth* (1606), where the witches' influence on the hero's mind is conveyed through his susceptibility to hallucination. This was the predominant intellectual position in early modern Europe. The incredible powers claimed by, and popularly attributed to, witches were dismissed by the learned as mere illusions. Satan was no illusion, however, and his real power manifested itself by making the witch's illusory power appear to be real. King James concedes that the devil controls the world of the senses, which he distinguishes from natural, divine creation:

And yet are all these thinges but deluding of the senses, and no waies true in substance, as were the false miracles wrought by King Pharaoes Magicians, for counterfeiting Moyses: For that is the difference betuixt Gods myracles and the Deuils, God is a creator, what he makes appeare in miracle, it is so in effect. As Moyses rod being casten downe, was no doubt turned in a natural Serpent: where as the Deuill (as Gods Ape) counterfetting that by his Magicians, maid their wandes to appeare so, onelie to mennes outward senses. (14)

In the Platonic tradition, James insists that sense-perception is not real. To believe in the ontological reality of sense-perception is to leave oneself open to Satan's illusions. This position bespeaks a profound fear of representation's performative effects. That fear was not irrational. It was demonstrably true that signs were becoming performative in what we would call the 'financial sector,' through the monetization of the economy and the legitimization of usury. It was also evident that the presence of religious icons, rituals, incense, and other sensual paraphenalia in liturgical observance could tempt many participants to adore these symbols and forget the non-apparent deity to which they refer. It was obvious that people could be falsely persuaded that signs could do things, the only question was how, and the most plausible answer available to the early modern mind was 'by magic'.

4.3 Reproduction and Inflation

The literary evidence suggests that the people of early modern England were especially preoccupied by 'sympathetic' magic, which rests on the belief that what is done to an image will also affect its referent. As the anonymous *The Lawes Against Witches* (1645) puts it: 'as the picture consumes, so may the parties bewitched consume' (62). In Thomas Middleton's *The Witch* (1615), the *maleficia* inflicted by Hecate and her followers depend on the efficacy of symbols:

Hecate: Is the heart of wax
        Stuck full of magic needles?
Stadlin: 'Tis done, Hecate.
Hecate: And is the farmer's picture, and his wife's,
        Laid down to th' fire yet?
Stadlin: They're a-roasting both, too.
Hecate: Good. Then their marrows are a-melting subtly,
        And three months' sickness sucks up life in 'em. (1.2.46–52)

Here the treatment of images has a precisely determinate effect on their referents: sticking needles in an image of someone's heart causes a stabbing pain to their actual heart. This is arguably the basic principle of all magic, and it dominated popular perceptions of witchcraft in early modern England. Perkins expounds orthodox opinion when he explains that the sign itself—the 'bare word' or 'bare picture'—has no performative power. Whenever it appears that magic has an efficacious force, whenever the laws of nature seem to have been suspended by the manipulation of images, we can recognize the practical working of Satan. Perkins describes how witches:

> ... make an impression into the said picture, by pricking or gashing the heart or any other place, with intent to procure dangerous or deadly pains to the same parts. This is a mere practice of Inchantment, & the making of the image, and using of it to this end, is in virtue a Charme, though no words be used. For the bare picture hath no more power of it selfe to hurt the body represented, then bare words. All that is done commeth by the worke of the deuill, who alone by the using of the picture in that sort, is occasioned so or so, to worke the parties destruction.[15]

According to Perkins, Satan's main purpose is to use the apparent efficacy of witchcraft to convince people that signs can alter the objective condition of the world. This point was entirely conventional. It had been made previously by King James, who repeatedly notes that the fatal effects of image magic were not achieved by the images, but by the devil, as part of his effort to fool humanity into crediting the performative power of signs:

> They can be-witch and take the life of men or women, by rosting of the Pictures, as I spake of before, which likewise is verie possible to their Master to performe, for although, (as I saide before) that instrumente of waxe haue no vertue in that turne doing, yet may hee not verie well euen by that same measure that his conjured slaues meltes that waxe at the fire, may he not I say at these same times, subtilie as a spirite so weaken and scatter the spirites of life of the patient... (266)

But murder was not the crime most often associated with witchcraft. In fact, several fictional treatments of the subject show Satan explicitly denying that he can kill human beings. In Thomas Dekker, John Ford and William Rowley's *The Witch of Edmonton* (1621), the incarnate devil tells the witch that he cannot take her enemy's life: 'Until I take him, as I late found thee,/ Cursing and swearing' (2.1.164–65). When it does occur, murder by witchcraft generally takes the form of infanticide. In Middleton's *The Witch* Hecate boils an 'unbaptised brat' (1.2.19), while in *Macbeth* the witches cook a 'birth-strangled babe.'[16] Ben Jonson's learned notes to *The Masque of Queens* (1609) comment that witches 'killing of Infants is common, both for confection of their Oyntment... as also out of a lust to do murder.'[17] The practice of infanticide is part of witchcraft's opposition to natural reproduction, which is a common theme of fictional portrayals. Receiving a visitor to her lair in *The Witch*, Hecate asks if he wants her 'to starve up generation? To strike a barrenness in man or woman?' (1.2.150–151). Once her suspicion is confirmed, she applauds his 'villainous, barren ends,' and eagerly furnishes the supernatural equipage to ensure that '[n]either the man begets nor woman breeds' (1.2.157).

Infanticide was commonly practiced *in lieu* of birth control, and many people executed for witchcraft were actually abortionists or 'midwives;' indeed contraception and abortion were widely considered to be subspecies of witchcraft.[18] According to John T. Noonan, the medieval Latin word for the malign effects of magic, *maleficia*, was used in Classical Latin specifically for abortion and contraception.[19] Several historians have recently argued that the witch-hunters' campaign against birth control was, at least originally, part of an official campaign to revive the population of Europe following the Black Death. Between 1350 and 1450 the population fell by approximately one-third, and authorities felt compelled to act. According to Gunnar Heinsohn and Otto Steiger:

> shortly after the Great Plague, secular and clerical aristocrats began to execute so-called wise women, often midwives, in their villages. This procedure gained momentum through the late 14th and most of the 15th century until it was coordinated–as will be shown below–for the entire Catholic world by the 'Witch-Bull' of 1484.[20]

Campaigns against abortion and contraception may have begun as almost instinctive, local responses to suddende population but Pope Innocent VIII gave them pontifical sanction in the 'Witch Bull.' The Bull's most significant innovation was that it included the prevention of reproduction under the category of witchcraft, condemning:

... persons of both sexes ... who by their incantations, spells, conjurations, and other accursed charms and crafts, enormities and horrid offenses, have slain infants yet in the mother's womb ... they hinder men from performing the sexual act and women from conceiving, whence husbands cannot know their wives nor wives receive their husbands.[21]

Thus it became official church policy that witches hindered sexual reproduction and that, in order to do so, they encouraged unnatural concupiscence of every description. A popularizing commentary on the Bull, published in 1487 as the *Malleus Maleficarum* by Heinrich Kramer and Jacob Sprenger, soon became the foundation of scholarly discussion. The authors stressed that 'in relation to the duty of human nature and procreation' they had identified 'seven methods by which [witches] infect with witchcraft the venereal act and the conception of the womb' (47). These included incitement to concupiscence ('inclining the minds of men to inordinate passion'), 'procuring abortion' and 'offering children to devils' (infanticide). Kramer and Sprenger announce that their investigation will focus specifically on 'midwives, who surpass all others in wickedness. The number of them is so great that, as has been found from their confessions, it is thought that there is scarcely any tiny hamlet in which at least one is not to be found' (269). The traditional village 'wise-woman' was thus declared a criminal.

The subsequent witch hunts were designed to eliminate, among other things, folk knowledge of abortion and contraception, and they were not limited to the Pope's jurisdiction. Protestant Europe was at least as vigilant in witch-hunting as Catholic states. Martin Luther called witches 'shameless whores of the devil ... who torture the newborn in the cradle, bewitch the sexual organs et cetera.... I myself would burn all of them.' In spite of such intemperance, the 'witch craze' was more than a primitive, irrational hysteria. Europe's most prominent intellectuals were as fearful of witchcraft as the most superstitious peasant, and this fact has puzzled many modern historians. The case of Jean Bodin has proven especially confusing. Bodin was among the sixteenth century's most ferocious witch-hunters; his *Demonomanie* (1580) ranks among the era's most authoritative texts on the subject. Yet he is also famous as the inventor of the 'quantity theory' of money. His *Response de Malestroit* (1568) is regarded today as a seminal breakthrough in the history of economics. To the modern mind it can be hard to understand how the same man could hold such 'rational' and 'irrational' beliefs simultaneously. Bodin's modern admirers have generally denied any connection between his economics and his witch-hunting, thus giving rise to the 'paradox of the two Bodins.'

In 1969 however, E. W. Monter achieved the kind of intellectual breakthrough that had previously been unavailable to post-Enlightenment thought. In an essay entitled 'Inflation and Witchcraft: The Case of Jean Bodin,' Monter was able to think far enough outside twentieth-century categories to notice the homology between Bodin's attack on magic and his attack on inflation. Witchcraft and inflation both cause dramatic effects by mysterious, impalpable means that seemed strikingly similar to Bodin. Monter reveals 'a common pattern of concern underlying both polemics endowing them with a common purpose and even at times with a common method.'[22] He notes that Bodin viewed both witchcraft and inflation as 'clear and present dangers' to the 'Commonweale.' Monter therefore argues that to separate Bodin's demonology from his economics is anachronistic: 'Bodin confronts us as an intellectual monolith.... The paradox of two or more Bodins–a Bodin of dazzling inconsistencies–is a paradox created by us and not by him' (375).

The paradox evaporates once we recall that, for Bodin and his contemporaries, money and magic did not occupy separate spheres of experience. The burgeoning independence of financial signs was just one manifestation of the general rise of representation to power and influence. The autonomous power of representation was magical by definition, and Bodin viewed his economic theories as inseparable from his campaign against witchcraft. He was among the first economists to take account of money's non-referential status. The sixteenth-century influx of American gold and silver into Europe caused unprecedented inflation, which clearly revealed that financial value was independent of precious metal. Bodin therefore conceived of financial value as relative and fluctuating, rather than as fixed or permanent. It fluctuated, he claimed, according to the proportionate relation between the amount of gold and silver possessed by a polity and its population.

Bodin was what historians of economics call a 'bullionist.' He assumed that financial value was identical with the physical body of precious metals. In this conception, value is imagined as literally inhabiting the body of an object; its symbolic form has not yet won its independence. Like Midas, Bodin believed that '[t]he abundance of gold and silver is money... and the wealth of the country' ('[l]e abondance d'or est d'argent ... et la richesse d'un pays').[23] Unlike Midas, however, Bodin was familiar enough with economic history to recognize the dangers of inflation caused by 'the abundance of gold and silver.' He identifies the 'abundance' of precious metals in sixteenth-century France as '[t]he principal and almost only reason' for the 'dearness that we see.' Anticipating twenty-first century theorists of 'financialization,' Bodin muses on inflation's cyclical destruction of empires: 'Thus it comes to all states … to go into decadence, to the point when they are wholly ruined.'[24] The invisible, revolutionary influence of inflation revealed a disjunction between financial signs and their referents, suggesting that money possessed a hitherto-unsuspected autonomy. It made money seem, and act, like magic.

This kinship between money and magic was confirmed, according to Heinsohn and Steiger, by Bodin's discovery of the causal connection between the decline in population and the increase in prices. If gold and silver flowed into a polity whose population was declining, prices must inevitably rise. Inflation was thus the result of infertility, which was in turn the work of witches, who practiced contraception, abortion and infanticide, while perverting natural sexuality towards barren concupiscence. Inflation also prevented natural reproduction by stimulating unnatural reproduction. To forestall the ruinous inflation that had destroyed ancient Rome and weakened contemporary Spain, Bodin believed it was necessary to increase the population, and he saw the witch-hunts as a necessary police action to enforce such an increase. In his *Republic* (1576) Bodin praised the Roman Emperor Augustus for having introduced laws to 'punish whoredom, adultery and sodomy, and also force everyone to seek him a lawful wife and children.' Augustus understood that a growth in the money supply demanded a corresponding growth in population. The demand for money must be increased to meet the increased supply. The true source of value in human labor power must remain proportionate in quantity to the symbolic expression of value in the form of coinage. If coinage proliferated while labor power remained static, the value of coins would rapidly decrease. Population growth was therefore necessary to avoid inflation, and like many others Bodin regarded witchcraft as the main obstacle to such growth. Witches opposed natural reproduction by birth control, and also by fostering unnatural sexuality.

The campaign against practical magic was induced by the fear that signs can be autonomously powerful. This idea is frightening because it removes any source of meaning from human experience, leaving no essence underlying appearance: no *logos*. The reproduction of financial signs in inflation and usury reminded many people of the magician's performative deployment of spells, rituals and icons—what Marlowe's Dr. Faustus calls '[l]ines, circles, signs, letters and characters' (1.1.50). In *The Witch of Edmonton*, Mother Sawyer has easy recourse to the language of usury when she describes how she became convinced of her own supernatural powers. Her enemies accuse her of witchcraft: 'This they enforce upon me, and in part/ Make me to credit it' (2.1.14–15). She seeks vengeance through magic which, like Simon Magus, she assumes can be bought for money: 'by what art learned,/ What spells, what charms, or invocations,/ May the thing called Familiar be purchased?' (2.1.36–38). Mother Sawyer consistently conceives her predicament in terms of credit and debt, describing the landowner who denies her charity as:

> ... this miser, this black cur,
> That barks and bites, and sucks the very blood
> Of me and of my credit. 'Tis all one
> To be a witch as to be counted one. (2.1.131–134)

Here Mother Sawyer reveal her understanding that image has displaced reality. Although she is not yet actually a witch, that makes no difference to the way she is treated. What matters is her public image, her 'credit.' When the devil finally appears in the shape of a dog, he vows to carry out her commands if she will 'put credit in my power' (2.1.169). In financial value's symbolic power, the people of early modern England recognized social and psychological tendencies that their culture had ascribed to Satan's influence for over a thousand years. Autonomous financial value is the embodied antithesis of human activity. When it reproduces, this symbolic form of human life achieves a spectral agency of its own. In Renaissance England, for the first time since antiquity, the commodification of labor power, and the concomitant reproduction of financial value, were becoming active forces in people's lives. Millions were making the uncomfortable transition between the peasantry, who lived by subsistence farming, and the proletariat, who lived by selling their labor power. Gradually deprived of access to the commons, with their small-holdings incrementally enclosed, peasants found themselves reduced to exchanging more and more of their labor power for money—or rather, since physical coinage was often lacking, for credit.

Although 'Lady Credit' would not become a fully-fledged, literary personification for almost a century, this surge in the mysterious but formidable power of credit coincided with, and arguably produced, an epidemic of magical thinking. Accounts of magical ceremonies invariably compare their idolatrous manipulation of symbols and images with their perverted sexuality. R.W.'s translation of Lambertus Danaeus's Latin *The Dialogue of Witches* (1575) is typical:

> So are sorcerers plainly miserable slaues vnto Satan, & in subiection vnto him, him doe they worship, to him doo they cōmit themselues, yea & offer vnto him cādles of waxe in token of honour. Yet some of thē doo séeme far more abiecte & fil|thily seruisable. For when Satan sheweth himself vnto them in yᵉ likenes of a man, yᵉ which is to shamful to speak, they kisse his buttocks, which thīg certē of thē afterward haue frāckli cōfessed thēselues to haue don.[25]

Skeptics often pointed out that such fantastic events cannot really have taken place. The witch-hunters retorted that, in that case, the accused showed such a pronounced tendency to hallucination that he or she was obviously under Satanic influence. Indeed, that influence consisted precisely in the attribution of practical potency to hallucinations. In *The Advancement of Learning* (1605), Francis Bacon's ethical objection to magic is that it can be used as a symbolic surrogate for human labor power. Bacon is skeptical regarding the intervention of supernatural agents, but he nevertheless deplores the manipulation of images to achieve the kind of practical effects that can naturally only be attained by human activity:

> For it may be pretended that ceremonies, characters, and charms do work, not by any tacit or sacramental contract with evil spirits, but serve only to strengthen the imagination of him that useth it; as images are said by the Roman Church to fix the cogitations and raise the devotions of them that pray before them. But for mine own judgment, if it be admitted that imagination hath power, and that ceremonies fortify imagination, and that they be used sincerely and intentionally for that purpose; yet I should hold them unlawful, as opposing to that first edict which God gave unto man, *In sudore vultus comedes panem tuum.* For they propound those noble effects, which God hath set forth unto man to be bought at the price of labour, to be attained by a few easy and slothful observances.[26]

Bacon is indifferent as to whether the effects achieved by magic are good or evil. The ethical objection to performative representation remains equally strong for beneficent magic as for *maleficia*. The moral problem lies in magic's substitution of symbols for labor. The labor theory of value was quite familiar to the early modern mind. It is elaborated in Roger Bieston's *The Bait and Snare of Fortune* (1556), which presents a dialogue between the figures 'Man' and 'Money.' This conversation, which seems to show the influence of Aristophanes' *Plutus*, soon turns to a debate concerning agency, with 'Money' claiming to act independently, and 'Man' replying that money is merely an objectified form of his own activity. 'Money' arrogates performative power to himself: 'What man of hymselfe by myght or wise inspeccion/ Without my mean can wurke a worthy deede?/ None doubtless, for I set all in good direccion...' He boasts of founding entire cities by his autonomous power: 'Who builded London that named was newe Troye,/ But I, puissant penny...?' In response, 'Man' declares that money is nothing but empty representation: 'Thou art false money, full of deceit and fraude/ In haunting wordes is set thy full content.' 'Man' tells 'Money' that human labor is the only truly potent force: 'never was noble Citie made by thee/... [but rather by] mankynde by great subtletie/ By diligent laboure and politike prudence..../ Not by thy means....' He demands to know the true source of the power that 'Money' claims to possess:

> Thou sayest that by thy maisterie thou bringest muche aboute
> And of thy wurthie valour great bost (?) doest thou blowe
> What is thy puissaunt power, I praie thee speake it oute:

In response, 'Money' disarmingly concedes that his 'puissant power' is actually 'Man''s own agency in objectified form: 'I as of my selfe can nothing doe ne say,/ In thee [i.e. Man] lieth al the dede....' Indeed, it is only because 'Man' acknowledges 'Money''s power, or 'knoweth my puyssaunt excellence,' that he is capable of even illusory agency. This argument serves to acquit 'Money' of the various crimes with which 'Man' has charged him. The true culprit is 'Man' himself, as he eventually confesses:

> If man with his money woulde be so reasonable
> To use it in virtue and with a good entent
> The usage thereof shall never be dampnable.
> But when man of hym selfe is so insatiable
> To covet worldly goods without reason or measure
> Full wretched is he doubtles...

The problem is not with money per se, but with the irrational and fetishistic 'use' to which man has put money. This 'dampnable' form of 'usage' alludes to usury, which transfers 'Man''s 'puissance' onto 'Money,' transforming a symbol into an active agent. Human labor power appears as an alien force to the extent that financial value acquires the capacity to reproduce. Having acquired this definitive characteristic of life, financial value inexorably develops subjective agency and volition. People then personify this power, conceiving it as the walking, talking incarnation of objectified subjectivity, human life's antithesis. Hence the popular perception, in the sixteenth and seventeenth centuries, that 'Satan' was rapidly extending his influence throughout the social, economic and political orders, from the Papal Antichrist in Rome to the hedge-witches of rural Lancashire.

Satanic or 'black' magic is anathema to monotheism by definition, and *maleficia* have always been illegal in monotheistic states. What changed in early modernity was that *any* manipulation of magical signs, for *any* purpose, was *ipso facto* adjudged Satanic. In fact any *attempt*, no matter how feeble or futile, to magically alter the objective condition of reality might legally constitute a pact with the devil. Since magical power derived from signs, and since signs naturally have no performative force, the only possible source of magic's efficacy was demonic—so the witch had necessarily entered a 'pact' with Satan, whether consciously or not. In addition to the official persecution of witches, the newly practical power of signs also produced more spontaneous, popular reactions. These sometimes took a form that we can recognize as 'economic,' such as vigilante justice against usurers, or riots against enclosure of the commons. Yet resistance to the money power was only one element in a range of protests against the rise of representation in areas of quotidian life like religious liturgy, sexual intercourse, poetic representation and such new forms of popular entertainment as the commercial theater.

4.4   Concupiscence on Stage

The public theater seems to have been generally recognized as a site where various forms of performative representation converged. Modern readers may be surprised by the close connections that were once clearly visible between these 'fields' of experience, but the antitheatrical campaigners who sprang up in reaction to the popularity of the stage routinely denounced the theater for inculcating sodomy, idolatry and commodity fetishism at the same time.[27] The theater, as Stephen Gosson put it, was a 'school of abuse.' The antitheatricalists also argued that, by inviting the audience to regard images as reality, the theater helped to inculcate magical thinking. Many playwrights acknowledged the ethical dangers inherent in their medium, but this only encouraged them to study the social, mental and moral implications of the autonomous sign. In Dekker and Middleton's *The Roaring Girl* (1611), Moll Cutpurse exhibits a concise conflation of rhetoric, magic, money and concupiscence when she defies 'all men... And their best flatteries, all their golden witchcrafts...' (3.1.92–93). The Renaissance stage is crowded with characters who are shown to be determined by their practice of magic, their unnatural sexuality or gender, their delight in punning rhetoric, their usurious pursuit of money, and very often by all four at once.

Like such debauched 'money-bawds' as Jonson's Sir Epicure Mammon or Middleton's Harry Dampit, the literary witches of early modern England display an ostentatiously sodomitical sexuality. Contemporary witch tracts dwell on their perverted practices, placing special emphasis on the *motif* of inversion. Ben Jonson's *Masque of Queens* claims that witches 'at their meetings, do all things contrary to the custom of Men,'[28] and they were commonly supposed to be especially addicted to kissing Satan's anus. This carnal concupiscence was easily blended with the spiritual whoredom of idolatry. John Jewel's *Third Homily Against the Perils of Idolatry* (1571) finds it:

> very agreeable... that they which fell into idolatry, which is spiritual fornication, should also fall into carnal fornication and all uncleanness by the just judgments of God, delivering them over to abominable concupiscence. (95)

In Platonic psychology the dominant, rational principle is figured as male, while the subordinate, passionate principle is figured as female. Effeminacy was the result of passion's unnatural usurpation of dominion over reason, which led to political tyranny in the macrocosm of the state. The homology between carnal sensuality and political tyranny inspired revolutionary, republican discourse from Cato to Castro. Milton deployed it against Henrietta Maria, and Marat used it against Marie Antoinette. As John Webster explained in 1677, the Biblical Jezebel was the archetypal figure for the nexus of sexual concupiscence, tyrannical politics and religious idolatry:

> Now what whoredoms or fornications had Jezebel committed? Spiritual
> whoredomes, and not Carnal ones; for she had her selfe gone a whoring
> after Idols.... From this it is plain that all her Witchcrafts were only
> impostures and delusions whereby the people were led into idolatry....[29]

Webster assumes that the relation between sexual and spiritual 'whore-
domes' is homologous. On the early modern stage, magicians are
consistently portrayed as libidinous but infertile, because they substi-
tute the unnatural reproduction of symbols for natural generation. Thus
Mephistopheles forbids Marlowe's Dr. Faustus from participating in the
genuinely efficacious, divinely ordained Sacrament of marriage, providing
him instead with images of demons disguised as courtesans. As he tells
the Doctor, these figures have no soul, no interior reality, no meaning.
They are purely performative:

> *Faustus*: Speak, Mephistopheles, what means this show?
> *Mephistopheles*: Nothing, Faustus, but to delight thy mind withal,
>   And to shew thee what magic can perform. (2.1.83–85)

Faustus eventually loses his natural desire for real women altogether and
selects for his 'paramour' the empty image of Helen of Troy, which he
knows to be the product of his own magic. He adores 'the works of
his own hands' in an erotic as well as a liturgical sense. In twenty-first
century terms, we might say that Faustus becomes addicted to pornography, with the predictable consequence that his soul is destroyed by the
sexual idolatry of concupiscence:

> Sweet Helen, make me immortal with a kiss:
> Her lips suck forth my soul, see where it flies!
> Come, Helen, come, give me my soul again.
> Here will I dwell, for heaven be in these lips,
> And all is dross that is not Helena! (5.1.99–103)

The plot of Middleton's *The Witch* hinges on the contradiction between
natural generation and the unnatural reproduction of the witch's kitchen.
Like Faustus, Middleton's witches are unabashedly lecherous. They pick
out handsome young men to use as *incubi*, and Hecate herself enjoys
an incestuous affair with her demonic son Firestone. The witches are
also happy to stimulate lust in others through commodified love potions,
but they stand firmly opposed to conception. The human characters also

conceive of pregnancy as a problem. Finding herself with child out of wedlock, Francisca laments: 'twas my luck, at the first hour forsooth,/ To prove too fruitful' (2.1.39–40). Her lover promptly disposes of the baby by leaving it on a tailor's doorstep.

Magic is connected with carnality in polytheism as well as in Christianity, and John Marston's *Sophonisba* (c.1606) places witchcraft in the pagan context of ancient Carthage. The villain Syphax is a libertine, given to such declarations as 'my wisdom is my sense' (4.1.188) and 'that's lawful that doth please' (4.1.191). Syphax has inverted Plato's ethical psychology, subordinating his reason to passion and appetite, and this inevitably leads him to the tyrant's conclusion that: 'Passion is reason when it speaks from might' (1.2.76). Marston portrays Syphax as an idolator ('Blood's appetite/ Is Syphax' god' (4.1.186–87) who naturally has recourse to magic. He commands the witch Erictho to use the 'potent sound' of her 'charms' to seduce the beautiful Sophonisba. Erictho duly takes on the appearance of Sophonisba for long enough to satisfy her own lust with Syphax, before revealing her true self to his horror ('O my abhorred heat! O loathed delusion!' (5.1.3). In Marston's polytheistic Carthage, it is 'Love' rather than the monotheistic deity which occupies the place of *logos*. Erichto warns Syphax that 'Love is the highest rebel to our art' (4.1.170) and following his downfall she mocks him for imagining '[t]hat 'tis within the grasp of heaven or hell/To enforce love....' (5.1.5–6).

In Marston's play, magic is used to satisfy concupiscent lust, which is presented as the opposite of virtuous love. Similarly, the main plot of Heywood and Brome's *The Witch of Edmonton* concerns the *maleficia* caused by Mother Sawyer's traffic with demons, but it is accompanied by a sub-plot involving Frank Thorney's supposed impregnation of his mistress. The two narratives proceed in tandem but are never explicitly connected, so we can presume that the link would originally have needed no elucidation. Mother Sawyer's opening monologue confirms the essentially verbal nature of her crimes. She reports that her neighbors blame their misfortunes on 'my bad tongue,' and she vows to retaliate by means of 'curses, imprecations,/ Blasphemous speeches, oaths, detested oaths' (2.1.13–14). She displays a predictably voracious sexual urge, which is rendered especially grotesque because the object of her affections is a large black dog she calls 'Tommy:'

Stand on thy hind-legs up—kiss me, my Tommy,

> And rub away some wrinkles on my brow
> By making my old ribs to shrug for joy
> Of thy fine tricks. What hast thou done? Let's tickle. (4.1.174–177)

Mother Sawyer's initial appeal to 'Tommy' blends sexual, magical and financial inducements. She envisages her intercourse with the devil as transactional: part seduction, part commodification: 'What is the name, where and by what art learned,/ What spells, what charms, or invocations,/ May the thing called Familiar be purchased?' (2.1.36–38). The allusion is to the story of Simon Magus, the paradigmatic magician who assumed that St. Peter's miraculous powers could be purchased for money in Acts 8.9–24. The sin of 'simony' consists in illegitimate commodification. Simon's mistake was to assume that Peter was a magician like himself for, unlike divinely ordained miracles and Sacraments, Satanic magic could indeed be bought and sold. Commentators on witchcraft frequently warned that it was spread through commodification, as when King James' *Demonologie* notes that the devil 'giues them [the witches] power to sel such wares to others, whereof some will bee dearer, and some better cheape; according to the lying or true speaking of the Spirit that is conjured therein' (19). Like the rhetoric of the ancient sophists, the ritual signs of black magic are rendered performative through commodification. They must be conceived as efficacious, because they are objects of exchange.

The commercial public theaters were themselves the object of a fierce debate concerning the ethics of representation. Pamphleteers like Gosson and Phillip Stubbes protested against the commodification of entertainment, arguing that the need to sell tickets must inevitably degrade the quality of the product for sale. Since female roles were taken by boys, the theater was also assumed to invite the audience to participate in homosexual desire. Some of the most prominent theologians of the seventeenth century, such as William Perkins and William Prynne, composed voluminous treatises against the stage that revived the argument (made in such ancient polemics as Tertullian's *De Spectaculiis* and also in such postmodern diatribes as Guy Debord's *Society of the Spectacle*) that the commodification of spectacle on stage leads inevitably to theological idolatry, concupiscent sexuality, and political tyranny.

While the authorities debated the legitimacy of their medium, the popular dramatists of Renaissance London embarked on a parallel attempt to develop an ethics of representation. They found themselves perfectly positioned to consider the aesthetic, implications of the performative sign. Much like the internet today, the public theater provided a unique, fleeting opportunity for ordinary voices to make themselves widely heard, and the era's playwrights responded with energy and enthusiasm. Surprisingly often, they endorsed the antitheatrical criticisms. In Shakespeare's *The Tempest* (1610) Prospero combines the roles of playwright and sorcerer, and his manipulation of illusory images serves his own, private ends as much as the disinterested moral good. The prefaces to Ben Jonson's plays frequently echo the antitheatricalists on the deleterious aesthetic effects of commodification. In *Bartholomew Fair* a Scrivener reads a contract to the audience:

> It is further agreed, that every person here have his or their free-will of censure, to like or dislike at their own charge, the author having now departed with his right: it shall be lawful for any man to judge his sixpen'-worth, his twelvepen'worth, so to his eighteen-pence, two shillings, half a crown, to the value of his place; provided always his place get not above his wit. And if he pay for half a dozen, he may censure for all them too, so that he will undertake that they shall be silent. He shall put in for censures here, as they do for lots at the lottery: marry, if he drop but six-pence at the door, and will censure a crown's-worth, it is thought there is no conscience or justice in that.

The Witch of Edmonton carefully compares the moral status of magical and financial signs. Mother Sawyer describes Old Banks, her main persecutor, as: 'this black cur,/ That barks and bites, and sucks the very blood/ Of me and of my credit' (2.1.132–133). The devil promptly enters, disguised as precisely such a black dog. Mother Sawyer's verbal image manifests itself in the real world, ready to perform her will, but she has already misconceived its nature. She imagines the dog as the literal incarnation of her own magical words, not as the embodiment of a spirit entirely independent of her, and vastly more powerful. The devil-dog's first words explain that his presence has been conjured by her speech: 'Ho! have I found thee cursing? now thou art mine own' (2.1.120). He leads her to believe that the autonomous power of her spell has caused his presence. In reality, however, it is her explicit repudiation of God—which was generally figured as 'selling' the soul—that interests the devil sufficiently for him to make an appearance. The impression that her magic is efficacious is dangled in front of Mother Sawyer as an illusory temptation.

Marlowe's Mephistopheles is summoned by the same means, and he entraps Doctor Faustus by the same method. On his first appearance, Faustus assumes that his magical incantations are inherently powerful: 'I see there's virtue in my heavenly words...Such is the force of magic and my spells' (1.3.23, 27). He appeals to the demon for confirmation: 'Did not my conjuring speeches raise thee?' (1.3.42). However Mephistopheles replies 'that was the cause, but yet *per accidens*' (1.3.43). Faustus' magic was only the accidental cause of his appearance. As with Mother Sawyer, the final or ultimate cause of the devil's presence is the magician's repudiation of *logos*: 'when we hear one rack the name of God,/ Abjure the Scriptures and his Saviour Christ,/ We fly, in hope to get his glorious soul' (1.3.44–46).

In *The Witch of Edmonton* Mother Sawyer cannily uses her trial as an opportunity to expand the definition of magic. She follows the example of Reginald Scot and countless others, claiming that witchcraft includes any use of representation to performative effect, especially in the spheres of money and sex. 'A witch!' she exclaims. 'Who is not?... What are your painted things in princes' courts,/ Upon whose eyelids lust sits, blowing fires/ To burn men's souls in sensual hot desires....?' (4.2.122–124). Taken aback, the Justice protests: 'But those work not as you do.' 'No,' replies the newly eloquent crone:

> ... but far worse
> These by enchantments can whole lordships change
> To trunks of rich attire, turn ploughs and teams
> To Flanders mares and coaches, and huge trains
> Of servitors to a French butterfly.
> Have you not city-witches who can turn
> Their husband's wares, whole standing shops of wares,
> To sumptuous tables, gardens of stolen sin;
> In one year wasting what scarce twenty win?
> Are not these witches? (4.2.126–135)

It is an excellent question. If witchcraft is defined as the use of representation to subvert the rule of *logos* over the *psyche*, then erotic seduction certainly qualifies. We may recall here Gorgias' *Encomium of Helen*, which blames Helen's elopement on the power of Paris' seductive rhetoric. We have also seen how the correspondence between concupiscent sexuality and magic had been commonplace from antiquity. Here Mother Sawyer argues, with unaccustomed fluency, that everyone in contemporary England practices witchcraft in one form or another. Her own trial is simply scapegoating: the projection of a widely practiced vice onto the most defenseless members of society. Nor does she discriminate by gender; seduction is witchcraft when perpetrated by men as well as on them:

> Dare any swear I ever tempted maiden
> With golden hooks flung at her chastity
> To come and lose her honour; and being lost,
> To pay not a denier for't? Some slaves have done it.
> Men-witches can, without the fangs of law
> Drawing once one drop of blood, put counterfeit pieces
> Away for true gold. (4.1.148–154)

As Mother Sawyer's final image suggests, early modern Europe saw counterfeiting and coin-clipping as conceptually akin to both magic and usury, since all these practices assume the efficacy of symbols.[30] Christopher Marlowe was convicted of counterfeiting in 1592, and the accusations that Richard Baines leveled against him are typical of the age in their combination of sexual and financial transgression. The accusatory 'Baines note' mingles sodomy, usury, idolatry, and magic to the extent that they become indistinguishable. Marlowe had allegedly claimed that 'Saint John the Evangelist was bedfellow to Christ and leaned always in his bosom; that he used him as the sinners of Sodoma,' that 'Moses was but a juggler,' and that Marlowe himself 'had as good a right to coin as the Queen of England.'[31] The common factor uniting Marlowe's various assertions is their confidence in the performative power of symbols, which supposedly led him to say that 'if there be any God or any good religion, then it is in the Papists, because the service of God is performed with more ceremonies, as elevation of the mass, organs, singing men, shaven crowns, etc.'

The public stage remained a prominent venue for the study of witchcraft until the mid-seventeenth century. Richard Brome's *The Late Lancashire Witches* (1634) opens with a debate concerning the existence of witches. A group of huntsmen have seen their prey apparently vanish into thin air. Most of them advance 'natural' explanations: the hare must have jumped into a foxhole and so on. But Arthur, the most articulate among them, insists that witchcraft must be to blame:

> … Well, well, gentlemen,

> Be you of your own faith, but what I see
> And is to me apparent, being in sense,
> My wits about me, no way tossed nor troubled,
> To that will I give credit. (1.1.34–38)

It might seem surprising today that Arthur 'credits' magic on the purely empirical grounds of sense-perception, but this was typical of seventeenth-century reasoning. Magic works precisely by the alteration of appearances; it can have no real, substantive effect on divine creation. In 1645 an account of a witch trial credited to 'H.F.' reminded readers that: 'The Devill cannot create any nature or substance but in juggling show, or seemingly only' (8). Pamphlets, plays and parliamentary debates ceaselessly emphasize that the effects of magic are illusory, and that any 'credit' given to them is due to the working of Satan in the *psyche*. The financial sense of 'credit' informs such discussions, for to believe that non-material money possesses efficacious power is a mistake of the same order and nature as the magician's belief that icons and images can achieve objective effects. Later in the play the huntsmen make bets on their sport, and one insists that the wagered coins should be held by a neutral observer. At this Whetstone is outraged: 'Do you think my word and my money is not all one?' (2.4.16–17). Although he is a fool, his question is pertinent in context, for *The Late Lancashire Witches* focuses on the homology between financial and magical signs with special intensity. 'I'll have none of your money, Gammer, because you are a witch,' (2.5.29–30) declares a boy on being offered a coin to keep Goodie Dickenson's magic secret, and throughout the play the disruptive impact of exchange-value is indistinguishable from the effects of witchcraft.

The huntsmen proceed to dinner at the house of Master Generous, who personifies the old-fashioned virtue of hospitality. Generous is presented as the antithesis of exchange-value: he is 'one who sells not/ Nor covets he to purchase' (1.1.40–41), and therefore '[a] character not common in this age' (1.1.44–45). It turns out, however, that he is typical of the age in at least one respect: his house is infested with witches, and his wife is one of them. In similar fashion, Robert Wilson's allegorical drama *The Three Ladies of London* (1581) shows the murder of Hospitality by Usury. The predictable economic effects of usury are accompanied by homologous developments in the sphere of sexuality. Love for example is transformed into the two-headed monster Lust, and Conscience becomes a 'bawd' for Lady Lucre's house of prostitution.

Recapitulating the standard opposition of witchcraft to wedlock, *The Late Lancashire Witches* features a lusty young bridegroom rendered impotent by a bewitched codpiece, as well as the disruption of the wedding-feast by demonic magic. In the words of Arthur: 'these hags had power to make the wedding cheer a *deceptio visus*' (3.1.165). The witches' ultimate triumph occurs when every man of the hunting party is revealed to be illegitimate by the supernatural apparition of their real fathers. As Arthur accurately remarks: 'It is plain witchcraft.' Legitimate reproduction is always opposed, through the entire canon of witch-literature, to the illegitimate reproduction that follows from sexual concupiscence, autonomous exchange-value and ritual magic. In a conclusion typical of English Renaissance drama, idolatry, usury, and sodomy are thus united under the rubric of witchcraft.

NOTES

1. Augustine of Hippo, *On Christian Doctrine*, in *Readings in Medieval History*, vol. I, 5th Edition, ed. Patrick Geary (U of Toronto P, 2016), 26.
2. Christopher Marlowe, *Dr. Faustus* (1.1.51).
3. St. Thomas Aquinas, *Summa contra gentiles*, cit. Brian P. Levack, *The Witchcraft Sourcebook* (Routledge, 2004), 37.
4. Anonymous, *The Lawes Against Witches* (London, 1645), in *English Witchcraft 1560–1736*, vol. 3, ed. Malcolm Gaskill (Pickering & Chatto, 2003), 61.
5. H.F., *A True and Exact Relation* (London, 1645), in *English Witchcraft 1560–1736*, vol. 3, ed. Malcolm Gaskill (Pickering & Chatto, 2003), 6.
6. Cit. Alan Charles Kors and Edward Peters, *Witchcraft in Europe: 400–1700: A Documentary History* (U of Pennsylvania P, 2001), 109.
7. King James I, *Daemonologie* (Woodstock, ON, 2016), 13.
8. Reginald Scot, *The Discoverie of Witchcraft* (New York: Dover Publications, 1972), 3. Subsequent references are to this edition.
9. Cit. David J, Davis, *From Icons to Idols: Documents on the Image Debate in Reformation England* (Eugene, OR: Pickwick Publications, 2016), 16.
10. Marion Gibson, Introduction to *English Witchcraft: 1560–1736*, vol. 2 (Pickering & Chatto, 2003), x.
11. Cit. Brian P. Levack, *The Witchcraft Sourcebook: Second Edition* (New York: Routledge, 2015), 110.
12. Edward Poeton, *The Winnowing of White Witchcraft*, ed. Simon F. Davies (Tempe, AZ, 2018), 34.

13. John Gaule, *Select Cases of Conscience Touching Witches and Witchcraft* (London, 1646), in *English Witchcraft 1560–1736*, vol. 3, ed. Malcolm Gaskill (Pickering & Chatto, 2003), 139.

14. Cit. Kors and Peters, 170.

15. William Perkins, *A Discourse of the Damned Art of Witchcraft*, in *English Witchcraft 1560–1736*, vol. 1, ed. James Sharpe (Pickering & Chatto, 2003), 265.

16. William Shakespeare, *Macbeth* (4.1.29), in 7 in *The Oxford Shakespeare: The Complete Works*, 2nd Edition, ed. Gary Taylor and Stanley Wells (Oxford UP, 1997). Subsequent references to Shakespeare are to this edition.

17. *The Works of Ben Jonson*, vol. VII (London: G. and W. Nicol, 1816), 150n6.

18. See Pauline Jackson, 'Abortion Trials and Tribulations,' *The Canadian Journal of Irish Studies* 18.1 (July 1992), 112–120.

19. John T. Noonan, *Contraception: A History of Its Treatments by the Catholic Theologians and Canonists* (Harvard UP, 1986), 156.

20. Gunnar Heinsohn and Otto Steiger, 'Birth Control: The Political-Economic Rational Behind Jean Bodin's *Demonomanie*,' *History of Political Economy* 31.3 (1999), 423–448. For a critique of Heinshon and Steiger's conclusions, see J.M. Riddle, *Eve's Herbs: A History of Contraception and Abortion in the West* (Harvard UP, 1997).

21. Heinrich Kramer and James Sprenger, *Malleus Malificarum* (New York: Dover Publications, 1971), xliii.

22. E.W. Monter, 'Inflation and Witchcraft: The Case of Jean Bodin,' in *Action and Conviction in Early Modern Europe: Essays in Memory of E.H. Harbison*, ed. T.K. Rabb and J.E. Seigel (Princeton UP, 1969), 371–389, 377.

23. Cit. Jerome Blanc, 'Beyond the Quantity Theory: A Reappraisal of Jean Bodin's Monetary Ideas,' in *Money and Markets: A Doctrinal Approach*, ed. Maria Cristina Marcuzzo and Alberto Giacomini (New York: Routledge, 2007), 147n3.

24. Jean Bodin, *Response to the Paradoxes of Malestroit*, ed. Henry Tudor (Thoemmes Pr., 1997), 32.

25. Lambertus Danaeus, *The Dialogue of Witches* (1575), trans. R.W., retrieved April 1, 2020: http://tei.it.ox.ac.uk/tcp/Texts-HTML/free/A19/A19798.html.

26. Sir Francis Bacon, *The Advancement of Learning* in *The Works of Lord Bacon*, vol. 1 (London: Henry G. Bohn, 1854), 45.

27. See David Hawkes, 'Idolatry and Commodity Fetishism in the Antitheatrical Controversy,' *Studies in English Literature* 39.2 (Spring 1999), 255–273.

28. Ben Jonson, *The Masque of Queens*, in *The Works of Ben Jonson* (London: George Routledge and Sons, 1869), 572.

29. John Webster, *The Displaying of Supposed Witchcraft* (London, 1677), in *English Witchcraft 1560–1736*, vol. 3, ed. James Sharpe (Pickering & Chatto, 2003), 221.

30. Although Teresa Nugent argues for a temporal sequence as opposed to a conceptual connection: 'as moneylending gained legitimacy, counterfeiting became ideologically charged with the illicit connotations traditionally evoked by usury as a threat to economic transactions and social stability.' 'Usury and Counterfeiting in Wilson's *The Three Ladies of London* and *The Three Lords and Three Ladies of London*, and in Shakespeare's *Measure for Measure*,' in *Money in the Age of Shakespeare: Essays in the New Economic Criticism*, ed. Linda Woodbridge (Palgrave Macmillan, 2003), 201–217, 201–202.

31. Cit. David Riggs, *The World of Christopher Marlowe* (New York: Henry Holt & Co., 2004), 77.

CHAPTER 5

Commodification and the Performative Sign in Eucharistic Ethics

5.1 LOGOS IN THE SACRAMENT

The moral status of signification has recently been discussed in relation to the sacraments by several commentators on religion, most notably Louis-Marie Chauvet.[1] David Power has described a 'symbolic crisis' in postmodern religion, and some theologians have attempted to extend sacramental hermeneutics into a generalized morality. Paul Matthew Burgess bases his reading of the sacraments on the semiotic theory of C. S. Peirce which, as he notes, 'offers a general frame-work for … relating these understandings and their objects to specialized areas of study at a far distance from theology.'[2] Yet modern theologians generally neglect to note that recent semiotic developments are reflected most clearly in the economy, or that it is the mutation of the economy into a network of signifying systems that makes the development of an ethics of representation the most pressing intellectual task of our era.

The people of early modern Europe, in contrast, were thoroughly cognizant of the connections between financial and liturgical fetishism. Idolatry is closely connected to commodification throughout the English Reformation. A typically didactic attitude to images is presented as early as John Ryckes' *The Image of Love* (1525), where the narrator seeks 'the very image of love' among the 'artificers.' Although he does not find it, he does discover manufactured icons:

© The Author(s) 2020
D. Hawkes, *The Reign of Anti-logos*, Palgrave
Insights into Apocalypse Economics,
https://doi.org/10.1007/978-3-030-55940-3_5

I set my mind to buy one of those and as I was choosing out one of the godliest there came to me a holy, devout doctor rebuking me greatly and said, 'Why do you cast away your money upon these corruptible and vain things....'[3]

In his *Answer unto Sir Thomas More's Dialogue* (1532) William Tyndale returns to this opposition between the true 'image of God' and the artificial images manufactured by human beings. Like Ryckes, he constructs the polarity on the fact that, unlike the true 'image of God,' the artificial icons can be commodified, drawing a further distinction between monetary price and 'the price of Christ's blood.' Tyndale notes that images are 'not made after the image of God nor are they the price of Christ's blood, but the workmanship of the craftsman and the price of money and therefore inferior to man.'[4] He goes on to warn that we dishonor God when 'we care more to clothe the dead image made by man and the price of silver, than the lively image of God and the price of Christ's blood' (27). The proper role of 'images, relics, ornaments, signs or sacraments, holidays, ceremonies or sacrifices' is 'to do man service,' but the prevalent 'abuse' of icons turns them into idols, reducing man to a servant of his own fetishized works.

This 'abuse' consists in taking a referential sign for a performative. Tyndale considers that carrying a crucifix or wearing a cross on one's forehead is admirable, so long as it is used as a 'remembrance' of Christ's sacrifice. It is 'abused' and becomes an 'idol' only when it is imagined as efficacious. Thus 'to bear a piece of the cross about a man thinking that so long as that is about him spirits shall not come at him, his enemies shall do him no bodily harm, all causes shall go on his side even for bearing it about him... is plain idolatry' (27). Tyndale extends his criticism to any liturgical rite that is non-referential: without 'signification' or 'true meaning':

And such is holy bread, holy water and the serving of all ceremonies and sacraments in general without signification. And I pray you how is it possible that the people should worship images, relics, ceremonies and sacraments, save superstitiously, so long as they know not the true meaning, neither will the prelates suffer any man to tell them? Yea, and the very meaning of some and right use, no man can tell. (28)

Tyndale stresses that idolatry is anti-logocentric, reminding the reader that an image is 'not God's Word' and 'neither God nor his Word.'

The Jews do not recognize *logos* because '[t]hey let the significations of their ceremonies go, and lost the meaning of them and turned them unto the works to serve them' (28–29). He conceives the idolatrous *psyche* as servile: 'then the image serves not thee, but thou the image; and so thou art an idolater, that is to say, in English, a serve-image' (28). This English iconoclasm was partly domestic and descended from the Lollards, but it is also a response to the continental theology of Martin Luther and John Calvin. As we shall see, Calvin's fashioning of the Eucharist into an efficacious sign is conceptually based upon Luther's attack on the Catholic Mass as fetishized human activity. Calvin's notion of performative representation emerges out of Luther's critique of abstract labor-power, and the sacramental controversy can thus provide the intellectual basis for an ethical critique of efficacious power when attributed to any kind of sign.

The sacramental controversy caught and held the public's attention because it raised the question of precisely how representation can cease to be merely referential and become performative. Can signs alter the condition of the human mind, or even of the objective world? How do they do so? To what extent should they be allowed to do so? The early modern rise to cultural prominence of performative signs marked an epochal departure in Western thought. A challenge to referentiality is a challenge to *logos*. When signs were seen to be efficacious in themselves, the ancient and medieval worlds regarded them with deep suspicion, generally designating them as magical and demonic. The sacraments were sacred because they were exceptions to this rule. Unlike the icons and images of the magician, whose effects were illusory, the sacraments actually achieved an objective effect in the real world. The *Catholic Encyclopedia* summarizes the canonical view of the Eucharist as a performative speech-act:

> The total conversion of the substance of bread is expressed clearly in the words of Institution: 'This is my body.' These words form, not a theoretical, but a practical proposition, whose essence consists in this, that the objective identity between subject and predicate is effected and verified only after the words have all been uttered, not unlike the pronouncement of a king to a subaltern: 'You are a major', or, 'You are a captain', which would immediately cause the promotion of the officer to a higher command. When, therefore, He Who is All Truth and All Power said of the bread: 'This is my body', the bread became, through the utterance of these words, the Body of Christ; consequently, on the completion of the

sentence the substance of bread was no longer present, but the Body of Christ under the outward appearance of bread.[5]

The Eucharist was medieval Christianity's paradigmatic performative sign. The question at issue in the Reformation controversies was the source of this performative power. Did it derive directly from the *logos*, or was it inherent in the sign? Was priestly mediation a necessity? Was the volition of the communicant a pertinent factor? The answers one gave to such questions determined one's view of representation in general, and also of the individual self, as well as of the relations between the two. This in turn held profound implications for what we would now call 'politics' and 'economics'. Because they were aware of the inter-relations between these 'spheres' of society—or rather because they did not conceive them as different spheres—the people of early modern Europe debated the semantics of the sacraments with a passionate intensity that did not stop short of continental warfare.

The term *sacramentum* was coined by Tertullian, who used it to translate the Greek *mysterion*. This latter word originally referred to the esoteric knowledge imparted by pagan mystery cults, and it usually designated a magical icon or image. It retained much the same sense when imported into Christian discourse. Tertullian found *sacramentum* an appropriate equivalent for *mysterion* because of its additional legal implications: it could refer to an oath sworn in court, or to a soldier's declaration of fealty, as well as to the external sign of such an oath—usually the brand or tattoo that marked a legionnaire's body. Such signs were legally enforceable and thus objectively efficacious in the same way as Tertullian understood the sacramental food to be efficacious. By the fourth century, both the Greek and the Latin were being used to designate specifically Christian liturgical signs such as Baptism and the Eucharist.[6] In this tradition, a sacrament is the paradigm of a performative image. As St. Thomas Aquinas put it: 'the sacraments of the New Law *cause* grace'.[7] The Council of Trent pronounced: 'a sacrament is a thing subjected to the senses, which has the power not only of signifying but also of effecting grace'.[8] This understanding of the sacraments remains current in most Christian confessions today. The *Catechismus Catholicae Ecclesiae* declares '*Sacramenta sunt signa efficacia gratiae*',[9] which is translated into English as 'the sacraments are efficacious signs of grace'.[10] Nor is this reading confined to Catholics. Paul Tillich announces that: 'Christian liturgy, at the center of which lies the Eucharist, is irreducibly performative ....'[11]

The Eucharistic debate historically veers between those, like Berengar of Tours, John Wycliffe and Huldrich Zwingli, who claim that the bread and wine are commemorative symbols of Christ's body and blood, and those like Tertullian, Aquinas and Luther, who hold that Christ is objectively and literally present in the sacrament. The doctrine of Calvin, who believed in both the symbolic nature of the Eucharist and the objective presence of Christ, constitutes a dialectical synthesis of these antithetical positions. Although he denies that the bread and wine undergo a transubstantiation, agreeing that they are Christ's body and blood in a purely symbolic sense, Calvin nevertheless asserts that the *logos* is objectively incarnate in the sacrament. In Calvin's theory of the Eucharist, then, Christian theology acknowledges and assimilates the performative power of signs.

All sides in the debate agreed that the Eucharist allows believing participants to experience a substantial, spiritual essence underlying physical appearances, thus enabling them to perceive an ultimate meaning designated by the symbols of empirical existence. The bread and wine make the *logos* objectively present in the mind of the communicant. The question is how this is possible. Realists argue that the Eucharistic bread and wine become *logos* in essence, while symbolists claim that they stimulate an association with *logos* within the mind of the communicant. Edward Kilmartin describes how the pre-scholastic discussion:

> ... oscillated between the more realistic theology of somatic real presence characteristic of the fourth-century school of Antioch exemplified by St. John Chrysostom and the more symbolic theology of St Augustine whose Neoplatonic philosophy prevented him from interpreting the sacraments as more than signs pointing to a spiritual reality.[12]

The Neoplatonism of the early Patriarchs offered a means of reading the sacramental sign (*signum*) as 'participating in' its prototypical referent (*res*) without being identical with it. This prepared the way for the first fully symbolist account of the Eucharist, which was formulated in the eleventh century by Berengar of Tours. His doctrine was anathematized at the Council of Rome in 1050, initiating a bitter controversy over the effects of the sacramental ritual. Berengar did not deny the real presence of Christ in the sacrament, but he held that this presence depended on and was thus caused by faith in the recipient. By implication, an unworthy recipient would receive no benefit. The efficacy lay in the interpretation, not in the signs themselves. In contrast, the victorious party, headed by Pope Leo IX, held that the actions of the priest effected a transubstantiation, altering the essence or substance of the bread and wine, although their appearances or accidental forms remained unchanged. This doctrine was affirmed by the Fourth Lateran Council in 1215:

> [Christ's] body and blood are truly contained in the sacrament of the altar under the forms of bread and wine, the bread and wine having been changed in substance, by God's power, into the body and blood ... . Nobody can effect this sacrament except a priest who has been properly ordained ....[13]

The exclusive right of the ordained clergy to administer the Mass was a central element in the dispute from its earliest stages. It remained a prime target of heretical sects like the Albigenses and Waldenses throughout the Middle Ages. Long-standing controversies like the railing off of altars or the withholding of one kind from the laity were rooted in efforts to bolster or diminish priestly authority. From the symbolist perspective, the belief that the priest effects a transubstantiation by his incantatory words or ritualistic actions seemed dangerously close to magic. This was the oldest and most dangerous charge ever laid against monotheism. By Luther's time, theologians had spent well over a millennium in the exegesis of Exodus, drawing a firm distinction between the demonic magic of Pharaoh and the divine miracles performed by Moses and Aaron.[14] We have already seen how Simon Magus offered to buy St. Peter's healing power, under the blasphemous assumption that it was magical. The accusation that Jesus's miracles were magical was the unforgiveable sin 'against the Holy Ghost' (Mark 3:29) committed by the Biblical Scribes when they claimed that Jesus 'hath Beelzebub, and by the prince of the devils casteth he out devils' (Mark 3:22). The ritualistic labor of the magician acquires a financial value at the same time as it imposes a performative power upon signs. Unlike genuine miracles, magical power can be exchanged; it is susceptible to commodification.

5.2   Martin Luther: Against the Commodification of Ritual

Martin Luther consistently opposed commodification. He saw it as a form of idolatry, because it involves the imposition of symbolic exchange value upon inherent use-value. He opposed it in the ecclesiastical and the secular sphere alike. In *Of Trade and Usury* (1525) he naively fantasizes about eliminating exchange value altogether when he imagines that an official just price (*pretium justum*) might be established by a 'commission' made up of 'honest people who might consider all wares and the outlay upon them and set accordingly the mete and limit of their value' (20). Although he concedes that such measures are impractical ('we Germans are too busy with drinking and dancing'), Luther does not seriously question the assumption that an object's 'value' is inherent in and inseparable from its physical body, nor does he doubt that exchange value is a 'reward' that ought, as closely as possible, to refer to a determinate amount of labor:

> But how high thy reward is to be set, which thou art to have from such trade and labor, this canst thou not reckon and judge better than by considering the time and the greatness of the labor, and taking comparison with a common day-laborer, who does any other work, see what he earns a day; then reckon how many days thou hast spent in getting and fetching the ware, and how great labor and risk thou hast undergone, for great labor and much risk should have a greater reward. (21)

Luther's 'just price' rests upon a labor theory of value. For him, instances of culpable 'usury' do not generally involve money-lending at all; any exploitation of a disjunction between use-value and market price is condemned under the same rubric. His examples of 'usurers' include traders who 'raise the price of their wares for no other reason than that they know that there is no more of them in the land' (26). Any conception of exchange value as independent of 'pains and labor,' and therefore as separable in principle from the natural world of use-value, was to Luther unnatural, irrational, and immoral. As late as the 1520s, he still assumes his readership will be shocked to learn of trickeries like 'deaconing,' 'cornering,' or 'bearing a market,' which he castigates in terms that anticipate the witch-hunts. He denounces a particularly nefarious financial instrument known as 'futures':

> ... this is a knavish performance: when one sells to another in words the wares in his sack which he really has not. Thus to-wit: A strange merchant comes to me and asks whether I have such and such wares for sale. I say yes, though I really have none, and sell him such wares for ten or fourteen florins, whereas they can be bought for nine or less, and promise to deliver

them in two or three days. Meanwhile I go and buy such wares where I well knew beforehand that I could buy them cheaper than I sell them to him, and deliver the wares to him and he pays me for them, and thus I deal with the money and goods of other people without any risk, pains, or labor, and become rich. That is a cunning way of living on the street by other people's goods and money without needing to travel land and sea.

Luther finds trading in 'futures' morally egregious because it exchanges mere 'words' instead of substantial commodities. He describes usury as a relentless circling from cash through 'words' to 'credit' and back again, writing in the voice of a bankrupt: 'I... give my creditors good words, and claim that I will pay them honestly. Meantime I go and obtain as much more on credit as I can and turn this into money, or otherwise get money on my draft, or borrow as much as I can' (30–31). Luther clearly understands this 'knavish performance' and 'cunning' attribution of power to financial signs as magical thinking, and the liturgical form of magical thinking is idolatry. As Simon Magus realized, the ritualistic labor of the magician acquires a financial value at the same time, and to the same degree, as it imposes a performative power upon signs. According to Luther, the consequent tradition of 'simony' had sunk deep roots in the church. He was convinced that the Catholic understanding of the Mass was magical, because the exclusive right of the priesthood to administer the sacrament led directly to the idolatrous confusion of sign and referent. As he put it in *The Babylonian Captivity of the Church* (1520):

> We priests are so mad that we arrogate to ourselves alone the right of secretly uttering the words of consecration … . Under the influence of some superstitious and impious notion we do reverence to these words instead of believing them.[15]

To 'reverence' the Words of Institution rather than 'believing' them was to focus on the sign to the exclusion of the referent—the paradigmatic error of magic and idolatry. It was to forget that the words had a meaning, a referent, which consisted in the promise of salvation. The magical, fetishistic attitude to the priestly labor of the Mass therefore became, for Luther, the paradigm of works righteousness in general. Works righteousness was the inevitable result of idolatry, the worship of 'the works of men's hands', and the sin from which all other sins grew. From Luther's perspective the most objectionable consequence of this conception of the Mass was that it became exchangeable—it could be performed on behalf of people other than the direct recipient. In the words of the Council of Trent: 'If any one saith, that the Mass ... profits only the recipient, and that it ought not to be offered for the living and the dead for sins, punishments, satisfactions, and other necessities; let him be anathema.'[16] As Luther pointed out, this view of the Mass as a 'finished work' (*opus operatum*) which took its efficacy from the priest's actions (*ex opere operato*) laid the ideological foundation of an entire ecclesiastical market economy:

> there is no opinion more generally held or more firmly believed in the church today than this, that the mass is a good work and a sacrifice. And this abuse has brought an endless host of other abuses in its train, so that the faith of this sacrament has become wholly extinct and the holy sacrament has been turned into mere merchandise, a market, and a profit-making business. Hence participations, brotherhoods, intercessions, merits, anniversaries, memorial days and the like wares are bought and sold, traded and bartered, in the church. On these the priests and monks depend for their entire livelihood.[17]

Once reified as an *opus*, the Mass could remit the punishment of sins for offenders who were not present, or even aware of the sacrifice made on their behalf. This belief inspired the bestowal of 'mass-stipends,' whereby priests were paid money for performing Masses on behalf of the absent or the dead, on the assumption that the efficacy of their ritualistic actions was transferrable in symbolic form. Luther explained the logical consequence of this doctrine in his *Commentary on Galatians*:

> The pope has taken away the true use of the Mass and has simply turned it into merchandise that one must buy for the benefit of another person. There stood the Mass priest at the altar, an apostate who denied Christ and blasphemed the Holy Spirit; and he was doing a work not only for himself but for others, both living and dead, even for the entire church, and that simply by the mere performance of the act.

Luther agreed with the Catholics that Christ's body was physically present in the bread and wine: he interpreted the image '*hic est meum corpus*' as a metonomy, on the grounds of Christological ubiquity. Luther believed that Jesus's union with *logos* had bestowed upon his human body the divine attribute of omnipresence. As an inevitable logical consequence, Christ's body was literally present in the sacramental bread, just as his essential divinity was present along with his human essence.[18] This presence was not, however, the result of the priest's words or actions, and nor was it dependent on his ordination. It was perceptible through faith alone, but it was nevertheless real for that.

In *The Babylonian Captivity*, Luther distinguishes between the 'word' or 'testament,' which is God's verbal promise of salvation, and the visible 'signs' by which God reminds the faithful of the word, such as Noah's rainbow, Abraham's circumcision or the bread and wine of the mass. As Luther notes with reference to Baptism: 'signs are added to the divine promises to represent that which the words signify.' In a gesture that would inspire Protestantism's notion of *sola scriptura* and its emphasis on the salvationary power of textuality, Luther prioritizes the word over the sign, on the grounds that its efficacy does not depend on external accoutrements: 'as there is greater power in the word than in the sign, so there is greater power in the testament than in the sacrament; for a man can have and use the word, or testament, apart from the sign, or sacrament.' One can therefore effect the mass simply by reading the word of the testament and this, says Luther, 'is the truly spiritual eating and drinking.'

Luther's quarrel with the Catholics concerned the manner of the Eucharist's efficacy (*modus eficiendi*). The church claimed that the priest himself performed a transubstantiation, but Luther claimed to have uncovered the base motive behind this fetishization of 'works'. As an *opus* that could only be performed by a priest, the Mass represented alienated labor power that could be exchanged for money: it became a commodity. As Luther explains in *The Babylonian Captivity*, the Mass:

> … has been converted by the teaching of godless men into a good work, which they themselves call an *opus operatum* and by which they presumptuously imagine themselves all-powerful with God. Thereupon they proceeded to the very height of madness, and having invented the lie that the mass works *ex opere operato*, they asserted further that it is none the less profitable to others, even if it be harmful to the wicked priest celebrating it. On such a foundation of sand they base their applications, participations, sodalities, anniversaries and numberless other money-making schemes.[19]

Rather than its efficacy being contained in the material action, Luther argued that the sacrament worked 'by virtue of the agent': *ex opere operantis*. Although Christ's body was physically present in the sacramental food, the subjective condition of the communicant was therefore an indispensable condition for the Mass's efficacy, for although it was objectively present, not everyone could perceive Christ's body in the sacramental signs. From the 'Papist' perspective, this doctrine was an obstacle to the commodification of the Mass. Luther was only too well aware that, by attacking the idea of the sacrament as an *opus operato*, he was destroying the conceptual source of the church's financial wealth:

> But you will say: How is this? Will you not overturn the practice and teaching of all the churches and monasteries, by virtue of which they have flourished these many centuries? For the mass is the foundation of their anniversaries, intercessions, applications, communications, etc.—that is to say, of their fat income. I answer: This is the very thing that has constrained me to write of the captivity of the Church, for in this manner the adorable testament of God has been subjected to the bondage of a godless traffic ...[20]

The connection between magic and commodification was the spark that fired Luther's original protest against indulgences. According to the concept of 'works of supererogation', stored-up good works performed by the saints formed a repository of labor-power that could be released in symbolic, financial form and sold as indulgences for money. The penitential labor required to ameliorate the soul's condition in purgatory could be replaced by a performative token—a certificate of indulgence.[21] Protests against the sale of indulgences were not unprecedented: in 1415 the Hussites of Prague smeared a chest intended to hold the indulgence money with mud, before dragging it into the cathedral where, as Malcolm Lambert reports, 'the treasure chest received a pronouncement addressed sardonically to the disciples of the evil demon Asmodeus, Belial and Mammon.'[22] Thomas Fudge argues that for Jan Hus 'indulgences were more about economics than salvation.'[23] However Luther focused more specifically than Hus on the denunciation of 'works righteousness,' claiming that it made a fetish of human activity and projected it onto the efficacious power of signs.[24]

In Luther's anti-indulgence rhetoric, the secular and the ecclesiastical markets are simply indistinguishable. The effects of marketing on the *psyche* do not depend on the nature of the commodity for sale. Phillipp Rossner observes that by the late fifteenth century the invention of the printing press meant that 'the indulgence campaigns attained the characteristics of big advertising sprees.'[25] The campaign led by Johann Tetzel, which initially outraged Luther, was administered in the German lands by the banking house of Fugger, which naturally also received a handsome share of the profits. Tetzel's *Ablasszettel* or 'indulgence note' promised remission from an offensively indiscriminate variety of sins, including 'whoring, adultery, usury, and all other sorts of wrongdoing.'[26] Luther's fateful audience with Cardinal Cajetan actually took place in Jakob Fugger's Augsburg residence. Secular and ecclesiastical commodification thus converged strikingly in the sale of indulgences, and this merger shaped Luther's theory of ecclesiastical commodity fetishism. As he expostulated in his *Appeal to the German Ruling Class* (1520):

> the business is now to be transferred, and sold to Fugger of Augsburg. Henceforward bishoprics and livings for sale or exchange or in demand, and dealings in the spiritualities, have arrived at their true destination, now that the bargaining for spiritual or secular properties has become united into a single business. But I would like to hear of a man who is clever enough to discover what Avarice of Rome might do which has not already been done. Then perhaps Fugger would transfer and sell to someone else these two lines of business which are now to be combined into one.[27]

In *The Babylonian Captivity* Luther carefully details the psychological homology between the idolatry of sacramental signs and the fetishization of financial signs. Alluding to the Biblical declarations that 'covetousness is idolatry', he claims that, correctly interpreted, sacramental idolatry is itself a sign of its financial equivalent. Why, he asks, is the sign of the sacrament in both kinds withheld from the laity?

> For in every sacrament the sign as such is of far less importance than the thing signified. What then is to prevent them from conceding the lesser, when they concede the greater? I can see but one reason; it has come about by the permission of an angry God in order to give occasion for a schism in the Church, to bring home to us how, having long ago lost the grace of the sacrament, we contend for the sign, which is the lesser, against that which is the most important and the chief thing; just as some men for the sake of ceremonies contend against love. Nay, this monstrous perversion seems to date from the time when we began for the sake of the

riches of this world to rage against Christian love. Thus God would show us, by this terrible sign, how we esteem signs more than the things they signify.[28]

Those rites and rituals to which no salvationary promise is attached require no subjective faith for their efficacy and are therefore not sacraments, despite the claims of the Roman church. For example, the ceremony of marriage involves a performative statement—'I now pronounce you man and wife'—that is efficacious regardless of the participants' attitude towards it. The couple will be objectively married, even if they and the priest all intend them to remain single. Since it does not require subjective faith, Luther does not consider marriage a sacrament. Sacraments, in Luther's view, are precisely defined by the fact that they require the subjective assent of faith. They can be efficacious only in the kind of subject equipped to offer such autonomous volition, and they thus implicitly refute the idea that representation can be autonomously efficacious. But the false claim that the actions of the priest gave the sacramental sign an independent efficacy allowed the Eucharist to be conceived as an *opus* and thus exchanged for money. By an identical process of thought, marriage's status as a performative statement, actually effected by the priestly declaration, logically enables its commodification:

> the Romanists of our day have ... become merchants. What is it they sell? The shame of men and women—merchandise, forsooth, most worthy of such merchants grown altogether filthy and obscene through greed and godlessness. For there is nowadays no hindrance that may not be legalised upon the intercession of mammon ... . O worthy trade for our pontiffs to ply ....[29]

Luther makes a further distinction between 'legal types... such as the priestly rites concerning robes, vessels, meats, dwellings, and the like' and 'efficacious signs,' on the grounds that the latter require faith in the promises attached to them before they can take effect. Interpreted in this way, the efficacy of the sacraments is purely internal: 'Their whole efficacy, therefore, consists in faith itself, not in the doing of a work; for whoever believes them fulfils them, even if he should not do a single work.' Far from being efficacious signs, the sacraments constitute logical and experiential demonstrations that representation alone can never be efficacious:

> It cannot be true, therefore, that there is in the sacraments a power effi-cacious for justification, or that they are effective signs of grace... the sacraments accomplish what they do not by their own power, but by the power of faith, without which they accomplish nothing at all.... (264)

It follows that priestly mediation is unnecessary for the sacraments' effi-cacy: '[t]he sacraments... are not fulfilled when they are observed, but when they are believed. It cannot be true, therefore, that there is in the sacraments a power efficacious for justification....' Since the efficacy emerges not from the visible sign but from faith in the verbal promise, each believer is his own priest. Luther castigates the Roman church for stressing the visible sign over the written word, and he connects this preference to works righteousness. The idolatry of the sign and the fetishization of priestly labor are thus fused inseparably in Luther's theology:

> ... the principal and chief thing, namely, the testament and word of promise, is not treated by one of them; thus they have obliterated faith and the whole power of the mass. But the second part of the mass, - the sign, or sacrament, - this alone do they discuss, yet in such a manner that here too they teach not faith but their preparations and *opera operata,* participations and fruits, as though these were the mass.... (204)

Luther pointed out that, if the Eucharist was conceived as effected by the priest, it would always potentially be subject to commodification. The specificity of Luther's Eucharistic doctrine thus lies in his objection to the fetishization of priestly labor. He traces all idolatrous belief in perfor-mative representation to this fetish. For Luther, the illusion that signs are performative is made possible by a magical attitude to human activity. *The Babylonian Captivity* explains how works righteousness leads inexorably to the fetishization of performative representation:

> if the sacrament confers grace on me because I receive it, then indeed I obtain grace by virtue of my work and not of faith; I lay hold not on the promise in the sacrament, but on the sign instituted and commanded by God. Do you not see, then, how completely the sacraments have been misunderstood by our sententious theologians? They have taken no account, in their discussions on the sacraments, of either faith or the promise, but cling only to the sign and the use of the sign, and draw us away from faith to the work, from the word to the sign.[30]

Performative representation leads to works righteousness because the power projected onto the sign is human subjective activity in alienated form. The 'Papist' error was to assume that the efficacy of the Eucharistic signs is consequent on their embodying the abstract labor-power of the priest. For Luther this kind of fetishized human activity, or works righteousness, can only produce idolatry. In contrast, Luther located the sacrament's efficacy in the *psyche* of the communicant. He nevertheless insisted that Christ was objectively present in the physical body of the signs themselves. By doing so he broke with the Roman church, but also distinguished his own position from the *schwarmer* of the radical Reformation.

5.3   John Calvin and the Radical Reformation

Iconoclast *schwarmer* like Andreas Karlstadt claimed that religious images exerted an objective effect on the soul of the observer. Karlstadt's *On the Removal of Images* (1522) claimed that 'images bring death to those who worship and venerate them' on the grounds that: 'Pictures are loathsome. It follows that we also become loathsome when we love them.' He mocks the popular practice of making *ex voto* offerings to religious images, in order to thank them for their beneficent actions, as a form of sympathetic magic, and therefore also of idolatry:

> You bring them wax offerings in the form of your afflicted legs, arms, eyes, head, feet, hands, cows, calves, oxen, tools, house, court, fields, meadows, and the like, just as if the pictures had healed your legs, arms, eyes, heads, etc. or had bestowed upon you fields, meadows, houses, honours and possessions. Therefore you confess other gods.[31]

Karlstadt's thought was structured around a rigid polarity between *logos* and *eidolon*. He inveighs at length against Pope Gregory the Great's description of images as 'the books of the poor.' Karlstadt despised the idea that images might benefit the condition of the soul: 'How can a piece of wood or a lump of stone teach? It may well be decorated with silver or gold, but there is no spirit in it' (29). He cites Habbukuk to show that 'there is no spirit in a likeness. When God rises up, all likenesses fall. Where images sit, God cannot be' (29). He is not ashamed to admit that he regards idols as physical enemies: 'I stand in fear that I might not be able to burn idols. I would fear that some devil's block of wood [i.e.

an idol] would do me injury' (39). Images were also dangerous because they enticed people to worship them using a quasi-sexual appeal to the senses. Thus Karlstadt warns 'we can be violated by them in an instant,' and calls them 'knavish and seductive blocks of wood' which must be 'driven' from the churches 'under pain of appropriate punishment' (40). He also claims that 'in many places the godless commit whoredom with images as whores do with youths' (37). Idolatry was itself a sexual perversion, so that 'all who venerate images or seek help from them or worship them are whores and adulterous women' (37) and 'churches in which images are placed and venerated ought in all fairness to be regarded as whorehouses' (38). In short, the radicals saw *eidolon* and *logos* as mutually exclusive. Unlike Tyndale they would not tolerate images even as referential 'remembrances.' Their position is summarized in Karlstadt's declaration: '[t]he believer shall live according to the Word and disregard appearance' (35).

This radicalism even extended to sacramental images. For Huldrich Zwingli the verb *esse* in Christ's phrase '*Hic est corpus meum*' implicitly meant '*significat*'. He pointed to similar 'sacramental expressions' (*locutiones sacramentales*) in Scripture, where Christ is compared to a rock, a vine, a path and so on. Zwingli claimed that the effect of the Eucharist consisted in the correspondence it demonstrated between sign and referent. As he explained, when celebrating the Eucharist: 'You do inwardly what you represent outwardly, your soul being strengthened by the faith which you attest in the tokens.'[32] All confessions agreed that the sacraments caused psychological moments at which the noumenal was actually experienced in the phenomenal. They differed over how that experience was possible. Luther objected to the idea that the priest caused this experience, claiming rather than it was down to the faith of the communicant, which itself consisted in the ability to experience sacramental figures as efficacious. Although Luther vigorously insisted on the Real Presence in opposition to Protestant 'Sacramentarians' like Zwingli, he also rejected the Catholic doctrine of transubstantiation, on the grounds that it presupposed a magical view of the priestly ritual.

In his 'Letter to the Princes of Germany' (1530), Zwingli came close to denying the real presence altogether: 'I have no use for that notion of a real and true body that does not exist physically, definitely and distinctly in some place, and that sort of nonsense got up by word triflers.'[33] Such sentiments horrified Luther as much as they outraged the Catholics. The performative power the *schwarmer* bestowed on what they admitted to be mere signs led Luther to charge them with an idolatry yet more egregious than the Pope's. Iconoclasm was an especially culpable form of works righteousness that lacked even the excuse of authoritative sanction. He castigated the iconoclasts for believing that the physical destruction of icons could obliterate their power. He pointed out that this assumed that the icons (the 'works of men's hands') actually possessed this power: '[t]heir idea that they can please God with works becomes a real idol and a false assurance in the heart. Such legalism results in putting away outward images while filling the heart with idols'.[34]

Luther's realism and the symbolist interpretations of Zwingli and the iconoclasts formed a dialectical contradiction. Calvin's Eucharistic theory forged an intellectually coherent synthesis that assimilated performative representation into Protestant hermeneutics. Although he argued that the sacrament represents Christ's body and blood in a purely symbolic sense, Calvin nevertheless claimed that the *logos* is objectively communicated. In Calvin's theory of the Eucharist, then, the symbolic becomes the substantial. Like Luther, Calvin recognized that the fetishistic form taken by the Roman Mass was determined by its commodification. In order to acquire exchange value, the Mass had to be conceived as an *opus*, a sacrificial work that repeated the efficacy of Christ's original sacrifice. Calvin rails against 'that opinion with which the Roman Antichrist and his prophets have imbued the whole world, viz., that the mass is a work by which the priest who offers Christ, and the others who in the oblation receive him, gain merit with God ....'[35] Priests who conceive of the Mass as an *opus* are followers of Judas: 'He sold for thirty pieces of silver: they, according to the French method of computation, sell for thirty pieces of brass. He did it once: they as often as a purchaser is met with' (566).

However, Luther remained firmly logocentric in his insistence that the presence was literal, and that the bread and wine were signs that designated a referent beyond themselves. In Calvin's sacramental theory, by contrast, the labor theory of value elaborated by Luther is assimilated into an account of representation as autonomously performative. Calvin echoes Luther in noting that the commodified Eucharist takes no account of the condition of the individual conscience. He attacked those who sell the Mass 'to anyone who is willing to purchase their merchandise from them for a price paid.' The abstract subject posited by a commercial transaction obscures the culpability of the individual soul, so that sinners are emboldened to continue in their transgressions by the apparently magical nature of redemption: 'the only thing which gives them so much courage is, that by the sacrifice of the mass as a price paid, they trust that they will satisfy God, or at least will easily find a means of transacting with him' (566). The idea that the sacrament would retain its efficacy even for the unworthy was for Calvin unambiguously magical:

> [The Papists] could not have been so shamefully deluded by the impostures of Satan had they not been fascinated by the erroneous idea, that the body of Christ included under the bread is transmitted by the bodily mouth into the belly. The cause of this brutish imagination was, that consecration had the same effect with them as magical incantation. They overlooked the principle, that bread is a sacrament to none but those to whom the word is addressed just as the water of baptism is not changed in itself, but begins to be to us what it formerly was not, as soon as the promise is annexed. (596)

This 'spiritual' efficacy was not derived from the ritual actions of the priest—Calvin concurred with Luther on that point. Unlike Luther, however, Calvin did not conceive of the presence as physical. The sacrament's efficacy was contained within the bread and wine, without being identical with the physical signifiers:

> there would be no aptitude in the sign, did not our souls find their nourishment in Christ ... . That sacred communion of flesh and blood by which Christ transfuses his life into us, just as if it penetrated our bones and marrow, he testifies and seals in the Supper, and that not by presenting a vain or empty sign, but by there exerting an efficacy of the Spirit by which he fulfils what he promises (594).

Calvin's Eucharistic theory anticipates the doctrine of 'transignification' as it has been developed by recent Catholic commentators, who draw on Saussure's linguistics to read the sacrament as a sign containing both signifier (the bread and wine) and signified (Christ's divine nature). As Calvin describes it, the Eucharist is designed to inculcate the idea that signs can be efficacious in a spiritual rather than a physical manner:

> But as this mystery of the secret union of Christ with believers is incomprehensible by nature, he exhibits its figure and image in visible signs adapted to our capacity, nay, by giving, as it were, earnests and badges, he makes it as certain to us as if it were seen by the eye; the familiarity of the similitude

giving it access to minds however dull, and showing that souls are fed by
Christ just as the corporeal life is sustained by bread and wine. (521)

Failure to understand the nature of the sacrament is evidence that the
recipient is unworthy to receive it. The unworthy receive the sign without
the referent, and this division robs the sacrament of its character as a
sign and turns it into an idol. For Calvin, in contrast, the presence of
Christ in the Eucharist is both real and symbolic—in fact, it is real *because*
it is symbolic, in the sense that its reality consists in the acceptance of
the symbolic nature of its truth.[36] In Calvin's understanding, the experience of Christ's real presence consists in the acknowledgement that
symbolic truth can be objective. He carefully positions his doctrine as
a middle way between the antithetical readings of the 'Papists' and the
'Sacramentarians':

> ... bare forms are not exhibited to us in the sacrament, but the reality is
> truly figured at the same time. For God is not so deceitful as to nourish us
> in empty appearances. A sign is indeed a sign, and retains its own substance.
> But just as the Papists, on the one hand, are ridiculously dreaming of
> some sort of transformation, so, on the other hand, we have no right to
> separate the reality and the figure which God has joined together. The
> Papists confounded the reality and the sign, unbelievers like Schwenkfeld
> and men like him [i.e. the *schwarmer*] separate the signs from the realities.
> Let us preserve a middle position, that is, let us keep the union made by
> the Lord, but at the same time distinguish between them so that we do
> not, in error, transfer what belongs to one to the other. (564)

This attempt to forge a 'middle position' earned Calvin the ire of
confused opponents from both sides. As an anonymous attack published
in Bordeaux in 1577 declared: 'One minute he is a Lutheran, the next,
in contrast, he takes on the personage of a Zwinglian, and like a juggler,
a buffoon, now says he is inside, now affirms that he is outside.'[37] In
fact, however, Calvin was outlining a distinctive third position. For him,
belief in the verbal promise, represented in the sacramental sign, constitutes an 'efficacy of the Spirit', a meaning that is at once symbolic and
real. The metaphoricity of the sacrament, in short, constitutes its efficacy.
As Calvin explains in the *Short Treatise on the Holy Supper* (1540), the
body and blood are 'signs,' but they are also 'instruments':

> Now, if it be asked whether the bread is the body of Christ and the wine his blood, we answer, that the bread and the wine are visible signs, which represent to us the body and blood.... the communion which we have in the body and blood of Jesus ... is a spiritual mystery which can neither be seen by the eye nor comprehended by the human understanding. It is therefore figured to us by visible signs, according as our weakness requires, in such manner, nevertheless, that it is not a bare figure but combined with the reality and substance. It is with good reason then that the bread is called the body, since it not only represents but also presents it to us.[38]

This is the figural, 'spiritual' hermeneutic sense that Paul opposes to the literalistic 'letter' of the law when he declares: 'the letter killeth but the spirit giveth life' (2 Corinthians 3:6). This is also what Calvin means in the *Institutes*, when he describes Christ's working in the sacrament as 'an efficacy of the Spirit, by which he fulfills what he promises' (594). The sacrament reminds the believer of essence underlying appearance, and of the spiritual truths concealed beneath the visible signs of empirical reality:

> I admit, indeed, that the breaking of bread is a symbol, not the reality. But this being admitted, we duly infer from the exhibition of the symbol that the thing itself is exhibited. For unless we would charge God with deceit, we will never presume to say that he holds forth an empty symbol. ... The rule which the pious ought always to observe is, whenever they see symbols instituted by the Lord, to think and feel surely persuaded that the truth of the thing signified is also present. For why does the Lord put the symbol of his body into your hands, but just to assure you that you truly partake of him. (594)

By learning to view corporeal bread and wine in a figurative, or spiritual sense, we allow them to have a spiritual effect: 'by the corporeal things which are produced in the sacrament, we are by a kind of analogy conducted to spiritual things' (595). Calvin has thus divided the sacrament into the 'signifier' (the word or icon) and the 'signified' (the concept). The 'signified' is part of the 'sign;' it is not to be confused with the 'referent'. Thus, in the sign 'cow', the signifier is the letters C, O, and W arranged in this particular form; the signified is the idea evoked by that word in the mind. These two elements together constitute the 'sign'. Although the signified is objectively present within the sign, it is possible to ignore it— just as it is possible to hear the word 'cow' and think of an elephant. Citing St. Augustine, Calvin asserts that 'in the elect alone, the sacraments effect what they figure' (634). Because the presence is conceptual rather than physical, a sacrament only works if it is acknowledged as working: 'The bread is not a sacrament to itself, but to those who receive it' (594).

Calvin's position might appear to recall Zwingli's, as expressed in statements like: 'We believe that the true body of Christ is eaten in the communion, not in a gross and carnal manner, but in a sacramental and spiritual manner by the religious, believing and pious heart.'[39] However Zwingli and his followers refused to accept that the spiritual or figurative eating of Christ, though real enough, could operate within an unworthy individual. The efficacy of the Sacrament depended upon the belief of the recipient for Zwingli, whereas Calvin saw it as operative objectively in the elect. Due to this difference, and in spite of concerted efforts from all sides, it proved impossible to mend the sacramental rift among Protestants. In 1536 the Lutherans signed the Wittenberg Concord with south-German former Zwinglians, but Heinrich Bullinger refused to participate, objecting to the insistence that the body and blood are 'substantially' expressed in bread and wine, and to the consequent conclusion that Christ would be received even by the unworthy. This was confirmed by the 1549 *Consensus Tigurines* between Bullinger and Calvin, in which article seventeen pacifies Bullinger by connecting the sacrament's efficacy to the Calvinist concept of election: 'While the signs are administered to the reprobate and elect, the truth of the signs reaches only the latter.'[40] The sacrament's efficacy remained objectively true, but its truth did not 'reach' the reprobate.

Both Zwingli and Calvin hold that only the believer is able to perceive the *logos* within the sign, but for Zwingli that is a psychological action and not caused by the tokens themselves. The difference is that for Calvin the efficacy resides in the signs. In other words, the signs are performative. The symbolic becomes substantial. Representation becomes reality. Calvin explains his difference from the Zwinglians thus:

> According to them, to eat is merely to believe; while I maintain that the flesh of Christ is eaten by believing, because it is made ours by faith, and that that eating is the effect and fruit of faith; or, if you will have it more clearly, according to them, eating is faith, whereas it rather seems to me to be a consequence of faith. (592)

When Calvin says that the sacrament is 'eaten by believing', he indicates that its effect is just as objective in the soul as the effect of food on the physical body—and this despite the fact that Christ is not physically but only symbolically present. It is in this sense, I think, that Calvin expresses the 'spirit of capitalism'. Max Weber's famous phrase has often been criticized, because he located its emergence in eighteenth-century Pennsylvania, where actual, empirical capitalism was practically non-existent. However, Weber was not interested in capitalism's empirical birth, but in the birth of its 'spirit' (the German word *Geist* also means 'essence' or 'soul'). Weber found this 'spirit' struggling to consciousness in the mind of Benjamin Franklin, expressing itself in such declarations as 'time is money,' and 'money is of the prolific, generating nature. Money can beget money, and its offspring can beget more.'[41] The equation of 'time', of human life itself, with its symbolic representation in financial form, and the attribution of subjective agency to this alienated symbol, provide the true psychological preconditions of capitalism.

Calvin's ethical endorsement of performative representation extended beyond sacramental to financial hermeneutics. Collapsing the distinction between use-value and exchange value, along with the homologous distinction between *phusis* and *nomos*, he dismissed Aristotle's opinion that money was sterile in *De Usuris* (1545): 'Indeed, I concede that *children* perceive that if you shut money up in a box it will be sterile.'[42] He worries that if 'we so completely forbid usuries we bind consciences with a tie more strictly than God himself,' and points out that 'there is no witness of scripture by which all usury is totally forbidden.'[43] In *Commentaries on the Prophet Ezekiel* Calvin concludes: 'we shall not find all interest contrary to the law, and hence it follows that interest is not always to be condemned.'[44] His willingness to tolerate usury springs from his conception of money as an active agent. In apparent disregard of any ethical objection, he happily personifies exchange-value as fertile: 'When does one ever buy a field thinking that money does not father money?'[45] As J. B. Sauer points out, this is a momentous intellectual breakthrough: '[t]he distinction that Calvin has made is between transactions for consumption and transactions for production. This is a profound theoretical differentiation.'[46] This vital distinction becomes possible to the extent that money is conceived as productive: an agentive symbol or a performative sign. The groundwork for this attitude to representation was laid in the sacramental controversies, and the message it inculcates—that symbols contain performative power—is now instinctively accepted by millions of people to whom the name of Calvin is unknown.

NOTES

1. See Mervyn Duffy, *How Language, Ritual, and Sacraments Work: According to John Austin, Jürgen Habermas, and Louis-Marie Chauvet* (Rome: Gregorian University, 2005).
2. Paul Matthew Burgess, *Play, Metaphor, and Judgment in a World of Signs: A Peircean Semiotic Approach to Christian Worship* (Ann Arbor, MI: University Microfilms), 1991, 87.
3. John Ryckes, *The Image of Love* (1525) in David J.Davis, *From Icons to Idols: Documents on the Image Debate in Reformation England* (Cambridge: James Clarke & Co., 2015), 21.
4. William Tyndale, *An Answer unto Sir Thomas More's Dialogue* (1532) in Davis, 26.
5. *The Catholic Encyclopedia*, http://www.newadvent.org/cathen/05573a.html. Retrieved March 31, 2020.
6. See Edward Foley, *From Age to Age: How Christians Celebrated the Eucharist*, revised and expanded edition (Collegeville, PA: The Liturgical Press, 2008).
7. Mary T. Clark, *An Aquinas Reader* (New York: Fordham University Press, 2000), 485. Emphasis added.
8. Cit. Regina Schwartz, *Sacramental Poetics at the Dawn of Secularism* (Stanford UP, 2008), 7.
9. *Catechismus Catholicae Ecclesiae* (CCE) (Vatican City: Vatican, 1997) no. 1131.
10. Cit. William P. O'Brien SJ, 'The Eucharistic Species in Light of Pierce's Sign Theory,' *Theological Studies* 75 (2014), 74–93, 75. See also Andrew Robinson, *God and the World of Signs: Trinity, Evolution, and the Metaphysical Semiotics of C.S. Peirce* (Leiden: Brill, 2010).
11. Paul Tillich, *The Meaning and Justification of Religious Symbols*, in *Religious Experience and Truth*, ed. Sidney Hook (New York: New York University Press, 1961), 23.
12. Edward Kilmartin SJ, *The Eucharist in the West: History and Theology*, ed. Robert J. Daly (Collegevile MN: The Liturgical Press, 1998), xxiii.
13. Cit. Phillip Kennedy, *Christianity: An Introduction* (New York: Taurus, 2011), 129.
14. See Simon During, *Modern Enchantments: The Cultural Power of Secular Magic* (Harvard UP, 2002), 4.

15. Martin Luther, *The Babylonian Captivity of the Church*, in *Luther's Primary Works*, ed. Henry Wace and C.A. Buchheim (London: Hodder and Staughton, 1896), 323.
16. Council of Trent, Sess. XXII, can. III, cit. *Catholic Encyclopedia:* http://www.newadvent.org/cathen/. Retrieved April 1, 2020.
17. Martin Luther, *Works*, ed. Jaroslav Pelikan and Helmut T. Lehmann (Philadelphia, PA: Fortress Press, 1959) XXVI, 135.
18. See Wolfhart Pannenberg, *Systematic Theology*, vol. 3, trans. Geoffrey Bromiley (Wm. B. Eerdmans Publishing Co., 1998), 312.
19. Ibid.
20. Ibid., 209.
21. A rare analysis of religious indulgences in economic terms can be found in Alberto Cassone and Carlo Macchese, 'The Economics of Religious Indulgences,' *Journal of Institutional and Theoretical Economics* 155.3 (September 1999), 429–442.
22. Malcom Lambert: *Medieval Heresies: Popular Movements from the Gregorian Reform to the Reformation* (Blackwell, 1992), 304.
23. Thomas Fudge, *The Trial of Jan Hus: Medieval Heresy and Criminal Procedure* (Oxford UP, 2013), 156.
24. See Philip Schaff, 'The Eucharistic Controversy,' *History of the Christian Church, vol. 7, Modern Christianity. The German Reformation* (Electronic Version, Christian Classics Ethereal Library), sections 103ff.
25. Phillipp Robinson Rossner, Introduction to Martin Luther, *On Commerce and Usury (1524)* (Anthem P, 2015), 19.
26. Cit. Rossner, 20.
27. Martin Luther, *An Appeal to the Ruling Class of German Nationality* (1520), in *Martin Luther: Selections From His Writings*, ed. John Dillenberger (New York: Random House, 1962), 470.
28. Martin Luther, *The Babylonian Captivity of the Church*, trans. Albert Steinhaeuser (Philadelphia: A.J. Holman Company, 1915), 181..
29. Ibid., 262.
30. Ibid., 229.
31. Andreas Karlstadt, *On the Removal of Images* in *Karlstadt, Emser and Eck on Sacred Images: A Reformation Debate*, ed. Bryan Mangrum and Giuseppe Scavizzi (Toronto: Center for Reformation and Renaissance Studies, 1998), 21–44, 23.
32. Cit. Carrie Euler, 'Huldrych Zwingli and Heinrich Bullinger,' in *A Companion to the Eucharist in the Reformation*, ed. Lee Palmer Wandel (Boston: Brill, 2014), 57–74, 64.
33. Ulrich Zwingli, 'Letter to the Princes of Germany' (August 27, 1530), in *On Providence and Other Essays*, ed. William John Hinke (Durham, NC: The Labyrinth Press, 1983), 105–127, 120.

34. Martin Luther, *Against the Heavenly Prophets* (1525), in *Theological Aesthetics: A Reader*, ed. Gesa Elsbeth Thiessen (Grand Rapids, MI: William B. Eerdmans, 2004), 132.
35. John Calvin, *Institutes of the Christian Religion Book IV*, trans. Henry Beveridge (Grand Rapids, MI: Wm. B. Eerdmans Publishing Co., 1989), 607.
36. Thus in 'The Eucharist in the Theology of Martin Luther and John Calvin,' *Perichoresis* 8.2 (2010) Dan Botica concludes that Calvin views the Eucharist as an 'analogy', and therefore as objectively true in the 'spiritual' sense. On the performative in Calvin, see Melvin Tinker, 'Language, Symbols and Sacraments: Was Calvin's View of the Lord's Supper Right?' More generally, see Robert Corrington, *A Semiotic Theory of Theology and Philosophy* (Cambridge UP, 2000) and Stephen Moore, *Post-structuralism and the New Testament: Derrida and Foucault at the Foot of the Cross* (Augsburg Fortress, 1994).
37. Cit. Ann W. Ramsey, *Liturgy, Politics and Salvation: The Catholic League in Paris and the Nature of Catholic Reform, 1540–1630* (U of Rochester P, 1999), 38.
38. John Calvin, *Short Treatise on the Holy Supper*, in *John Calvin: Selections From His Writings*, ed. John Dillenberger (Scholars Press, 1975), 515.
39. Huldrich Zwingli, 'Confession to King Francis', cit. Schaff, *History of the Christian Church Volume VI* (Charles Scribner's Sons, 1916), 677.
40. Cit. Emidio Campi, *Shifting Patterns of Reformed Tradition* (Bristol, CT: Vandenhoeck and Ruprecht, 2014), 105.
41. Benjamin Franklin, *Advice to a Young Tradesman* (1748), cit. Max Weber, *The Protestant Ethic and the 'Spirit' of Capitalism*, trans. Peter Baehr and Gordon Wells (New York: Penguin Books, 2002), 9.
42. Cit. Michael Wykes, 'Devaluing the Scholastics: Calvin's Ethics of Usury,' *Calvin Theological Journal* 38 (2003), 27–51, 44.
43. Cit. Wykes, 42.
44. John Calvin, *Commentaries on Ezekiel*, trans. Thomas Myers (Edinburgh, 1850), 226.
45. Cit. Wykes, 44.
46. Cit. Wykes, 45.

CHAPTER 6

The Two Usuries: Performative Representation in the City Comedies

6.1 Usury and Lust

This chapter examines the treatment of performative representation in the Elizabethan and Jacobean public theaters. That means studying the new prominence of efficacious signs across the social totality—in aesthetics, economics, sexuality, and religion—as it was expressed in the vibrant popular medium of the drama. The plays performed, especially the 'city comedies' that focused on the daily life of London's mercantile class, were constructed around elaborate conceptual and linguistic analogies between usurious finance and concupiscent sexuality.[1] The systematic convergence of sex and money may initially seem arbitrary to modern minds, but it is perfectly in accordance with the canonical Aristotelian tradition that formed the sixteenth-century intellect. Aristotle conceived of usury as a mode of reproduction that was unnatural, irrational, and unethical because it treated money as if it were a sexual being. The Aristotelian and Thomistic traditions regard usury as a quasi-sexual perversion, and early modern literature often employs sexual perversion as an 'instructive synecdoche'[2] for usury's psychological and moral ramifications.

The monetization of the European economy, the raising of the legal rate of interest, the dispossession of the peasantry, the primitive accumulation of capital, and the spread of wage labor are best conceived as different aspects of a single process. Over the sixteenth century, that process created the conditions for symbolic value to emerge as an autonomously

© The Author(s) 2020
D. Hawkes, *The Reign of Anti-logos*, Palgrave
Insights into Apocalypse Economics,
https://doi.org/10.1007/978-3-030-55940-3_6

powerful agent. Between 1580 and 1640 England's playwrights under-
took a sustained study of the social, spiritual, and sexual consequences of
representation's rise to power. These dramatists frequently compared, or
even equated, the emergent power of finance with the power of the devil.
Satan, the 'opponent' or 'opposite' of humanity, was often conceived as
identical with the objectified representation of human activity that was
achieving animation in the form of self-reproducing money.[3] This dual
power of usury and the devil was exercised stealthily, invisibly, within the
mind, but it displayed itself externally in the manipulation of performative signs, which it induced humanity to fetishize and to worship. The
agency of money and the agency of the devil both tried to obscure the
creative power of *logos*, displacing it with the illusory efficacy of images.
People therefore understood usury as a force that, in its invisibility and its
irresistibility, was similar in nature to the power of demonic magic.

Over the sixteenth century the power of representation, as well as
the reaction against that power, unleashed a whirlwind of creation and
destruction that leveled the feudal order in England. The process known
to economic historians as 'financialization' germinated in the city-states of
Renaissance Italy, before exploding across western Europe as the sudden
influx of American gold transformed society 'like an acid dissolving all
customary relationships.'[4] The profoundest and most subtle effects of the
financial revolution were semiotic. The Hispanic discoverers of American
gold were semantic literalists. Accustomed to identifying sacramental wine
with the substantial blood of Christ, the Dons naturally equated physical
bullion with financial value, thus insuring their nation's speedy impoverishment. In contrast, having grown accustomed to the moral legitimacy
of performative representation through the kind of sacramental debate
we discussed in the last chapter, Calvinist Holland and England avoided
Spain's fate by liberating financial value from its confinement in matter,
and acknowledging it as an abstraction that could be represented by
worthless paper just as effectively as by precious metal. Money, in short,
was recognized as a symbol capable of effecting changes in the objective environment: a performative sign. As Sir Moth Interest, the 'usurer
or money-bawd' of Ben Jonson's *The Magnetic Lady* (1632) observes:
'Wealth … doth inable him that hath it, / To the performance of all real
Actions.'[5]

In Jonson's day, the inexorable spread of the money-power, the
church's alleged lapse into liturgical idolatry, and the resort of the peasantry to ritual magic were understood as various manifestations of the

growing autonomy of signs. Strange as it may seem to the modern mind, sexual concupiscence was perceived as a similar manifestation of symbolic power. Etymological traces of the connection between magic and sexual attraction still linger in words like 'glamour.' Deriving from the Scots 'gramarye' and the French 'gramaire,' it originally meant 'learning' or 'logic' in a general sense. However, it gradually came to evoke specifically the occult logic of black magic, a kind of *anti-logos*. The term crossed the English border in the early sixteenth century, and was used to describe the way things appear under the influence of either magic or sexual attraction. These two influences were conceived as fundamentally similar, insofar as they evaded the rational faculties and exerted a powerful effect by the manipulation of appearances alone.

Reginald Scot's *Discoverie of Witchcraft* (1584) discusses the convergence of witchcraft and sexual attraction in detail. The false objectification by which a woman's body is fetishized in the male gaze is, for Scot, simultaneously a false subjectification, in which the body itself acquires an intent and a volition that it expresses, for instance through the invisible power of syphilis:

> The venom or poison of an harlot. Vertue conteined within the bodie of an harlot, or rather the venome proceeding out of the same maie be beheld with great admiration. For hir eie infecteth, entiseth, and (if I maie so saie) bewitcheth them manie times, which thinke themselves well armed against such maner of people. Hir toong, hir gesture, hir behaviour, her beautie, and other allurements poison and intoxicate the mind: yea, hir companie induceth impudencie, corrupteth virginitie, confoundeth and consumeth the bodies, goods, and the verie soules of men. And finallie hir bodie destroieth and rotteth the verie flesh and bones of mans bodie.[6]

Early modern playwrights constantly utilize the vocabulary of witchcraft to evoke sexual passion. The word 'charm' is employed by Shakespeare exclusively in the sense of magic or witchcraft, although often in a sexual context. In *The Tempest*'s masque, Venus plans to lay '[s]ome wanton charm' (4.1.95) on Ferdinand and Miranda; Tarquin rapes Lucrece while 'bewitched with lust's foul charm' (224), Romeo is 'bewitched by the charm of looks' (2.0.785) and Antony twice calls Cleopatra his 'charm' (4.12.2920, 2929). In Thomas Dekker's *The Shoemaker's Holiday* (1599) Jane remarks: 'I could be coy, as many women be,/ Feed you with sunshine smiles and wanton looks,/ But I detest witchcraft' (9.65–67).

As the Earl's servant perfumes his bed-chamber and prepares a banquet for the purpose of seduction in Dekker and John Webster's *Westward Ho* (1607), he asks: 'Does my lord mean to conjure, that he draws these strange characters?' (4.2.10). The Earl does not reply directly, but he muses on the kinship of magic and lust: 'But to do thus, what spell can us excite?/ This, the strong magic of appetite' (4.2.30–31). The magical language of the body could repel as well as attract. Sir Phillip Sidney's 'A Remedy for Love,' features the hideous Mopsa: 'Whose lips of marble, teeth of jet,/ Are spells and charms of strong defence,/ To conjure down concupiscence.'[7]

It was often observed that, through the forces of sexual repulsion or attraction, the body effectively communicated or 'spoke.' In Shakespeare's *Troilus and Cressida* (1602), Ulysses describes Helen of Troy: 'There's language in her eye, her cheek, her lip,/ Nay, her foot speaks' (4.5.55). As we have seen in previous chapters, Helen is the traditional symbol of erotic beauty's idolatrous efficacy, and she is consistently opposed to *logos* in early modern literature. Marlowe's *Dr. Faustus* (1592) is the most famous example of Helen's fetishization: 'Sweet Helen, make me immortal with a kiss./ Her lips suck forth my soul' (5.1.83–84). The language of the body is strongly efficacious–it can launch a thousand ships–but it is not referential. It ends in surface appearance. Like magic, sexual concupiscence circumvents reason and the will, the higher elements of the soul, causing people to follow appetite alone.

In Webster's *The Duchess of Malfi* (1613) Ferdinand asks Bosola whether, despite his Christianity, he believes in the power of love-magic to over-ride the will: 'Can your faith give way/ To think there's power in potions or in charms,/ To make us love whether we will or no?' (3.1.66–68). A majority of sixteenth-century English people would have answered with Bosola: 'Most certainly!' (3.1.69). The performative powers of usury, magic and sexual concupiscence were effectively homologous. Usury fetishizes money, magic fetishizes rituals, icons and incantations, and concupiscence fetishizes the body which, according to canonical philosophy, should properly be regarded as the sign of the soul. The imaginary reproduction of financial signs fetishizes 'the works of men's hands,' by treating a conventional or 'customary' symbol of human activity as if it were an independent agent and a natural creature. Usury and concupiscence are parallel violations of natural teleology, they divert money and sex away from their proper purposes. Furthermore, they both commit the basic epistemological and ethical error of confusing nature with custom: usury treats an artificial sign as if it were a natural creature, while concupiscence treats cultured human subjects as if they were mere physical bodies.

The people of early modern England were hardly the first to remark on the affinity between reproductive money and non-reproductive sexuality. Plato's *Republic* describes predatory usurers who 'recover the parent sum many times over multiplied into a family of children.'[8] Aristotle provides another early description of usury as unnatural reproduction when he points out that the Greek word for usury—*tokos*—also means 'birth.' Yet he already seems to be commenting on an established axiom, rather than arguing an original or controversial point:

> ... usury is most reasonably hated, because its gain comes from money itself and not from that for the sake of which money was invented. For money was brought into existence for the purpose of exchange, but interest increases the amount of the money itself (and this is the actual origin of the Greek word: offspring resembles parent, and interest is money born of money); consequently this form of the business of getting wealth is of all forms the most contrary to nature.[9]

It is reasonable to hate what is irrational, and usury is irrational because it perverts money away from its natural *telos*. Concupiscent sexuality was also deemed unnatural to the degree that it departs from the natural *telos* of sex, which is reproduction. In the *Laws* Plato remarks: 'when male unites with female for procreation the pleasure experienced is held to be due to nature, but contrary to nature when male mates with male or female with female'[10] (1.636c). The end, purpose and final cause of money—the reason for its existence—is to serve as a common denominator facilitating the exchange of objects other than itself. Financial value is a medium, not a thing. But usury does not regard money as a medium for exchange; it treats money as an object of exchange. Usury treats money as a *rei*, a thing: it objectifies the medium of exchange. Once money becomes a commodity it necessarily attains a value. Yet in the traditional conception money *is* value. In Thomistic scholasticism, Aristotle's argument is refracted into the observation that, since its *telos* was realized in consumption, money could not be separated from the 'use' of money. As St. Thomas Aquinas put it:

> ... the use of money... is nothing other than its substance, therefore either the lender sells something which doesn't exist, or he sells the same thing twice, namely the money itself whose use is its consumption, and this is manifestly against the principles of natural justice.[11]

If value itself is subjected to evaluation, then no value—whether economic, epistemological, or ethical—can avoid becoming relative. The anonymous author of *The Ruinate Fall of Pope Usurie, Deriv'd from Pope Idolatrie* (1580) finds this a threatening prospect. The tract protests against money's independence, warning that that having been established by the political sovereign, financial value must remain fixed,. It must not fluctuate autonomously:

> Money was ordained to passe between man and man, as a thing made having his full value, neither to be diminished nor augmented, as the pound is said be be xx shilling... because the Prince hath set eche sundry valew. (3)

Money is the standard by which all other value is measured, 'the cheef, which equall value governeth all unequall values.... Money is once valued which may not bee altered' (3). The author distinguishes between money and commodities or 'wares,' whose value is indeed flexible '[w]ares rise and fall, and no continued certaintie abideth of their prices' (3). His conclusion is unequivocal: 'Money must not be used as wares, nor wares as money' (3). But usury did treat money as ware, and it was this departure from *telos* that made it homologous with sodomy. In *Usuries Spright Conjured* (1604) Thomas Pie lists several objections to usury, including unnatural reproduction, but he reserves the term 'sodomy' for usury's neglect of 'commutation,' the rendering equal of different commodities, which is money's proper purpose.

> Fourthly, the Usurer maketh that breed, gender and increase which by nature is barren and unapt to increase; for in usurie money genders, gets, or bringes foorth money; whereupon Plutark saith that the Usurer maketh something of nothing, mauger the head of the naturall Philosopher.
> Fifthly the Usurer perverteth that end and use of money, which is agreeable to nature: namely commutation, for commutation was the end wherefore money was ordeiened in humane societie, and is the use of it; which natural use the Usurer turneth into that which is against nature. Therefore it is called a kinde of Sodomie. (19)

We might have expected him to connect 'sodomy' to his fourth objection against usury, rather than to his fifth. But money's *telos* is to be a mediating symbol, and Pie labels as 'sodomy' the process by which that symbol ceases referring to external commodities, and is instead idolized as an end-in-itself. Because every object of exchange must pass through the medium of commutation, moreover, the reification of money is highly contagious. It tempts humanity into other kinds of fetishism, provoking an irresistible impulse to perverse reproduction. Usury assumes that the purpose of money is to produce more money, and it induces human beings to act on that assumption. Aristotle notes that the belief that money can breed has even become embedded in language through the word *tokos*. His description of interest as the fruit of unnatural reproduction established a conceptual homology between usury and sexual concupiscence that grew axiomatic with the empirical verification derived from their reliably simultaneous historical advancement.

6.2 SOCIETY OF SHOWS

According to John T. Noonan, the traditional ecclesiastical prohibition of usury reached its height around 1450. Over the subsequent century and a half, 'the leading moral theologians worked out the modifications, alternatives, and changes which effectively sapped the force of the old rule so that by the seventeenth century almost every modern credit transaction could be accommodated within the revised framework.'[12] This legitimization of usury, unprecedented since antiquity, was made possible by a new way of understanding money. As Odd Langholm reminds us, the Aristotelian case against usury 'was a theory based on the conception of money as coin.'[13] If financial value is conceived as inhabiting the physical bodies of gold and silver, then money clearly is not fruitful. Gold and silver visibly do not reproduce. In that case, it makes financial sense to plunder and hoard precious metals, since they are identical with wealth itself. Only by conceiving of financial value as symbolic does it become possible to imagine it as fertile. If financial value is symbolic, it can and indeed must reproduce. If value is symbolic, it must be invested in order to survive. To hoard money is then to destroy it: 'caves/ Dam miser's gold' (4.2.106), as Mistress Openwork puts it in Middleton and Dekker's *The Roaring Girl* (1611).

This re-conception of value produced several common literary conceits. The need to 'put out' or invest money in order for it to reproduce was incessantly used metaphorically, to demand that a woman circulate her sexual favors in order to bear children. This trope is invariably constructed by a morally dubious character. Most frequently, as in Shakespeare's *Sonnets* (1609) and Milton's *Comus* (1634), it appears as the suave ploy of a seducer. In Shakespeare the seduction is homosexual, in Milton it is magical, in both it is ethically transgressive—not least because both writers use the seductive force of magic as a vehicle for female self-assertion. Milton's Lady wins her crown of virtue by spurning Comus' claim that '[b]eauty is Nature's coin, must not be hoarded' (738), while Shakespeare's aggressive Venus uses the seducer's argument on Adonis: 'Foul-cankering rust the hidden treasure frets/ But gold that's put to use more gold begets' (789–790). This trope also features in more openly financial calculations, as in *The Taming of the Shrew* (1592) when Tranio congratulates Baptista Minola for having off-loaded his daughter: ''twas a commodity lay fretting by you; / 'Twill bring you gain or perish on the seas' (2.1.322–323). 'Beauty's for use' (1.2.149) exclaims Malheureux in John Marston's *The Dutch Courtesan* (1604) and Shakespeare's Venus resorts to a similarly fallacious teleology: 'Torches are made to light, jewels to wear,/ Dainties to taste, fresh beauty for the use' (183–184).

Although neither term was available to them in today's sense, the people of early modern England were thus accustomed to use 'sexual' imagery in 'economic' contexts, and vice versa. Developments in what we would consider the 'economic sphere' inevitably carried implications for what we would regard as the 'sphere' of 'sexuality,' and the period's most prominent economic development was money's incremental acquisition of reproductive power. That power was consolidated when London's goldsmiths realized that they could accrue interest on bank-notes whose nominal value far exceeded the physical gold in their coffers. Although some historians argue that the process of 'financialization' is inherently cyclical and recurrent,[14] it was in seventeenth-century England that the expression of financial value as a performative symbol first acquired the official endorsement of a global imperium, whose wealth and power rapidly increased as the immediate result of that intellectual breakthrough.

As Craig Muldew has shown, sixteenth-century England witnessed the rapid growth of a monetized, exchange-based economy, combined with a severe shortage of physical coinage.[15] Carl Wennerlind estimates that 'during the second half of the sixteenth-century demand for money grew by approximately 500%, while the supply of coins expanded by only 63%.'[16] As a result, most small-scale transactions necessarily took place through the medium of credit. Elizabethan finance was mostly a money of the mind. This mental money was coined out of the intimate relations between individuals, and such financial relations as credit, debt and confidence were interiorized and experienced as psychological phenomena. Money's effects on the mind were thus readily perceptible, and this in turn exposed financial representation's kinship with other kinds of sign. For example, Francesca Trivellato stresses the influence of the financial instruments known as 'bills of exchange' on the developing understanding of value. These were originally encoded documents that could be redeemed for gold by a particular person, but by the seventeenth century they were increasingly transferable. A holder might endorse a bill and pass it on to someone else, who then had the right to collect the debt, and this process might be repeated several times. Trivellato observes that 'by abstracting value from any tangible referent, bills of exchange amplified widespread fears about social disintegration and the erosion of traditional hierarchies that accompanied the expansion of commerce.'[17]

Small-scale usury was ubiquitous in Renaissance England, as Shakespeare frequently indicates. King Lear laments that he lives in an age when '[t]he usurer hangs the cozener' (4.5.155). In *Timon of Athens* (1605), Alcibiades castigates 'usury/ That makes the senate ugly' (3.5.97–98) and 'the usuring senate' (3.5.108) who 'have told their money and let out/ Their coin upon large interest' (3.5.105–106). Participants in an economy based on small-scale credit, like Timon's Athens or Shakespeare's England, necessarily learned to equate words with currency. Promises to pay must be accepted as payment; words must be treated as legal tender. The symbolic nature of money is taken for granted when Timon's Steward laments that his master's 'promises fly so beyond his state/ That what he speaks is all in debt, he owes/ For every word' (1.2.197–199). Thomas Middleton, who collaborated with Shakespeare on *Timon*, makes a similar point in *A Trick To Catch The Old One* (1605): 'Are not words promises, and are not promises debts, Sir?' (4.4.182). The extent to which words were taken for coins inevitably brought home the affinity between the two media, and they advanced towards power in such close lockstep as to suggest their fundamental affinity.

The legitimization of usury was not conceived as a specifically 'economic' development, but rather as part of a more general growth in the practical power of autonomous symbols. Other symptoms of representation's burgeoning power included a dangerous increase in the popular practices of ritual magic and idolatry. In *The Advancement of Learning*

(1605) Francis Bacon distinguishes between the referential signs or 'types' of the Old Testament and the 'non-significant' signs of magic and idolatry: 'the very ceremonies and figures of the old law were full of reason and signification, much more than the ceremonies of idolatry and magic, that are full of non-significants and absurd characters.'[18] This was an ethic that could be applied to any form of representation. The *Ruinate Fall of Pope Usurie, Deriv'd from Pope Idolatrie* (1580) is a dialogue between the Flesh and the Spirit. The former opens by asking: 'Are none usurers but those men and women that occupy money?' The Spirit replies: 'Yes verily, as the Adulterers, Idolaters, witches, sorcerers, false forswearers and money usurers' (2). It appears that financial usury is just one among many of the forms taken by the vice. Capacious as it is, however, the list is by no mean arbitrary. The common factor among these miscreants is their fetishization of representation. Similarly in *The English Usurer* (1610) John Blaxton extends the well-known Biblical passages equating covetousness and idolatry to include usury:

> The Vsurer sinneth by Idolatrie. For seeing the roote of vsury is couetous-nesse (which is the roote of all euill) it cannot bee denied; but that euery Vsurer is couetous; and euery couetous man is an idolater *Eph.* 5.5. And a Seruant of *Mammon, Mat.* 6.24. And therefore no true Seruant of the Lord, now you must remember, that for couetous persons and idolaters, there is no inheritance in Heauen. (26)

The kinship of usury and idolatry seemed obvious to Blaxton. Although it may be obscure to modern perceptions, the people of Renaissance England found it no less obvious that 'adultery' or 'fornication' was essentially similar to both vices. By making sensual pleasure the end of desire, sexual concupiscence mistakes the appearance of a human being for the essence. It addresses itself to the body at the expense of the soul: to the sign rather than to the referent. In sixteenth- and seventeenth-century England, concupiscent sexuality was frequently designated by the term 'sodomy'—a word which designated a wide range of sins, not all of which were sexual in nature. As Michel Foucault observes, the resulting 'uncertain status'[19] of this 'utterly confused category' (101) made it a convenient figure for transgression in general.[20] Stephen Orgel observes that 'sodomy ... has no independent existence in the Renaissance mind,'[21] while Alan Bray notes that sodomy was 'also a political and a religious crime.'[22] The concept of 'usury' was equally versatile. As early as the thirteenth century, the future Pope Innocent IV declared that 'practically every evil stems from usury,'[23] and the grotesque 'money-bawds' who prowl the Renaissance stage provide ample confirmation of R. H. Tawney's observation that '[t]he typical usurer was apt ... to outrage not one but all, of the decencies of social intercourse.'[24]

The malleability of both 'usury' and 'sodomy' invited public interest in their convergence, which often took surprisingly quotidian forms. Thus Eliza Greenstadt observes that opponents of usury 'compared usury to sodomy because both violated communal values based on friendship' and that 'sodomy and usury converged as twinned antitheses to the virtue of friendship.'[25] The convergence of usury and sodomy, in turn, revealed their kinship with autonomous symbols of every description. The public theaters of Elizabethan London were places where all kinds of performative sign seemed to coalesce. They survived by charging admission, selling their art as a commodity, and the playwrights themselves frequently commented on the commodified condition of their product. The uniquely visual, sensual nature of the theater exuded an appeal that was acknowledged as erotic by the players and their puritanical opponents alike. Stage-players are sexually objectified in many cultures; in pre-Communist China female actors were literally prostitutes.[26] As a result, many societies, including early modern England, have prohibited women from performing on stage. This created a different problem, however. The erotic allure of the theatrical spectacle was considered especially egregious because women's roles were taken by boys, so that the audience was effectively invited to pederastic desire. A typical protest against a performance by the Children of Her Majesty's Chapel complains with disarming frankness of 'the lascivious writhing of their tender limbs, and gorgeous apparel.'[27]

Nevertheless, the stage's display of human beings in symbolic, objectified form enabled playwrights and audiences to reflect upon the subjective and ideological repercussions of performativity, especially in the convergent fields of sex and money. Dekker's *If This Be Not a Good Play the Devil Is in It* (1611) employs the usurer-bawd Bartervile as a specimen of performative identity. 'Pursued by kennels of barking creditors,' he 'turns Turk' to avoid paying his debts. Questioned as to the morality of this course, he replies that he is happy to replace 'nature' with 'art'—that is, to adapt his conscience to the pursuit of:

> Profit, that gilded god, commodity.
> He that would grow damn'd-rich, yet live secure,
> Must keep a case of faces, sometimes demure,
> Sometimes a grum-surly sir, now play the Jew,
> Then the Precisian. Not a man we'll view
> But varies so. Myself, of bashful nature,
> Am thus supplied by art. (4.1.9–15)

In Renaissance England, the theater was the 'art' best suited to investigate and exhibit the psychological effects of an economy based on credit. The theater's fascination with 'self-fashioning,' its obsession with disguise, multiple identity and 'shape-shifting,' reflect the fluid subjectivity demanded and molded by the power that Bartervile calls 'commodity.' To the extent that usury is tolerated, credit and credit-worthiness become financially valuable, and one's 'character' attains objective form in the opinion of others. Character becomes a commodity, and as such it can be expressed in terms of exchange-value, alienated and rendered external to its natural possessor.[28] When this occurs among a relatively small circle of people, as in early modern London, the disjunction between human being and economic actor is made clearly visible, and this raises new and disturbing questions about the nature of identity itself.

The theater was an ideal medium in which to evaluate such developments—so much so that any anti-theatrical critics believed that it actively encouraged them. The theater's public deployment of poetry to affect the passions of the audience seemed dangerously close to magic, and Sir Phillip Sidney's *Defence of Poesie* (1580) finds it necessary to defend 'poesie' against the charge. The poet is not a 'conjurer' because he 'nothing affirmeth… the poet never maketh any circles about your imagination, to conjure you to believe for true what he writeth.'[29] Although poetry may not have qualified, however, sixteenth-century England seemed full of magic to many. In *The Scourge of Villainy* (1598) John Marston expressed the fear that people were degenerating into simulations:

> These are no men, but *Apparitions,*
> Ignes fatui, Glowormes, Fictions,
> Meteors, Ratts of Nilus, Fantasies,
> Colosses, Pictures, Shades, Resemblances.
> ....
> ....Now raile no more at my sharpe Cynick sound
> Thou brutish world, that in all vilenes drown'd
> Hast lost thy soule, for naught but shades I see,
> Resemblances of men inhabite thee.[30]

According to Marston, the elimination of essence in favor of appearance not only destroys the soul, it leaves humanity permanently vulnerable to deception. The popular culture of early modern London was fascinated by the 'gulling' and 'coney-catching' facilitated by the urban environment. In Dekker's *If This Be Not a Good Play the Devil Is in It*, Pluto sends his devils into the world in disguise: 'For men are out-sides only; be you the same' (1.1.95).

Like Dekker and Marston, Ben Jonson saw the stage as a means of exposing, criticizing or parodying idolatrous spectacles in the very act of displaying them. Jonson's bitter dispute with the architect and set designer Inigo Jones produced a prototypical ethics of representation, as the playwright constructed a moral hierarchy between a masque's 'soul' (its story or narrative, composed by Jonson) and its 'body' (the physical, sensual spectacle for which Jones was responsible). Throughout his career Jonson was consumed by the conviction that an ulterior reality underlies phenomenal appearances. That conviction had been a philosophical commonplace since Plato, but the urgency with which Jonson propounds it indicates that he perceives it as under serious threat. In his dispute with Jones, Jonson returns repeatedly to the dichotomy between a masque's exalted 'soul' and its vulgar 'body,' invariably characterizing the latter as ontologically and ethically inferior. The worst insult Jonson could hurl at Jones was 'all thy work is show.'[31] In his 'Expostulation with Inigo Jones' (1631) Jonson denounces the entire genre of masques as excessively dependent on spectacle:

> O shows, shows, mighty shows!
> The eloquence of masques! What need of prose,
> Or verse, or sense to express immortal you?
> You are the spectacles of state! ....
> ...O, to make boards to speak! There is a task!
> Painting and carpentry are the soul of masque!
> Pack with your peddling poetry to the stage,
> This is the money-get, mechanic age! (39–42, 49–52)

The 'speaking,' significant stage-effects created by Jones communicate in the same language as Helen of Troy's 'speaking' body. Jonson associates such 'shows' with *banausic* or 'mechanic' crafts, which are designed to delight the groundlings and so make money. The pursuit of profit produces a sensual, commercial aesthetic, and this is one way in which money achieved an obvious agency in early modern England. Just as

Socrates traced the sophists' rhetoric to their need to commodify their thought, so here Jonson explains the masque's reliance on spectacle by its historical location in 'the money-get, mechanic age.'

Playwrights had frequent recourse to *prosopopoeia*, or personification, to convey the agency of financial entities—as when, in Shakespeare's *King John* (c.1596), Phillip the Bastard refers to '[t]hat smooth-faced gentleman, tickling Commodity' (2.1.573). Middleton in particular tends to embody usury in the form of semi-human, walking abstractions like Harry Dampit, and even to figure 'credit,' 'debt' and other usurious phenomena as independent agents. In *A Trick to Catch the Old One* (1607) Witgood exclaims 'I dare not visit the city: there I should be too soon visited by that horrible plague, my debts' (1.1.16–17). These duly appear in the person of three 'Creditors,' only one of whom is given a proper name. Such figures represent the same abstract force invoked by Middleton in *The Phoenix* (1603), when the Captain wishes 'I had lost my credit seven year ago. / 'T'as undone me; that's it that makes me fly…' (8.9–10). His wife ascribes a similar agency to 'chaste credit… Well may I call it chaste, for like a maid, / Once falsely broke, it ever lives decayed. / O, captain, husband, you name that dishonest / By whose good power all that are honest live' (8.19–23). The personification of 'credit' displayed usury's unnatural nature by showing how it confounded the categories of subject and object, displacing the activities, aspirations and interests of human beings with the very different demands of humanity's objectified representation.

The artificial agency acquired by 'credit' was sufficiently unnatural to invite comparison to the paradigmatic violation of nature, which was 'sodomy.' This concept evolved out of a scholastic teleology that castigated any direction of desire toward pleasure rather than procreation. This also provided grounds for the link between sodomy and idolatry, since idolatry abandons the naturally referential *telos* of signs by mistaking them for their referents. The connection found dramatic expression in 1538 when John Bale's *Three Lawes* presented the figure of Infidelity plotting: 'The law of Nature to Poison,/ With pestilent idolatry, /And with most stinking sodomy.'[32] Citing Biblical sanction ('As Paul to the Romans testify/ The gentiles, after idolatry,/ Fell to such bestial sodomy' [22]), a character named Sodomismus forms a close alliance with Idolatrie, whose performative power he describes as independent of *logos*:

So they bring money to the box
When they to her make moan
She can fetch again all that is lost,
And draw drink out of a rotten post,
Without the help of the Holy Ghost—
In working she is alone. (17)

Idolatrie is 'alone' in her 'working;' the source of her magical power is not *logos* and can therefore only be demonic. Nor is her 'working' limited to liturgy. She also operates through commerce, as Infidelitie explains: 'Here have I pretty gins,/ Both broches, beads, and pins,/ With such as the people wins/ Unto idolatry' (24). Although state and ecclesiastical authorities had condemned 'concupiscence' since before Christ, the term 'sodomy' emerged at a much later date.[33] However, Bale's play suggests that, by the sixteenth century, sodomitical, usurious, magical, and idolatrous transgressions had attained a general identity that transcended the differences between the areas in which it was made manifest. The people of Renaissance England conceived of experience as a totality, and this enabled them to see that the burgeoning power of usury was conceptually, figuratively and even empirically connected to the cultural prominence of performative signs in general. Along with magic and idolatry, usury and concupiscence were different manifestations of a unitary, consistent intent, the unfolding of a single process throughout society, the diffusion of a particular tendency through every cranny of the *psyche*. To acknowledge the autonomous power of representation was to be confronted with the traumatic possibility that there is no meaning or significance underlying the surface appearances of life as a whole.

6.3   THE BROKING KNIGHT OF TROY

Karl Marx's famous description of money as 'the common pimp of people and of nations' is far from original. In Shakespeare's *Measure for Measure* (1604) the pimp Pompey complains: 'Twas never merry world since, of two usuries, the. merriest was put down, and the worser allowed by order of law' (3.2.5–6). The 'two usuries' here are pimping (commonly known as 'bawdry') and money-lending. Shakespeare evidently assumed that his audience would easily understand Pompey's casual allusion to their affinity.[34] A familiar constellation of empirical associations connect prostitution and usury in the city comedies: whoremongers fund their vice with borrowed money, so that bawds are often usurers too, while prostitutes scorn financial as well as sexual propriety in their characteristic fetishism of commodities. As the anonymous *Hic Mulier (The Mannish Woman)* (1620) observed: 'she that hath pawned her credit to get a hat will sell her Smock to buy a Feather' (269).

In Shakespeare's England, the proposition that sexual concupiscence, ritual magic, liturgical idolatry and financial usury were different manifestations of a fundamentally identical underlying tendency was a basic premise, as well as a logical consequence, of an entire world-view. These vices violated natural teleology, preferring the means to the end. This was to prefer the body to the soul, the appearance to the essence, and the sign to the referent. The fundamental unity of bawdry and usury was axiomatic. In *Timon of Athens* even the Fool understands it: 'no usurer but has a fool to his servant; my mistress is one, and I am her fool. When men come to borrow of your masters, they approach sadly, and go away merry; but they enter my master's house merrily, and go away sadly' (2.2.103–7). Timon himself singles out usurers and bawds as appropriate targets for the vengeance of Alcibiades:

> Pity not honour'd age for his white beard;
> He is an usurer: strike me the counterfeit matron;
> It is her habit only that is honest,
> Herself's a bawd... (4.3.110–113)

Aristotle expands on the link between usury and pimping in the *Nicomachean Ethics*. He condemns 'those who ply sordid trades, pimps and all such people, and those who lend small sums at high rates. For all these take more than they ought, and from the wrong sources. What is common to them is evidently a sordid love of gain.'[35] As George Downame reminded his readers in 1604: 'The Philosopher matcheth the usurer with the baud.'[36] In an epigram as dense as it is brief, Ben Jonson argues: 'If, as their ends, their fruits were so the same, / Bawdry and usury were one kind of game.'[37] The 'ends' of bawdry and usury are different: one pursues sexual pleasure, the other financial profit. Yet their 'fruits' are 'the same,' because both of them produce illegitimate offspring. The bawd and the usurer are both mediators who fetishize mediation.

Early modern dramatists never tire of drawing attention to their basic identity. In *Timon of Athens*, Apemantus scorns 'poor rogues and usurer's men. / Bawds between gold and want' (2.2.6–7). In William Rowley's *A Match at Midnight* (c.1622) a character known only as 'Bawd' informs a usurer: 'As I have been bawd to the flesh, you have been bawd to your money.'[38] In 1614 Sir Thomas Overbury described a 'Devillish Usurer' as one who 'puts his money to the unnatural act of generation; and his scrivener is the supervisor bawd to't.'[39] Thomas Dekker repeats the commonplace that 'the Usurer lives by the lechery of mony, and is bawd to his owne bags.'[40] Of all the Elizabethan grub street hacks, Dekker was the most obsessed with the trope of usury as unnatural fertility. He employs it to describe not only the nature of usury, but also of usury's social effects. Addressing the city of London he declares:

> Thou doest likewise Lye with Usury: how often hast thou bin found in bed with her! Upon Usury hast thou begotten Extortion (a strong but unmannerly child), Hardnes of heart (a very murderer), and Bad conscience, who is so unruly, that he seemes to be sent unto thee, to be thy everlasting paine. Then hath she sonnes in law, and they are all Scriveners: those Scriveners have base sonnes, and they are all common Brokers; those Brokers likewise send a number into the world, & they are all common Theeves. (36–37)

Dekker asserts that usury effectively gives birth to a whole race of social undesirables. It causes the indebted to turn to theft, and thence to fences or 'brokers' who launder their money through 'scriveners.' The period's drama confirms that 'gallants' often financed their whoring with borrowed money, so that the pimp and the usurer were frequently the same person. Usury and prostitution are often simply synonymous: Castiza in Middleton's *Revenger's Tragedy* (1607) is content to 'prostitute [her] brest to the Dukes sonne, / And put herself to common Usury' (4.4.103–104). In Marston's *The Dutch Courtesan* (c.1604) Freevill is attacked for resorting 'to the stale use, / The common bosom of a money creature' (1.1.103–104) while Timon of Athens tells Timandra: 'Be a whore still: they love thee not that use thee' (4.3.82). The terms 'bawd' and 'broker' were also synonymous. 'Hence bawd, hence broker' (4.1.53) declares Susan Mountford in Heywood's *A Woman Killed with Kindness* (1603). Shakespeare's *King John* describes 'commodity' as '[t]his bawd, this broker, this all-changing word' (2.1.608). 'Hence, broker-lackey' (5.10.33) declares Shakespeare's Troilus to the bawd Pandarus. The word 'commodity' was a common synonym for 'prostitute.'[41] Dekker and

Middleton's *The Honest Whore Part One* (1604) opens with Matheo's disarmingly frank reflection on the logic behind the synonym: 'Here's a coil for a dead commodity! 'Sfoot, women when they are alive are but dead commodities, for you shall have one woman lie upon many men's hands!' (1.1.91–94). A 'dead commodity' is an unsaleable item, typically passed off *in lieu* of cash onto impecunious gallants by unscrupulous usurers, and Matheo's pun is ubiquitous in the city comedies.

Indeed, Valerie Forman remarks that 'the OED cites Dekker's phrase, "the whore is call'd the commodity," from his rogue pamphlet *The Belman*, as the first use of "commodity" to refer to something in which one deals or trades.'[42] Throughout early modern literature, prostitution is employed as a synecdoche for wage labor, the commodified form of human activity. In *The Honest Whore Part One* Hipolito denounces 'whores' as paradigmatic 'journeywomen' or proletarians, who sell themselves:

> Like bears and apes, y'are baited and show tricks
> For money, but your bawd the sweetness licks.
> Indeed you are their journey-women, and do
> All base and damn'd works they list set you to. (2.1.214–217)

Characters like Security in Chapman, Jonson and Marston's *Eastward Ho* (1605), Perfidious Oldcraft in Beaumont and Fletcher's *Wit At Several Weapons* (c.1613) and Bartervile in Dekker's *If This Be Not a Good Play the Devil Is in It* (1612) are simultaneously usurers and bawds, and their sexual sins blend imperceptibly into their financial transgressions. Bartervile gloats that 'there's little marrying, we ha' so much whoring,' as he takes receipt of '[t]he pension of the Stews... Stew-money, sir; stewed-prune cash, sir.' He encapsulates the convergence of economic, sexual, and liturgical fetishism when he calls gold '[t]he young man's whore, the saint of him that's old.' A common slang term for 'usurer' was 'penny-father,' and it came naturally to Middleton to remark that 'interest may well be called the usurer's bastard.'[43] Confronted with a pile of gold in *If This Be Not a Good Play*, Scumbroth exclaims: 'the devil and some usurer's money have been here at their lechery, and see what goodly children they have begot, if you will keep the bastards at burse' (3.2.108–109). It seems equally natural, in *Eastward Ho*, for Quicksilver to liken his recruitment of clients for the 'money-bawd' to the begetting of children, in payment for which he receives the 'use' of whores: 'I am now loose, to get more children of perdition into thy usurous bonds. Thou feed'st my lechery, and I thy covetousness; thou art pander to me for my wench, and I to thee for thy cozenages.'[44] The word 'pander' can be used as a verb, noun, or proper name, and the unity of these usages indicates that the fusion of bawdry and usury has become personified in a popular cultural figure.

The Trojan aristocrat Pandarus first appears in the *Iliad*, where he is a noted archer. This may foreshadow his later cupidity, though it was not until the Middle Ages that he acquired the features that are regarded as typically his today. The medieval Pandarus is more than a sexual go-between; he is also conspicuous as a rhetorician, deeply committed to the efficacy of verbal persuasion. In addition to his own delight in word-play, he constantly refers to old books, and in Chaucer's version he insists that Troilus and Cresidye conduct an epistolary affair. When Shakespeare's Troilus laments that he cannot know if Cressida intends to return, Pandarus exclaims 'she is to be tested by writing' and arranges for the lovers to exchange letters—at which Troilus is dismayed to discover that Cressida's missive is an insincere attempt to manipulate him through language: '[w]ords, words, mere words, no matter from the heart:/ The effect doth operate another way' (5.3.126–127). The audience is encouraged to see Pandarus' role as go-between as akin to, and arising out of, his commitment to rhetorical manipulation. The *Iliad* already hints at this, when Diomedes' impaling of Pandarus' tongue suggests the nature of his offence. By the sixteenth century, however, Pandarus has developed into a symbol of mediation in general.[45]

In Shakespeare's *Troilus and Cressida* (1602), Pandarus presents himself as agency embodied, lamenting 'thus is the poor agent despised' and demanding why is 'the performance so loathed?' In John Webster's *The White Devil* (1612), Vittoria banishes Flamineo—'Hence you Pandar!'—to which he responds: 'Pandar! Am I the author of your sin?' (4.2.138–139). To be a 'pandar' was to be an author, an agent, an actor. In binary, definitive contrast to Troilus, Pandarus performs. Yet he simultaneously represents: he is Troilus' representative to Cressida. In fact, he represents the externalized performance of Troilus' passive desire, and this leaves him vulnerable to a wide range of moralistic criticism. Between the twelfth and the seventeenth centuries, Pandarus came to embody a nexus of 'homoerotic, heterosexual, and incestuous'[46] perversions, as well as the convergence between sexual, linguistic, and economic 'abuse.' He provided a locus where discourses that today we conceive as distinct, or even mutually exclusive, were perceived to congregate. Throughout the medieval and early modern periods, the parallels between erotic, rhetorical, and financial exchange were embodied in the personage who Middleton called 'Sir Pandarus, the broking knight of Troy.'[47]

In Benoit de Sainte-Maure's *Roman de Troie* (c.1160) Pandarus is a relatively inoffensive messenger and general facilitator of relations between Troilus and Cresidye. He starts to take on darker tones in Boccaccio's *Il Filostrato* (c.1335), where his moral ambiguity is a major source of the poem's comic effect. Boccaccio's Pandarus is reprehensible because he cynically claims that real sincerity can be replaced by its symbolic form. Sincerity in love is supposed to be an expression of essential subjectivity, so that when it is equated with a rhetorical formulation, and exchanged from one man to another, it is ethically devalued. Pandarus achieves this devaluation by his skillful use of performative discourse, telling Troilus that he has 'so plied her with talk of thy sincere love that she loveth thee.'[48] He even employs his own ethical decay as a manipulative tool, reminding Troilus: 'I have for thy sake become a go-between; for thy sake I have cast mine honor to the ground' (239). Pandarus is an entertaining but fundamentally pernicious influence in Chaucer's *Troilus and Cresidye* (c.1381), where he uses his rhetoric to manipulate the *amours* of others for his own amusement. In Shakespeare's *Troilus and Cressida* (1602) Pandarus is a pox-ridden lecher lacking even the dignity of Chaucer's pimp.

The Pandar of Shakespeare's *Pericles* (c.1608) is worse still. Along with two other semi-allegorical figures named Bawd and Boult, Pandar conspires to advertise the charms of the kidnapped Marina, obliterating her identity in pursuit of her exchange-value. 'Performance shall follow' answers Boult when ordered to tout her availability in the marketplace. This 'performance' involves transforming a human being into a commodity—'a creature of sale' (4.5.78), in the words of her prospective client Lysimachus. The three pimps energetically construct a sexualized image of Marina until, as Boult says, he has 'drawn her picture with my voice' (4.2.91). But Marina's chastity proves impenetrable, and Lysimachus predictably vents his indignation on the go-between: 'Avaunt thou damned door-keeper!' (4.5.123). The original audience would presumably have viewed Pandar and his colleagues as realistic as well as allegorical characters, their wiles doubtless familiar to *habitues* of the Jacobean *demimonde* adjacent to the theaters in London's liberties.

In *Wit's Miserie* (1596) Thomas Lodge assumes that the exchange of labor for 'hire' is the definitive characteristic of a 'Pandar.' He calls attention to 'Earthly Deuils in humane habits, ... [who] become Panders if you hire them.'[49] This contradicts Chaucer's Pandarus, who protests 'never I this for coveitsye wrought.' But of course his argument is spurious: while it is true that he was not motivated by monetary greed, the reader knows that he achieves other kinds of satisfaction for his trouble. When Boccaccio's Pandarus shamefacedly describes himself as a pimp, Troilus protests: 'Don't call yourself such a vile name! Use it on those who work for money.' Troilus protests that his employment of a representative, his substitution of symbolic for subjective agency, is not in itself corrupt. But the fallacy of his argument is demonstrated by performative contradiction when he eagerly offers to reciprocate Pandarus' pimping: 'to show my gratitude, name the sister you wish, and I'll get her for you.' Chaucer employs the same device when Troilus proposes to bestow on Pandarus 'my faire suster Polixene,/ Cassandre, Eleyne, or any of the frape' (3.409–410). Pandarus is always paid for his labor although, like the boy prostitutes in Aristophanes' *Plutus* who we discussed earlier, he tries to disguise the transactional nature of his relations by preferring presents or favors to cash. In 'How To Use The Court,' the Earl of Surrey advises an aspiring courtier to pimp '[t]hy nece, thy cosyn, sister, or thy daughter' (2) but to avoid Pandarus' mistake by insisting on a suitable reward:

> But ware I say, so gold thee helpe and spede:
> That in this case thou be not so vnwise,
> As Pandar was in such a like dede.
> For he the sole of conscience was so nice:
> That he no gaine would haue for all his paine.
> Be next thy selfe for frendshyp beares no price. (7–12)

The 'frendshyp' of 'thy better' may not have a financial 'price,' but it assuredly brought other kinds of value in exchange for the lady's favors. Chaucer's Troilus is deceived by this hypocrisy. Pandarus' behavior might constitute 'baudrye,' he admits, if it were carried out 'for gold or for richesse,' but he knows that his friend his motivated only by 'gentilesse,/ Compassioun, and felawship, and trist' (3.402–403). Troilus' failure to discern his true motives is understandable for, by the sixteenth century, Pandarus had become a by-word for any discrepancy between external appearance and internal essence. In 'Hero and Leander' (1598), Christopher Marlowe establishes the heroine's capacity for disguise with a financial image. Hero 'held it for a very sillie sleight,/ To make a perfect mettall counterfeit:/ Glad to disclaime her selfe; proud of an Art,/ That makes the face a Pandar to the hart' (944–947). To be a 'Pandar' here is to impose an image on something real, as in a counterfeit coin. With this broadening of his significance, the archetypal nature of Pandarus' bawdry becomes a recurrent *motif*. In *Phillip Sparrow* John Skelton alludes to: 'Pandara, that went between.... He is named Troylus baud,/ Of that name he is rue/ Whyles the world shall dure.' Sir Phillip Sidney's *Apology* remarks of 'the Terentian Gnatho and our Chaucer's Pandar... that we now use their names to signify their trades' (108). Shakespeare's Pandarus even persuades the lovers to swear an oath:

> If ever you prove false one to another, since I have taken such pains to bring you together let all pitiful goers between be called to the world's end after my name: call them all Pandars. let all constant men be Troiluses, all false women Cressids, and all brokers-between Pandars! (3.2.197–199)

Pandarus is thus the personified paradigm of mediation. He forges unions between people who would not otherwise come together—like gold in *Timon of Athens* he 'solder'st close impossibilities/ And makest them kiss!' (4.3.387–388). This enables him to over-ride the distinction between erotic and financial mediation, and to symbolize their unity. John Stephens' *Satyrical Essayes* even ties Pandarus to pawnbroking with a false etymology: 'His Etymologie is Pawne-dare: which intimates; hee dares pawnes his soule to damnation.'[50] *Twelfth Night*'s Fool asks if a pair of coins might have 'bred.' 'Yes,' he is predictably told, 'being kept together and put to use.' His response—'I would play Lord Pandarus of Phrygia, Sir, to bring a Cressida to this Troilus' (3.1.44–46)—reveals the degree to which Pandarus had become a commonplace figure for the union of usury and bawdry. The mention of Phrygia is especially significant: a province of ancient Lydia and the homeland of Midas, Gyges and Croseus as well as Pandarus, it was also the place where coinage was invented.

In short, Pandarus personifies what Marx calls 'the alienated ability of mankind.' He represents representation, he stands for the surrogate: he performs his labor on behalf of somebody else. He can be startlingly self-aware about this. As he wryly remarks in Shakespeare: 'I have had my labour for my travail... gone between and between, but small thanks for my labour' (1.1.67–69). In fact, Pandarus spawns an entire, quasi-allegorical race of greedy sensualists in Renaissance literature—from Jonson's Sir Epicure Mammon, Milton's Mammon, Comus and Satan, Middleton's Harry Dampit and Phillip Massinger's Giles Over-reach to John Bunyan's Mr. Badman. The ferocious, insatiable appetite displayed by such figures operates without distinction in the sexual and financial arenas. They fetishize the financial signs that represent labor-power in the same manner, to the same degree, and for the same reasons, as they fetishize the body that represents the human soul. The 'money-bawds' of the early modern theater incarnate the Biblical and Platonic fusion of avarice and idolatry in a humanoid *persona* whose most striking feature is an insatiable and perverted *libido*.

6.4   FROM CUCKOLD TO WITTOL

Pandarus, Mammon, Dampit, Badman, and their ilk are half-allegorical, and clearly descended from the Vice, Lust, Avarice, and similar stock figures of medieval drama. Yet they are also given sufficiently individualized features to make them appear realistic, and there is no doubt that characters like them populated the less salubrious fringes of early modern London. The convergence of usury, prostitution and witchcraft in the urban underworld is evoked in texts like Dekker's *The Gull's Hornbook* (1609):

> There is another ordinary, to which your London usurer, your stale bachelor, and your thrifty attorney do resort; the price threepence; the rooms as full of company as a jail; and indeed divided into several wards, like the beds of an hospital.... if they chance to discourse, it is of nothing but of statutes, bonds, recognizances, fees, recoveries, audits, rents, subsidies, sureties, inclosures, liveries, indictments, outlawries, feoffments, judgments, commissions, bankerouts, amercements, and of such horrible matter; that when a lieutenant dines with his punk in the next room, he thinks verily the men are conjuring.[51]

In Jonson's *The Alchemist* (1610) Doll Common's prostitution business and Subtle's magical racket are conducted in the same house, and managed by the same pandar, Face. One of their gulls, Sir Epicure Mammon, declares his intention to use the philosopher's stone to facilitate a range of orgiastic indulgences. As his exchange with Face makes clear, what attracts him to such vices is their violation of nature. Maddened by lust, he insists that this violation be as extreme as possible:

> *Mammon*: Where I spy/ A wealthy citizen, or [a] rich lawyer,/ Have a sublimed pure wife, unto that fellow /I'll send a thousand pound to be my cuckold.
> *Face*: And I shall carry it?
> *Mammon*: No. I'll have no bawds, /But fathers and mothers: they will do it best,/ Best of all others. (2.2.54–61)

As large as 'punks,' 'conjurers,' 'bawds,' 'jugglers,' 'puffers' and similar small-scale traffickers in magic and prostitution loom in dramatic depictions of usury, early modern playwrights dwell at even greater length on a more surprising sexual correlative of money-lending. Mammon plots the use of his alchemical riches to 'cuckold' the bourgeoisie and, if the dramatic literature is any guide, the people of Renaissance England perceived an especially close connection between usury and 'cuckoldry.'[52] The 'money-bawd' in Chapman, Jonson and Marston's *Eastward Ho* (1605) enters declaring 'I am security itself, my name is Security, the famous usurer' (2.2.8–9). His bravado is short-lived, however, and he ends by singing a crestfallen ditty:

> Alas, I am a Cuckold,
> And why should it be so?
> Because I was a usurer,
> And bawd, as you all know.... (5.5.132–136)

Security's response to the question of why he should be a cuckold apparently seemed perfectly logical to the play's original audience: 'Because I was a usurer/ And bawd, as you all know.' He sees no need to explain further, and this suggests that cuckoldry, like bawdry, was connected to usury axiomatically, as a fundamental element in an ancient conceptual structure that was still extent, albeit crumbling, in the late sixteenth century. Unlike sodomy, moreover, bawdry and cuckoldry are not necessarily infertile. On the contrary, their kinship to usury lies in their illegitimate fertility. The key is their parallel violation of natural teleology. Usury ignores the natural *telos* of money as a medium of exchange, fetishizing its accumulation as an end-in-itself. In parallel fashion, bawdry and cuckoldry fetishize sexual pleasure as an end-in-itself, actively avoiding sex's natural *telos*, which is reproduction. Like the bawd, then, the cuckold became a figure for the violation of nature—hence his proverbial monstrosity, signaled by his horns. In Dekker and Webster's *Northward Ho* (c.1605), a visitor is announced who speaks "not like a man of God's making." Bellamont responds: 'Not of God's making? What is he? A cuckold?'[53]

Modern readers may be puzzled by the sadistic mockery to which cuckolds are endlessly subjected in Renaissance drama. After all, they were ostensibly the wronged party. The hostility directed toward them becomes easier to understand once we grasp the connection between cuckoldry and bawdry. In Jonson's *Volpone* (1606), Corvino's transformation from enraged cuckold to eager bawd is instantaneous enough to suggest that it involves no great distance. Indeed the bawd and the cuckold fuse in the figure of the 'wittol,' a complaisant cuckold, usually bawd to his own wife. Jennifer Panek cites the ballad of 'one Ieamie of Woodicock Hill' (1610): 'for lucre of money contended was he / To put up cuckold.'[54] Panek also finds 'tantalizing references to what may have been cases of wittolry in church court records of "bawdry"' (86n5).[55] John Harrington's *Epigrams* (1615) features 'a Wittol Broker' who is delighted that his 'wife's ware' is 'to divers daily sold.' By the seventeenth century the trope of cuckold as bawd had produced several well-known running jokes—the mere mention of a candle-stick was enough to induce gales of merriment in a knowing audience. In Middleton's *Anything for a Quiet Life* (c.1620) Mrs Knavesby tells her husband: 'For thy pander's fee,/ It shall be laid under the candlestick' (4.2.37); the wife in *The New Brawle* (1654) 'makes Hornes' and 'bids me goe look under the candle-stick' (4); in *The Rich and Flourishing Cuckold* (c.1680) a wittol exults 'under the Candlestick gold I could find;' in *Fifteen Comforts of Cuckoldom* (1706) we learn that 'A Groat (which always is a Cuckold's Fee) /Under the Candlestick I've laid for me;' the 'Golden Cuckold' from *Horn Fair Garland* (c.1770) is told to 'look under the candle-stick cuckold, /A single groat you'll find there, /I hid, for to put in your pocket, /Your charges to bear at Horn-fair.'

It was common for the wittol's wife to repay her husband's creditors with her sexual favors. William Fennor's *Cornu-copiae* (1612) describes the usual recourse of insolvent wittols: 'many which in prison have beene layd,/ In taking of the horne their debts have payd,/ That sure I thinke, though other hornes be daintie,/ A Cuckolds horne it is the Horne of Plentie.' As his name suggests, the supreme wittol of the age is Allwit, from Middleton's *A Chaste Maid in Cheapside* (c.1613).[56] He triumphs over his wife's lover, Sir Walter Whorehound, because he exploits the knight financially: "'a keeps me, / And all my family; I am at his table, / He gets me all my children, and pays the nurse' (1.2.17–19). With equal insouciance 'The Merry Cuckold' (1630) rejoices: 'Of all that she gets./ I share a good share,/ She payes all my debts,/ Then for what should I care?'[57]

Cuckoldry is firmly connected to commerce throughout the city comedies. In Middleton's *The Family of Love* (c.1607) we are told 'he that tends well his shop, and hath an alluring wife with a graceful *what d'ye lack?* shall be sure to have good doings, and good doings is that crowns so many citizens with the horns of abundance' (2.1.3–6). In *The Honest Whore Part One* (1604), Candido is not explicitly a cuckold, but he is certainly emasculated and androgynous, causing one gallant to exclaim: 'Is't possible that *homo*/ Should be nor man nor woman...' (1.5.114–115). Candido attributes his lack of aristocratic *machismo* to his mercantile social position: 'We are set here to please all customers,/ Their humours and their fancies, offend none' (1.5.29–30). He has been neutered by his role as an agent of commerce, and the retail trade in general could easily be included under the rubric of 'usury.' The anonymous author of *The Death of Usury* (1594) reminds his readers that '[b]y the opinion of the schoolmen, usurie is taken so largely that it comprehendeth buying and selling' (41).

In conclusion then, the people of early modern England understood usury, sorcery, idolatry, and sodomy as a single, universal temptation, which can be summarized as the fetishization of performative representation. All of these sins involve the fetishization of appearances and symbols, they all obscure essence and reference. They all replace nature with custom. They all deny the distinction between representation and reality. At root, they are all attacks on *logos*, and anti-logocentrism remains their philosophical expression today. The twenty-first-century economy is dominated by practices that were once known as 'usury,' while twenty-first-century culture is dominated by practices that were once known as 'sodomy.' This does not mean that sodomites or usurers are personally vulnerable to moralistic strictures. It means that anti-logocentrism is spreading throughout postmodern society and influencing the consciousness of postmodern humanity. It means that *logos* is becoming difficult to discern behind the fetishized images of sense-perception. It is at least worth inquiring whether these developments are worthy of approbation.

NOTES

1. Swapan Chakravortycalls this a 'sex-money calculus. What the merchant gains in money, he loses in virility, what the prodigal heir loses in estates, he gains in sex.' *Society and Politics in the Plays of Thomas Middleton* (Clarendon Press, 1996), 46.
2. The phrase is used in a different context by Jean Howard, in *The Stage and Social Struggle in Early Modern England* (Routledge 2003), 23.
3. As Dwight Codr reminds us, however, the early modern understanding of 'usury' was more capacious than our own. In *Raving at Usurers: Anti-finance and the Ethics of Uncertainty in England, 1690–1750* (U. of Virginia P., 2016) Codr makes a good case for interpreting 'usury' as 'an early modern approximation for *finance*' (4).
4. R.H. Tawney, *Religion and the Rise of Capitalism* (London, 1926), 137.
5. Ben Jonson, *The Magnetic Lady, or, Humours Reconciled* (Manchester UP, 2009), 2.6.82–83.
6. Reginald Scot, *The Discoverie of Witchcraft* (New York: Dover Publications, 1972), 172.
7. Sir Phillip Sidney, 'A Remedy for Love,' in *A Defence of Poesie: And Poems* (London: Cassell and Co., 1899), 142.
8. Plato, *The Republic* (8:555), trans. Benjamin Jowett (Clarendon Press: Oxford, 1887), 262.
9. Aristotle, *Politics* 1.1258b1–4, trans. Benjamin Jowett (Dover Publications, 2000).
10. Plato, *Laws*, trans. R.G. Bury (Loeb Classical Library, 1926), 1.636c.
11. St. Thomas Aquinas, *On Evil*, cit. Michael Wykes, 'Devaluing the Scholastics: Calvin's Ethics of Usury,' *Calvin Theological Journal* 38 (2003), 27–51, 35.
12. John T. Noonan, 'Authority, Usury and Contraception,' *Cross Currents* 16.1 (Winter 1966), 55–79, 55.
13. Odd Langholm, *The Aristotelian Analysis of Usury* (Universitetsforlaget AS, 1984), 60.
14. See Giovanni Arrighi, *The Long Twentieth Century: Money, Power and the Origins of Our Times* (London, 2010).
15. Craig Muldew, *The Economy of Obligation: The Culture of Credit and Social Relations in Early Modern England* (Palgrave Macmillan, 1998).
16. Carl Wennerlind, *Casualties of Credit: The English Financial Revolution, 1620–1720* (Harvard UP, 2011), 18.
17. Francesca Trivellato, *The Promise and Peril of Credit* (Princeton UP, 2019), 3.
18. Francis Bacon, *The Advancement of Learning*, retrieved April 1, 2020: https://oll.libertyfund.org/titles/bacon-the-advancement-of-learning.
19. Michel Foucault, *The History of Sexuality: Volume One: An Introduction* (Random House, 1978), 37.

20. E. Michael Jones aptly calls Foucault 'the Socrates of anti-Logos.' *Logos Rising* (South Bend, IN: Fidelity Press, 2020), 735.

21. Stephen Orgel, 'Nobody's Perfect; Or, Why Did the English Stage Take Boys for Women?' *South Atlantic Quarterly* (1989), 7–21, 20.

22. Alan Bray, 'Homosexuality and the Signs of Male Friendship in Elizabethan England,' in *Queering the Renaissance*, ed. Jonathan Goldberg (Durham, 1993), 41.

23. Cit. Lawrin Armstrong, *The Idea of a Moral Economy: Gerard of Siena on Usury, Restitution and Prescription* (U of Toronto P, 2016), 13.

24. R.H. Tawney, 'Historical Introduction,' in *A Discourse on Usury*, Thomas Wilson (London, 1962), 21–22.

25. Eliza Greenstadt, 'Strange Insertions in *The Merchant of Venice*,' in *Queer Shakespeare: Desire and Sexuality*, ed. Goran Stanivukovic (Bloomsbury, 2017), 197–226, 204.

26. See Jonas Barish, *The Antitheatrical Prejudice* (U of California P, 1981), 2.

27. Cit. Frankie Rubinstein, *A Dictionary of Shakespeare's Sexual Puns and Their Significance* (Palgrave Macmillan, 1989), xiv.

28. See Alexandra Shepard, 'Manhood, Credit and Patriarchy in Early Modern England 1580–1640,' *Past and Present* 167 (May 2000), 75–106.

29. Sir Philip Sidney, *The Defense of Poesie* (Boston: Ginn & Co., 1890), 36.

30. John Marston, *The Scourge of Villainy* 'Satire VII: A Cynic Satire' (13–16, 139–142), in *The Columbia Anthology of British Poetry*, ed. Carl Woodring and James Shapiro (Columbia UP, 1995), 145–146, 147.

31. Ben Jonson, 'To Inigo, Marquess Would Be, a Corollary,' 21.

32. John Bale, *Three Lawes* in *The Dramatic Writings of John Bale: Bishop of Ossory* (Charles W. Traylen, 1966), 16.

33. In *The Invention of Sodomy in Christian Theology* (U of Chicago P, 1998), Mark Jordan claims that '[s]odomy is a medieval artifact. I have found no trace of the term before the eleventh century' (1). Jordan does however identify several scholastic precursors of the term *sodomia*, including *luxuria, vitium sodomiticum* and *peccatum contra naturam*.

34. See E. Pearlman, 'Shakespeare, Freud, and the Two Usuries, or, Money's a Meddlar,' *English Literary Renaissance* 2 (1972), 218. Pearlman points out that the homology between usury and sodomy can be read as contradicting the Aristotelian association of usury with breeding, since 'sodomy' is defined precisely by its non-reproductive status. He argues that early modern English literature circumvented this contradiction by also connecting usury to bawdry.

35. Aristotle, *Nicomachean Ethics* (Oxford, 2009), 1120–22a.

36. George Downame, *Lectures on the XV Psalm* (1604), 258.

37. Ben Jonson, *Complete Poems*, ed. G. Parfitt (London, 1975), 52.

38. William Rowley, *A Match at Midnight*, in *A Select Collection of Old Plays*, vol. VI, ed. Robert Dodsley (London, 1845), 144.
39. Sir Thomas Overbury, 'Characters,' in *Miscellaneous Works* (John Russell Smith: London, 1856), 133.
40. Thomas Dekker, *News From Hell*, in *The Non-dramatic Works of Thomas Dekker*, ed. Alexander Grosart (The Huth Library, 1885), 2.136. 22.
41. See *2 Henry IV* (4.7.120), *Much Ado About Nothing* (3.3.1485), *The Taming of the Shrew* (2.1.322). On the use of the word 'commodity' in early modern England, see Heather Ackerman, *Accommodation Fetishism* (Ph.D. Dissertation, Arizona State University, 2017).
42. Valerie Forman, 'Marked Angels: Counterfeits, Commodities and *The Roaring Girl*,' *Renaissance Quarterly* 54.4 (Winter 2001), 1531–1560, 1533.
43. Thomas Middleton, *The Black Book, Works*, 275.
44. Thomas Middleton, *A Chaste Maid in Cheapside*, 2.1. in *Thomas Middleton: The Collected Works*, ed. Gary Taylor and John Lavagnino (Oxford, 2010).
45. Hyder E. Rollins, 'The Troilus-Cressida Story from Chaucer to Shakespeare,' *PMLA* 32.3 (1917), 383–429, 410.
46. Gretchen Mieszkowski, *Medieval Go-Betweens and Chaucer's Pandarus* (New York: Palgrave Macmillan), 2006, 142.
47. Thomas Middleton, *Your Five Gallants* (1607) (2.1.117). The word 'Pandar' could also refer to a 'kept gallant,' who lived off the earnings of a prostitute: what twentieth-century English would call a 'ponce.' This word originally meant 'pimp,' but it also suggested sartorial ostentation to the point of effeminacy. This association between pimping and fancy clothes appears in Spenser's *Mother Hubberd's Tale*, when it is said of a follower of 'lustie gallants' that 'for pleasure would he sometimes scorne/ A Pandares coate' (808). Robert Greene's *Notable Discovery* (1598) defines a female bawd as a 'pandar,' but insists that the proper term for a male pimp is 'Apple-squire.'
48. *The Filostrato of Boccacio*, trans. Nathaniel Edward Griffin and Arthur Beckwith Myrick (Biblo and Tannen, 1929), 241.
49. Cit. Rollins, 424.
50. John Stephens, *Satyrical Essayes, Characters and Others* (1615), E5.
51. Thomas Dekker, *The Gull's Horn-Book* (Bristol: J.M. Dutch, 1812), 124.
52. One study to remark on the cuckold's sexual pleasure is Katherine Eisaman Maus, "Horns of Dilemma: Jealousy, Gender and Spectatorship in Renaissance English Drama," *ELH* (1987), 561–83. Cuckoldry's broad scope in the period is conveyed by the range of essays in *Cuckoldry, Impotence and Adultery in Europe (15th–17th Century)*, ed. Sara Matthews Grieco (New York, 2014). For a specific treatment of cuckoldry's financial implications see Douglas Bruster, 'Horn of Plenty: Cuckoldry and Capital

in the Age of Shakespeare,' *Studies in English Literature, 1500–1900* (1990), 195–215.

53. Thomas Dekker and John Webster, *Northward Ho*, in *The Works of John Webster*, ed. David Gunby, David Carnegie and MacDonald P. Jackson (Cambridge, 2019), 4.1.10–13.

54. Jennifer Panek, '"A Wittall Cannot Be a Cookold": Reading the Contended Cuckold in Early Modern English Drama and Culture,' *Journal for Early Modern Cultural Studies* (2001), 66–92, 73.

55. Claire McEachern examines the cuckold's horns in the context of debates about the relation between "carnal signs" and the invisible soul in 'Why Do Cuckolds Have Horns?' *Huntington Library Quarterly* (2008), 607–631. See also Coppélia Kahn, *Man's Estate: Masculine Identity in Shakespeare* (Los Angeles, 1981), 119–150.

56. As Gary Kuchar observes, Allwit represents 'the dramatic and ideological limit point of the Jonsonian wittol': 'Rhetoric, Anxiety, and the Pleasures of Cuckoldry in the Drama of Ben Jonson and Thomas Middleton,' *Journal of Narrative Theory* (2001), 1–30, 3.

57. 'The Merry Cuckold' (1630), in *The Roxburghe Ballads*, ed. Charles Hindley (London, 1874), 464.

CHAPTER 7

Modernism, Inflation, and the Gold Standard

7.1 Modernism and Representation

This chapter examines the ways in which Anglophone literary modernism was influenced by economic developments of the inter-war period. Over the decades following World War One, such ostensibly economic matters as the international gold standard, the collection of war debts, and the runaway German inflation raised inescapable questions about financial semiotics: how money represents value. Such issues had clear implications for other kinds of representation. The major figures of British and American modernism were united in the conviction that, as Wallace Stevens put it, 'money is a kind of poetry.'[1] As Alec Marsh observes, Ezra Pound was one among many 'who struggled in poems to reconcile the implications of their sudden belief in economic determinism with the ancient priority of the poetic imagination.'[2] Here I will argue that, during the early 1920s, important differences between the economic opinions of Pound and T. S. Eliot either caused or reflected—but in any case paralleled—a significant divergence between their theories of the poetic symbol.

The philosophical chasm between the two poets was obvious by the 1930s, following Eliot's public avowal of Christianity and Pound's loud espousal of Fascism. Yet it grew out of economic and aesthetic differences that had been apparent ten years earlier. Between October 1923 and November 1925, Eliot supervised the publication—and was presumably the author—of twenty-six columns headed 'Foreign Exchange' that

© The Author(s) 2020
D. Hawkes, *The Reign of Anti-logos*, Palgrave
Insights into Apocalypse Economics,
https://doi.org/10.1007/978-3-030-55940-3_7

appeared in *Lloyds Bank Monthly*.[3] They adopt a position that directly contradicts Pound's economic theories, but which bears a close resemblance to Eliot's own poetics. Pound followed Aristotle in viewing usury as the veritable paradigm of unnatural thought and behavior. He conceived of usury as the artificial reproduction of symbols, and thus as the antithesis of natural production, whether economic, artistic, or sexual. Inspired by such economists as Brooks Adams, Jeffrey Mark, Arthur Kitson, and Richard Soddy, Pound regarded the gold standard as a ruse perpetrated by usurers, who needed to pretend that the money they created out of nothing referred directly to a determinate quantity of bullion. Scorning recourse to any ultimate *logos* in finance as he did in poetry, Pound invested value, meaning, and power in the image alone.

By publicly proclaiming the self-referentiality of the poetic image as the main doctrine of 'Imagism,' Pound attempted to make it a modernist *shibboleth*. In this he was resisted, quietly but firmly, by Eliot, who simultaneously practiced and advocated usury in both the financial and the verbal senses. It was therefore predictable that Eliot should strongly support the gold standard, and insist that money must refer to an external, objective *logos*. His poetic doctrine of the 'objective correlative' also tactfully but unequivocally departs from Pound's Imagist orthodoxy, being based on the distinction between symbol and referent that Pound's 'image' attempts to abolish. Although they usually refrained from criticizing each other in print, such differences annoyed Pound enough for him to seriously imperil their friendship through his strenuous efforts, both theoretical and practical, to liberate Eliot from his service to Lloyds Bank.

They agreed, of course, that the new century demanded new forms of representation, a fresh understanding of the relation between signs and things. Modernism was in revolt against the 'realist' aesthetic that had dominated Western literature in the eighteenth and nineteenth centuries, according to which the proper function of a verbal sign was accurately to represent a pre-semiotic reality. In economic realism too, paper money was supposed to be a referential sign that accurately designated an objective value incarnated in the material substance of gold. Ian Drummond explains:

> The paper currency was supposed to be convertible into gold coin or bullion, on demand in unlimited amounts, at a fixed price. Thus a hundred-pound bank note, or a hundred pounds in bank deposits, could always

be exchanged for a hundred gold sovereigns, giving the paper pound an assured value in terms of gold.[4]

This realist model attaches an economic, aesthetic, and even an ethical value to transparent representation. The same attitude manifested itself in economic thought. A typically moralistic tone pervades the declaration of Samuel Loyd, head of Lloyds Bank, in 1857: 'Precious Metals alone are money. Paper notes are money because they are representations of Metallic Money. Unless so, they are false and spurious pretenders.'[5]

This was the attitude against which modernism rebelled, in economics as well as in poetics and linguistics. In fact, modernism in general can be understood as a cultural turn toward performative representation. Alain Badiou's observation on Stephane Mallarme holds true for modernist aesthetics as a whole: 'what the poem says, it does.'[6] By taking this performative turn, modernism registered and reflected a newly autonomous power of the sign in every sphere of thought. Ferdinand de Saussure's structuralist linguistics posed a fundamental challenge to realism, by suggesting that verbal meaning was the product of relations between signs, rather than deriving from reference to an extralinguistic reality. In a homologous development, economic modernism involved the demise of the gold standard as a universal referent, and the concomitant rise of money as a performative sign. The wild inflation of the 1920s could not easily be reconciled with an economic *logos*. New forms of aesthetic representation were demanded—and embodied—by contemporary transformations of the money-form. As Jean-Joseph Goux describes the transition from realism to modernism:

> The bygone era of "gold-language," the basis for realist and expressive mechanisms of classical representation, has been succeeded by the present age of "token-language" with its vanishing frames of reference and floating signifiers.[7]

French literature had already registered the autonomous power of representation. The late-nineteenth-century 'symbolist' poetry of Mallarme, Verlaine and Rimbaud focused *avant garde* attention on the poetic symbol's relation to reality. A symbolist image was emphatically not a referential sign. It evoked a subjective response in the reader without mediation: 'immediately.' Its significance was connotative rather than denotative, rhetorical rather than logical, and derived from its own inherent properties rather than from any correlation with objective reality.[8] Such ideas were introduced into the Anglosphere by Arthur Symons' widely influential *The Symbolist Movement in Literature* (1899). Symons asked: 'What are words themselves but symbols, almost as arbitrary as the letters which compose them, mere sounds of the voice to which we have agreed to give certain significations....'[9] He observes that this 'arbitrary' quality of verbal symbols is shared by financial signs: 'In the modern world... money is more often a symbol than an entity...' (1). Modernist writers could agree on that much but, as we shall see, their reactions to the autonomy of financial representation varied as widely as their theories of the efficacious poetic symbol.

7.2   EZRA POUND: USURA CONTRA NATURAM

Pound was the first writer in English to grasp the timeliness of the French symbolist revolution. As Jacques Derrida observes, Pound's 'poetics was, with that of Mallarme, the first break in the most entrenched Western tradition.'[10] It was Pound's profound knowledge of economics that inspired his critique of realism in poetics. His grandfather had been a businessman who printed his own currency, his father was an assayer at the Philadelphia Mint, and the poet was familiar with the philosophy of money from earliest youth. He evidently absorbed a markedly moralistic attitude to finance. As James Wilhelm observes: 'Pound saw the false manipulators of money as the true traitors to any society, along with the polluters of language.'[11] Some have accused him of attributing too much performative power to money, and too little to the labor-power that money represents. Paul Morrison remarks, accurately enough, that 'Pound never progressed beyond a concern with financial surfaces—the signifier rather than the signified, money rather than social labor....'[12] It is true that Pound attributed performative power to financial signs, as he did to verbal signs. In doing so, however, he was acknowledging (and insisting that others acknowledge) the reality of the modern condition. He was far from celebrating it; on the contrary he aspired to educate society on the moral dangers inherent in performative representation.

Pound's reading of scholastic economics had taught him that '[a]ll value comes from labor and nature,'[13] and his economic tracts vigorously attack the usurious appropriation of value by self-generating, financial signs. His modernism was an attempt to assimilate the newly performative power of the symbol into traditional Western culture, by translating it from financial into poetic form. There is thus a sense in which Stuart Christie is right to claim that he 'rejects usury as an ideology, only to apply it aggressively as an aesthetic practice.'[14] Yet the lifelong, unrepudiated vehemence of Pound's hostility to usury shows how deeply he deplored the reproductive capacity of symbols—and he deplored it in poetry quite as much as in finance. As Alessandro Lanteri puts it: 'Pound's life and literary production are troubled by the doubt that poetry might be self-engendering, just like usury.'[15] Far from endorsing the unnatural fertility attained by symbols in modernity, Pound applied the ancient moral critique of usury to contemporary semiotics. In 'Gold and Work' (1944) he denounced the power of money as modern idolatry:

> The nineteenth century, the infamous century of usury, went even further, creating a species of monetary Black Mass. Marx and Mill, in spite of their superficial differences, agreed in endowing money with properties of a quasi-religious nature.... The error has been pecuniolatry, or the making of money into a god. This was due to a process of denaturalization, by which our money has been given false attributes and powers that it should never have possessed. Gold is durable, but does not reproduce itself—not even if you put two bits of it together, one shaped like a cock, the other like a hen. It is absurd to speak of it as bearing fruit or yielding interest. Gold does not germinate like grain. To represent gold as doing this is to represent it falsely.[16] (346–347)

Such passages reflect the influence of Jeffrey Mark's *The Modern Idolatry* (1934), a work Pound greatly admired,[17] which argues that 'the gold standard... is a direct psychological derivative from the gold-idol worship of barbarism.'[18] Indeed, Pound had initially been attracted to aesthetic modernism precisely because it laid bare this fetishistic power of the symbol. As Eugene Vance points out, his early, troubadour poems involved 'a fetishism of verbal signs whose economy depend[s] upon the poet's ability to sustain the body of the poem as a serious rival for the feminine object of desire whose absence the poem celebrates.'[19] Modernism appealed to Pound because it assimilated this performative power of the sign into its poetic form, transposing the autonomy of financial signs into aesthetics. In the words of Richard Sieburth:

> ... [Pound's] abandonment of his early troubadour manner in late 1912 for the modernist poetics of Imagism.... represented a fundamental attempt to get his poetry off the gold standard, to defetishize the signifier, as

it were, to establish a poetics whose economy would be based on the direct exchange between subject and object, language and reality, word and world.[20]

Just as economic life in the twentieth century was organized around financial usury so, Pound believed, twentieth-century aesthetics must foreground the performative sign, the symbol that contains its meaning within itself, the modernist 'image.' As he put it in 'Hugh Selwyn Mauberly' (1920): 'The age demanded an image/Of its accelerated grimace' (II, 1–2), and he was determined to answer its demand. In Pound's modernism, the verbal image attains an autonomous, immediate semiotic force, setting off subjective reactions in the reader without denotative reference to an objective reality.[21] Postmodernist philosophers like Jacques Derrida describe this self-generating power of representation as a 'linguistic surplus value' produced by 'verbal usury.' In 'White Mythology' (1971) Derrida argues that *usure* is 'systematically connected with the theme of metaphor.'[22] As Marc Shell explains:

> … "verbal usury" is an important technical term in the Talmud, the Christian church fathers, and in the Islamic Traditions. There it refers to an illegitimate—the church fathers say unnatural—supplement of verbal meaning by use of methods such as punning or flattering.[23]

In the Aristotelian tradition, usury is defined as unnatural reproduction, and thus as the enemy of natural reproduction. Because usury makes money breed, the sins of usury and sodomy are traditionally considered natural allies and mirror images: the former makes fruitful what is naturally barren, while the latter makes barren what is naturally fruitful. At first glance this logic might seem remote from modernity, but it was vital to the formation of cultural modernism. Pound took his view of 'usura' from Aristotle, via Aquinas and Dante. The *Cantos* firmly identify it with artistic and sexual infertility:

> Usura rusteth the chisel
>   It rusteth the craft and the craftsman It gnaweth the thread in the loom
> None learneth to weave gold in her pattern;
>   Azure hath a canker by usura; cramoisi is unbroidered
>   Emerald findeth no Memling

Usura slayeth the child in the womb It stayeth the young man's courting It hath brought palsey to bed, lyeth between the young bride and her bridegroom
CONTRA NATURAM[24]

The greatest usurious villain in Pound's version of economic history was Samuel Loyd, the mid-nineteenth-century head of Lloyds Bank. As we have seen, Loyd was an uncompromising adherent of the gold standard, and an impassioned advocate of the 'currency principle,' according to which: 'When... notes are permitted to be issued, the number in circulation should always be exactly equal to the coin which would be in circulation if they did not exist.'[25] Since the supply of bullion was limited, such an economy would be subject to deflation, which would benefit creditors at the expense of debtors. As Pound put it: 'the advantages of the gold-standard system lauded by the bankers are advantages for the bankers only—for some bankers only, in fact.'[26] These bankers were further able to increase the value of their loans by manipulating the price of gold. Because money was supposed to derive its value from gold, a rise in the price of gold increased interest rates. Therefore, as Mark explained, the gold standard also facilitated imperialism:

> ... if another country has its internal currency more than "covered" by gold, it can either sell its gold or hire its credit (i.e., create external debts through foreign investment) to other countries. This is the financial basis of the international gold standard, whose much-lauded "symmetry" has the ultimate effect of driving down the standard of living in all countries. (80)

To equate financial value with gold bullion is fetishism, for financial value is a symbol that we treat as an agent. In the words of Frederick Soddy, another of Pound's favorite economists: '[money] is imagined to exist for the purpose of charging interest upon it.'[27] In 'Gold and Work' Pound condemns 'interest on money that does not exist, on a mirage of money' (351). The gold standard is an idol, a spurious *logos* invented to facilitate the reproduction of financial signs that actually refer to nothing beyond the human imagination. This nefarious collaboration between usury and the gold standard was denounced by Arthur Kitson, another strong influence on Pound, in 1925: 'By the universal adoption of the Gold Standard... an irresponsible super-Government was created, composed of International Bankers.'[28] Willis Overholser, who Pound also admired, declared in 1936 that: 'The gold standard in reality is a gold fraud, and was conceived as a means of enabling the international banker to fleece and rob.'[29] Mark blames imperialist efforts to deprive India of its natural wealth on '[t]he recent efforts of bankers to put India on the gold standard...' (137n1). Pound echoes this point in 'Gold and Work': 'By returning to gold, Mr. Churchill forced the Indian peasant to pay two bushels of grain in taxes and interest which a short time before he had been able to pay with one only...' (338).

This depiction of the gold standard as a facilitator of usury harmonized closely with the views of another strong influence on Pound's economics, Brooks Adams—the great-grandson of John Adams, and thus the incarnation of the Jeffersonian political tradition that Pound admired. 'Gold and Work' includes several lengthy citations from Adams' *The Law of Civilization and Decay*:

> Perhaps no financier has ever lived abler than Samuel Loyd. Certainly he understood as few men, even of later generations, have understood, the mighty engine of the single Standard. He comprehended that, with expanding trade, an inelastic currency must rise in value; he saw that, with sufficient resources at command, his class might be able to establish such a rise, almost at pleasure; certainly that they could manipulate it when it came, by taking advantage of foreign exchange....[30]

Loyd was the main architect of the 1844 Bank Charter Act which, as Adams notes, ensured that 'the usurers became supreme' (338) and that 'debtors would have to surrender their property on such terms as creditors might dictate' (340). The hegemony of usury was achieved through the Act's enforcement of the gold standard, which Adams calls 'Loyd's principle... the rigid limitation of the currency to the weight of gold available for money' (336–337). Adams explains how 'men like Nathan Rothschild and Samuel Loyd... engrossed the gold of the world, and then, by legislation, made it the sole measure of values.' By thus handing power to usurers, 'Loyd's policy' constituted a 'catastrophe' that 'has changed the aspect of civilization' (337).

Pound's copious consumption of such material led him inexorably to conclude that, in the words of William Chace: 'The chief usurer was the British banker Samuel Loyd' (89n5). That was more than enough to convince Pound of Loyd's world-historical villainy. Nor was he slow to draw conclusions for aesthetics. He described usury as 'destroying the images' because it referred all financial signs to the single, standardized idol of gold.[31] As St. Augustine explains in *De Doctrina Christiana*, signs have referents by definition. To the extent that any sign is deprived of its referent, it ceases to be a sign. Pound accordingly announced that money should 'represent something, such, namely, AS Rams and Ewes.' The allusion is to *The Merchant of Venice*, where Shylock rationalizes usury by comparing it to the breeding of sheep. Antonio scoffs at his literalism: 'Was this inserted to make interest good?/Or is your gold and silver ewes and rams?' (1.3.92–93). In reply, Shylock boasts: 'I cannot tell, I make them breed as fast' (1.3.94).

Shylock thinks of money as if it literally were the cattle to which he compares it. His literalist conception of money displaces its referent from his mind. Thus it effectively ceases to be a symbol for him: he takes it literally. Like Antonio, Pound reminds us that the rams and ewes are only symbols of Shylock's money; they are not literally identical with the money, so the fact that they breed is no argument that money should also do so. In a 1935 essay for *Current Controversy* Pound points out that Shylock's mistaking of symbols for reality is not limited to sheep: 'Are we never to see that Shylock betrays his race, by hiding *behind it*? Charged as a usurer in attempt toward mayhem, he cried, "I am a jew."'[32] Ironically enough, Pound himself made precisely the same ethical and hermeneutic error, when his originally figural use of 'Jew' for 'usurer' also lapsed into literalism.[33] This was not an uncommon problem in modernism, as the early work of T. S. Eliot clearly reveals.[34]

7.3   T. S. ELIOT: THE GOLD STANDARD AS OBJECTIVE CORRELATIVE

Eliot spent the early 1920s in what Pound regarded as the belly of the beast. He was employed as an analyst of foreign exchange for Lloyds Bank, where he specialized in the collection of German war debts, including the reparations imposed after World War One.[35] During this period, the influence of his financial opinions on his literary theories grew pronounced Under his editorship, *The Criterion* often carried articles on the philosophy of money. A typical piece by G. Elliot Smith on 'The Glamour of Gold' (1925) alluded to the magical heritage of the term 'glamour' to speculate that the metal's life-giving properties in mythology sprang from the magical power of exchange-value, originally embodied in cowrie shells and then transferred to gold.[36]

At Lloyds, Eliot was personally charged with implementing the policies of the men Jeffrey Mark called the 'Shylock-driven statesmen at the Treaty of Versailles' who had humiliated Germany with 'external taxation by the foreign creditor powers' (38). He advanced rapidly at Lloyds, eventually taking charge of the bank's newly organized Intelligence Section, to his evident delight. He cited this promotion as his main reason for resisting the relentless insistence of his wealthy aesthetic acquaintances that he quit his job. He wrote to his brother on January 2, 1923:

> I cannot resign now without letting [Lloyds] down very badly and behaving with ingratitude. I am now head of an Intelligence Department with a number of clerks under me, and in sole charge… The bank is getting bigger and bigger, with interests practically all over the world, and affiliated banks everywhere, and there is the opportunity to create a service of Intelligence which would be quite unique.[37]

As Matt Seybold reminds us in his important study of Eliot's career at Lloyds, the campaign to persuade Eliot to leave the bank involved such luminaries as Hugh Walpole, Richard Adlington, Aldous Huxley, Wyndham Lewis, I. A. Richards, Herbert Read, Lytton Strachey and Virginia Woolf.[38] It is remarkable, today, to consider how easily London's literati assumed that Eliot's genius would be better expressed by editing small-circulation poetry journals than by leading a major restructuring of one of the world's largest financial concerns. Many of them were doubtless motivated by simple snobbery but Pound—the campaign's prime instigator and *eminence grise*—had more philosophical reasons for opposing Eliot's employment. He sincerely believed that the model of representation employed in fractional reserve banking was entirely incompatible with the symbolic practice of modernist poetry.

Yet Eliot steadfastly resisted Pound's pressure, well aware that his banking experience had given him a perspective unique among his literary circle. On November 7, 1922 he wrote to Pound: 'Of course I don't see England exactly as you do, it comes largely from having spent so much of my time among commercial people ….' Such differences came to a head when Pound informed Eliot that his job was irreconcilable with his literary career. On March 14, 1922 he warned his friend: 'if you try to do editorials as well as spend your days at Lloyds, I don't know that they will be very enlightening.' He told John Quinn it was 'a crime against literature to make him waste eight hours vitality per diem in that bank.'[39]

He declared to a wide circle of mutual acquaintances that Eliot's 'bank work has diminished his output of poetry, and that his prose has grown tired.'[40]

As we have seen, Pound held Lloyds Bank in special contempt, and Eliot could have been forgiven for taking this personally. His professional life involved following in the footsteps of Samuel Loyd, castigated by Pound for 'taking advantage of foreign exchange' by means of 'the mighty engine of the single Standard.' Eliot was implicitly among those abused by Pound as the 'men… of later generations' who continue the work of the 'early money-merchants'—the direct ancestors of his present employers. Pound even made an excruciating attempt to free Eliot from his day-job by setting up a charitable fund to support him, thus exposing his friend to considerable public and private ridicule. He went so far as to mention Lloyds by name in his appeal, possibly intending to force Eliot's hand. On January 22, 1922 Eliot wrote to Pound in a panic:

> If this Circular has not gone out, will you please delete Lloyds Bank, to the mention of which I strongly object. If it is stated so positively that Lloyds Bank interfered with literature, Lloyds Bank would have a perfect right to infer that literature interfered with Lloyds Bank. Please see my position—I cannot jeopardise my position at the Bank before I know what is best. They would certainly object if they saw this. If this business has any more publicity I shall be forced to make a public repudiation of it and refuse to have anything more to do with it.

It was not so much the time and effort that Eliot devoted to Lloyds that bothered Pound as the nature of his occupation: usury was antithetical to poetry. Eliot disagreed, assuring his mother that he was happy in his work 'and I can do my own work much the better for it.' He believed that his job at the bank complemented rather than inhibited his aesthetic endeavors. He was intrigued by money. On March 21, 1917 he told his sister: 'Anything to do with money—especially foreign money—is fascinating, and I hope to learn a little about finance while I am there.' Two days later he told Graham Wallas: 'I should like to think that I shall come to learn something of that extraordinary science of banking, if I can grasp any of it.' Seybold correctly observes that 'the record of poetry and prose from 1917 to 1925 clearly suggests that however exhausting, writing and banking were mutually beneficial pursuits for Eliot' (132).

As a financier, furthermore, Eliot exercised real power during an era when, as W. H. Auden observed, 'poetry makes nothing happen.'[41] He was soon working with the British Foreign Office to frustrate Germany's attempts to evade its obligations by presenting worthless *fiat* currencies as legal tender. The column in *Lloyds Bank Monthly*, which Eliot oversaw for over two years, regularly fulminated against this 'printing press paper.' It frequently expressed an economic semiotics that is analogous to Eliot's burgeoning theory of the poetic symbol. In 'Hamlet and His Problems' (1920), Eliot defines the 'objective correlative' as:

> ... a set of objects, a situation, a chain of events which shall be the formula of that particular emotion such that when the external facts, which must terminate in sensory experience, are given, the emotion is immediately evoked.[42]

There is a subtle but vital difference between Eliot's idea of a 'formula' and Pound's famous description of an 'image' as 'that which presents an intellectual and emotional complex in an instant of time.' In a 'formula,' a specific combination of ingredients brings about a transubstantiation: the transformation of one substance into another. A 'formula' is a relationship between two separate essences, in which one naturally produces the other. Eliot's notion of formulaic correlation thus retains a distinction between sign and referent, 'the external facts' and 'the emotion... evoked.' For example, he applauds Shakespeare's portrayal of Lady Macbeth's madness because it correlates with the crime she has committed, providing a 'complete adequacy of the external to the emotion.' By the same logic, *Hamlet* is 'an artistic failure' because the Prince's psychological turmoil lacks an appropriate external cause—Gertrude's re-marriage is not the appropriate 'formula' for his disproportionate reaction.

Eliot's doctrine of the 'objective correlative' thus evaluates figural representation according to the degree of correlation it achieves between subject and object. It is a means of connecting the objective symbol with the subjective emotion. In contrast, Pound's 'intellectual and emotional complex' is a unity, a fusion of diverse elements into a single whole. The 'Imagism' exemplified by Pound's 'In a Station of the Metro' acknowledges no Hegelian binaries: 'The apparition of these faces in a crowd;/ Petals on a wet, black bough.' As Ronald Schleifer has recently observed, this apparition is 'not a positive fact in [Pound's] experience of mass transit in Paris, but neither is it something beyond or "underneath" his experience.'[43] The petals and the faces are not symbol and referent, one does not designate or represent the other. They are not correlated; they are merely juxtaposed. As Pound himself put it:

> In a poem of this sort one is trying to record the precise instant when a thing outward and objective transforms itself, or darts into a thing inward and subjective.[44]

Such poetry attempts to elide linguistic mediation altogether, as James Dowthwaite argues: 'Pound's imagistic poetry shifts meaning from the interplay of words onto the interplay of the images they describe.'[45] 'Don't be descriptive' as Pound told aspiring Imagists in 1913, 'the natural object is always the adequate symbol.'[46] Pound's object is its own correlative. A modern poet does not concern himself with the correlation between objective symbol and subjective emotion, but with the 'direct treatment of the "thing" whether subjective or objective.'[47] The parable of Agassiz and the fish, which opens Pound's *ABC of Reading*, suggests that wisdom comes from contemplation of surface appearances, and from the reluctance to abstract from them, the refusal to explain them by looking beneath or beyond them.[48] As Emily Rich observes, he thus commits himself to a performative aesthetics in which:

> By eliminating poetry's symbolic elements, Pound removes poetry from the realm of language and transports it to the realm of physical action. This denial of the figurative represents an attempt to transform poetry from language to object and thus convert writing from a form of discussion to a form of action.[49]

In Pound's view, the nature of the modern poetic symbol is part of the same process as the modern dominance of usury. Usury reifies symbolic exchange-value by making it into an object of exchange, so modernist poetry transforms the verbal image into an object. The modernist image aspires to the iconic condition of the Chinese ideogram, as described in Pound's adaptation of Ernest Fellonosa's essay 'The Chinese Written Character as a Medium for Poetry' (1919):

> … Chinese notation is something much more than arbitrary symbols. It is based upon a vivid shorthand picture of the operations of nature. In the algebraic figure and in the spoken word there is no natural connection between thing and sign: all depends upon sheer convention. But the

Chinese method follows natural suggestion. First stands the man on his two legs. Second, his eye moves through space: a bold figure represented by running legs under an eye, a modified picture of an eye, a modified picture of running legs but unforgettable once you have seen it. Third stands the horse on his four legs.[50]

Similarly, according to Fellonosa as rendered by Pound, the Chinese express the verb 'to shine' with an ideograph representing the sun and the moon. They designate the adjective 'red' with the 'abbreviated pictures' (22) of iron rust, a cherry, a flamingo, and a rose. The Chinese refuse to treat language usuriously. They refuse to abstract from the material and then allow the abstraction to reproduce autonomously. Their language remains iconic rather than representational, meaning is not displaced into an absent referent but remains immanent with the sign. As Michael Kindellan and Joshua Kotin comment, 'the ideogrammic method juxtaposes discrete facts to make complex connections and communicate abstract ideas,' utilizing this immediate mode of communication to 'free us from the corrupting influence of usury, linguistic indeterminacy, and abstraction.'[51]

A 'phonetic word' in contrast 'does not bear its metaphor on its face' it does not contain its meaning within itself, but rather displaces its significance onto an external referent. Pound's modernist revolution demanded that poetic images should cease to be referential, that they should resemble Chinese characters, constituting objects in themselves, rather than function as a medium for the representation of anterior objects. The task of a modern poet is to express the modern condition, in accordance with Rimbaud's manifesto: 'if what he brings back from *down there* has form, he gives form; if it is formless, he gives formlessness. A language must be found.'[52] This desire to give poetic form to the autonomous, self-referential sign of modernity constitutes Pound's main difference from Eliot, whose Hegelian training never allowed him to forget that ideal essences underlie subjective appearances. Indeed, some critics are currently examining Eliot's modernist credentials with suspicion: for instance, Jason Harding refers to 'misleading accounts of Eliot as an aloof Modernist (a term he never embraced).'[53]

Certainly, if Pound represents modernist orthodoxy, Eliot was a heretic, a fact that their lifelong friendship has traditionally tended to obscure. In 1983, Christian Stough was among the first to discuss the 'skirmishes' between them, observing that in their later years the two pillars of modernism 'delighted in bickering over differences of opinion, most obviously over economics and religion.'[54] Stough cites the public quarrel that followed Pound's 1934 review of *After Strange Gods*, which attacked Eliot for avoiding 'the vital issue' of usury. Eliot responded with a letter to the effect that Pound apparently considered economics the 'only vital issue,' which elicited the following response from Pound:

> It is not that economics constitute 'the ONLY vital problem,' but the poverty and the syphilis of mind called the Finance-Capitalist system kill more men annually than typhoid or tuberculosis. I would not stop to discuss blue china in the midst of a cholera epidemic if I possessed means to combat the epidemic and, in the present circumstances, I consider certain kinds of aesthetic discussions on a par with such a course.[55]

In response to Eliot's charge that economics is not 'the only vital issue,' Pound claims that usury ('the Finance-Capitalist system') is not exclusively, or even mainly, 'economic' in nature. It is above all a corruption in thought, a 'syphilis of the mind.' So understood, usury is indeed 'the only vital issue.' Because usury manifests itself in poetics as well as in economics, Pound asserts that Eliot, and by extension poets in general, possess the practical means to combat usury. They are however failing to employ them, being distracted by the 'blue china' of their ivory-tower aesthetics. Stough rightly emphasizes the significance of this exchange, but the economic and aesthetic differences between Eliot and Pound long predate it. They diverge definitively by the early '20s, when Eliot's advocacy of the financial gold standard reflected a logocentrism that already verged on the theological.

Eliot's columns for *Lloyds Bank Monthly* are committed to a realist, referential model of financial signs, totally at odds with Pound's opinions. They argue that Germany–and eventually the entire world—should return as soon as possible to the gold standard.[56] The column dated January 1924[57] eagerly anticipates 'such date as the Bank of Norway again redeems its notes with gold,' and the one dated May 1925 declares that South Africa's return to the gold standard 'is an economic development that cannot but be interesting.' By August 1925 the tone becomes urgent:

> In connection with the return of so many European nations to the gold
> standard ... It is, perhaps, not too much to say that the well-being of
> the whole world depends, in a great measure, upon a speedy return by all
> countries to sound monetary conditions....

Such talk was anathema to Pound, who believed that the gold standard facilitated international usury. Indeed, that was precisely the reason
Eliot insisted it was indispensable. He had seen how, in the absence of
such a standard, governments could and did print reams of worthless
paper to avoid paying their debts. Germany had been especially remiss
in this regard. Eliot sniffs that 'the paper mark is nominally a token
currency, though it appears to retain a vitality to which it is not entitled.'
The authentic value of money—the value to which it is 'entitled'—lies
beyond the paper sign, in the gold standard to which it refers. The paper
money issued by the German government is nonreferential and therefore
fictional: 'inflation figures at the Reichsbank have become utterly fantastic,
the bank officials there have been working twenty hours a day—mostly
writing noughts, one would imagine....' Eliot also frowns upon the new
currencies issued by regional banks: 'these new issues are denominated
"gold" issues, with one qualification or another, but it is to be noted that
a "goldmark" of any kind is not necessarily backed by gold, and is never,
of course, convertible into gold.' He even reports a reversion to barter:
'a leather manufacturer in Saxony paid part of his wages in soles, stamped
with the date and the value at that date. It is not stated whether these
symbols were accepted by the local tradesmen.'

The Saxons were literally selling their soles, but Eliot warns that such
'symbols' are not real money. The value of financial signs is derived
from the *logos* of gold alone. Eliot put his faith in *logos* well before his
public conversion to Anglo-Catholicism. His youthful academic training
in philosophical idealism had convinced him that essential reality lay
beneath empirical appearances, and his financial columns applied this
ontological idealism to economics. In January 1924 Eliot even applauded
the Soviet *tchervonetz*, because it 'is only issued against definite cover in
the form of gold foreign money....' No friend of the Bolsheviks politically,
Eliot nevertheless admired the economic realism of their adherence to
the gold standard. His semiotic logocentrism thus transcended the widest
possible political differences, and it easily trumped any residual loyalty he
may have felt to the modernism espoused by his erstwhile mentor.

Pound did not suffer heretics gladly. He delighted in reminding his acolytes of the ancient association between usury and sodomy, recalling in 1934 how in Dante's *Inferno*: 'the usurer is damned with the sodomite. Usury judged with sodomy as "contrary to natural increase," contrary to the nature of live things (animal and vegetable) to multiply.' In view of recent suggestions about Eliot's putatively homosexual tendencies,[58] such allusions may have been pointed. They certainly recall Ernest Hemingway's digs at Eliot. Hemingway's short story 'Mr. and Mrs. Elliot' (1925) evoked Eliot's marriage through its focus on sterility: 'Mr. and Mrs. Elliot tried very hard to have a baby. They tried as often as Mrs. Elliot could stand it.'[59] Hemingway responded to news that Eliot had finished 'The Waste Land' by opining that he would have done better to 'buggar the brain specialist and rob the bank.'[60] In 'Death in the Afternoon' (1932), he includes Eliot among the 'Humanists' whose 'long preserved sterility' suggests that they reproduce through 'decorous cohabitation'[61] rather than sexual intercourse—in other words, they engage in reproduction by unnatural means.

7.4   Ernest Hemingway, Harold Loeb, and Anti-Semitism

It is hard to deny that, as Suzanne Churchill phrases it: 'Eliot's poetry and prose writings display an obsessive interest in sexual corruption and a particular fascination with homosexuality.'[62] But his poetry's 'queer' status does not depend on whether, for example, 'The Waste Land' mourns the death of a male lover, or on any other putatively biographical allusion. Jess Cotton argues that Eliot's collaboration with Pound itself constituted an asexual, artificial form of reproduction:

> Whereas the family romance in Eliot's pocket epic seems to have been rendered sterile within heterosexual relations ('What you get married for if you don't want children?' is an unanswered question that reverberates through the text), collaboration offers the potential for new, queer kinds of affective and erotic sensibilities that might be borne in this indeterminate space.[63]

Pound employs sexual imagery to represent his collaboration with Eliot in 'Sage Homme,' which half-seriously presents the consequent verse as the offspring of unnatural reproduction: 'These are the poems of

Eliot/By the Uranian muse begot;/A Man their Mother was,/A Muse their Sire.' The *motif* of sterility in 'The Waste Land' has often been remarked upon; the parallel theme of unnatural reproduction has been noticed less often. Yet Eliot alludes to the ancient association between sodomy and finance when Mr. Eugenides' implicitly homosexual proposition follows his euphemistic characterization as a 'Smyrna merchant.'[64] The association also appears elsewhere. 'A Cooking Egg' declares:

> I shall not want Capital in Heaven
> For I shall meet Sir Alfred Mond;
>   We two shall lie together, lapt
> In a five per cent Exchequer bond. (13–16)

The five per cent Exchequer bond had been issued as a war-time surrogate for the gold standard. The Bank of England had advertised the bonds with a disarming frankness: 'If you cannot fight, you can help your country by investing all you can in 5 per cent. Exchequer Bonds.... Unlike the soldier, the investor runs no risk.' Eliot had not fought in the war, and such language made the bonds sound distinctly usurious—it was a traditional criticism of usury that, unlike a legitimate investor, the money-lender did not share in the risk of the enterprise. The image of the Jewish financier Mond eternally embracing the poet suggests a degree of moral discomfort. Eliot appears to have salved his conscience with the usual modernist medicine: he projected his anxiety onto 'the Jew.'

In 'Burbank with a Baedecker, Bleistein with a Cigar' this symbol's referential significance is given as if in a footnote: 'The Jew is underneath the lot. Money in furs.'[65] Money is the underlying power supporting the new European order, in which 'Sir Ferdinand/Klein' has usurped social power. For Eliot, 'Jews' are not only literal Jews, they are also symbolic: money personified. When money is personified it takes on a figural life, and the definitive characteristic of life is reproduction. Money personified is money that breeds, and money that breeds is usury. The word 'Jew' functioned as a symbol for 'usury' throughout the century of Marx, Dickens, Trollope and Dostoevsky, and this trope reaches an apotheosis in modernism. As Gabriel Hankins has recently observed of Eliot's 'Gerontion': 'the "jew" is a prejudicial figure for usury... and more particularly a global usury of the kind practiced by Lloyds....'[66] Hemingway's *The Sun Also Rises* (1926), arguably the seminal Anglophone modernist novel, is perfectly explicit on the symbolic valence of 'Jews':

'She never has any money. She gets five hundred quid a year and pays three hundred and fifty of it in interest to Jews.'

'I suppose they get it at the source,' said Bill.

'Quite. They're not really Jews. We just call them Jews. They're Scotsmen, I believe.' (185)

Hemingway thus subverts the prejudice that the relation between 'Jews' and 'usury' is one of literal identity. In Ford Madox Hueffer's novel *A Call* (1910), for instance, a character is simply 'heavily indebted to the Jews.'[67] In contrast, the passage from Hemingway insists that the relationship between 'Jews' and 'usury' is figurative rather than literal. Anti-Semitism has often been called the socialism of fools, and its foolishness often consists in hermeneutic literalism. It projects phenomena that are actually the products of usury onto symbolic 'Jews,' and it mistakes this symbol for reality. In his lucid intervals, even Pound protested against anti-Semitism's literalist mistaking of sign for referent. In 1935 he commented in the *New English Weekly*: 'USURERS have no race. How long the whole Jewish people is to be the sacrificial goat for the usurer, I know not.'[68] In 'Gold and Work' (1944) he pronounced: 'It is, of course, useless to indulge in anti-Semitism, leaving intact the Hebraic monetary system which is their most tremendous instrument of usury' (351). Over the '30s' and '40s,' however, Pound increasingly equated the sign of 'the Jew' with the referent of 'usury,' in both financial and verbal forms. As Paul Morrison puts it: 'the Jew remains *the* privileged figure for figuration, the paradoxical (non)referent for a semiotic order, at once linguistic and economic, which eludes referentiality' (10). For Pound as for Eliot, and arguably for Anglophone modernism in general, the 'Jew' is a symbol of performative representation itself. As Andrew Parker perceptively observes: 'Pound's animus against Judaism ultimately will be legible as an animus against (his own) writing as such....' Parker explains the connection Pound perceived between usury and the hermeneutics of Talmudic Judaism:

In the same way that usury produces a "surplus value" without direct monetary reference to the world of tangible commodities, so do the texts of Judaism conspire to undermine the efficacy of immediate linguistic reference—to suppress "any interest in verbal precision...."[69]

The Sun Also Rises reflects at length on the moral dangers inherent in hermeneutic literalism. The Jewish character Robert Cohn is treated appallingly by the book's other figures. The obvious explanation, which Hemingway dangles in front of the reader like bait, is simple anti-Semitism. Bill Gorton calls Cohn a 'kike' and complains of his 'Jewish superiority,' Mike Campbell orders him to 'take that sad Jewish face away,' Jake Barnes remarks on his 'hard, Jewish, stubborn streak.'[70] But the word 'Jew' functions here symbolically as much as literally, as was common in Anglophone modernism. When Lady Brett exclaims of Cohn 'I hate his damned suffering,' he is transformed into an archetypal, symbolic Jew through the same modernist re-invention of tradition that elevates the quotidian wanderings of Leopold Bloom to mythical status in James Joyce's *Ulysses*.

'Robert Cohn' represents usury in both its financial and verbal manifestations. This becomes clearer on acquaintance with the published work of the real man represented by this figure in Hemingway's *roman a clef*. Harold Loeb was a well-known editor, little-known novelist and general fixture on the 1920s Left Bank. He was also a scion of one of the world's wealthiest Jewish banking families, and a major patron-cum-publisher of many rising modernist writers. These had once included Hemingway, but the two men appear to have fallen out after Loeb's romantic tryst with Lady Duff Twyson, lover of Hemingway's friend Pat Guthrie. During this ill-fated encounter, which set in motion the sequence of events immortalized by Hemingway's novel, Loeb apparently thrust upon Twyson his lengthy article, 'The Mysticism of Money.'[71] Although she remained unmoved, the episode suggests that Loeb regarded this article as his most impressive achievement.

Whatever its virtues for the purpose of seduction, 'The Mysticism of Money' is an intriguing piece of work. It rehearses the standard modernist position that the European art has entered its 'decadent period,' which is 'marked by the exhaustion of the traditional forms.' In contrast, Loeb claims that American aesthetics retains a primal energy that 'parallels the archaic expressions of less sophisticated races.' In America, he explains, this 'mystical' aesthetic is expressed in the fetishistic belief that an objectively powerful 'value' inheres in money. All societies require:

> ... that there should be no doubt at all concerning values. Thus it is necessary that something should be assumed to be true, not that it is true. This need has been satisfied in the past by what is termed religion. It is

filled to-day in America by the Mysticism of Money. Money, because that which was originally but a medium of exchange and a valuable metal, has become the measuring staff of all values and the goal and reward of all efforts conventionally accepted as proper. Mystic because the validity of the money standard and the intrinsic merit of money making are accepted on faith, extra-intellectually.[72]

Loeb portrays financial value as a surrogate religion. The 'money standard' is the god of modernity—it is only a symbol, but people accord it real power through their faith in its efficacy. In the twentieth century, money has become a performative sign, a symbol that refers to nothing, but exerts an objective effect nonetheless. As we have seen, Pound wholeheartedly agreed with the empirical accuracy of this description, which he attempted to reflect in his poetics. But whereas Pound deplores the usurious characters of modern representation, Loeb provocatively and enthusiastically celebrates it. He outrageously suggests that the 'mystical' money of capitalist America should be accorded the same sacred reverence that other 'primitive' cultures bestow on their fetishes. Whereas Pound saw the gold standard as an idolatrous facilitator of usury, Loeb presents it as an unnecessary, illusory obstacle to the autonomous reproduction of financial signs. He held onto this position in *Life in a Technocracy* (1933), where he notes that the money issued by war-time and post-war governments did not refer to gold, which was thus dethroned from its position as financial *logos*. Loeb applauds this 'realization that gold is not wealth.' He ridicules:

> ... [the] notion that gold and the paper or metal certificates supposedly entitling the holder to gold are wealth—a concept undermined, even among the people, during the late war and its aftermath, because every government was forced to spend money which did not exist if the gold basis had been strictly adhered to.[73]

Since its own value is determined by the market, gold cannot logically be the standard of value. Like Pound, Loeb believes that '[m]oney based on gold... will not do, because the value of gold like that of other commodities under the capitalist system depends on scarcity...' (38). However, Loeb remains finally convinced that money must have some transcendental signified. Having rejected gold and commodity-baskets, he rather eccentrically decides on the 'erg,' a unit that, he claims, can be applied to any form of energy. But the nature of the referent is less important than its necessity. The point is that money should refer to *something*, that it should be referential. Loeb is wary of the infinite fluctuation in value that flourishes in the absence of any financial *logos*. He understands that the autonomy of financial signs carries ominous ideological consequences, although he is rather naïve about their ethnic implications:

> Success is judged largely in money terms. Few realize how short a time this code has been in general force and how drastically it differs from the preceding aristocratic and peasant codes. The interloper, the middle-man shopkeeper, has imposed his mores on the entire commonwealth. (26)

For centuries, '[t]he interloper, the middle-man shopkeeper' who imposes his disruptive financial values on traditional society was symbolically figured as 'the Jew.' Loeb does not acknowledge this, any more than 'Robert Cohn' understands the reasons for his ostracism in *The Sun Also Rises*. When he came to reflect on the Pamplona trip in his autobiographical *The Way It Was* (1959), Loeb was still asking: 'What was it in me that set me apart?'[74] Perhaps his confusion is understandable, for it would be wrong to assume that Hemingway disliked Loeb for his Jewishness in any literal sense. Loeb's Jewishness was for Hemingway a symbol. He hated what it represented, and what it represented was usury.

Although he always remained on friendly terms with Pound, Hemingway's public stance toward Eliot conveys an implacable, though apparently unprovoked, hostility.[75] In 1924 the unknown Hemingway fantasized publicly about 'grinding Mr. Eliot into a fine dry powder and sprinkling that powder over Conrad's grave in Canterbury.' In 1950, the world-famous Hemingway described Eliot as '[a]damned good poet and a fair critic; but he can kiss my ass as a man.'[76] Since they never met, this asperity demands explanation. Several critics have diagnosed a Bloomian anxiety of influence. H. R. Stoneback remarks that 'the influence of "The Waste Land" on *The Sun Also Rises* (and much of Hemingway) is pervasive.'[77] Wendolyn Tetlow concludes that 'despite Hemingway's acid comments… he could not escape Eliot's influence.'[78] Joseph Flora notes the resemblance between 'The Waste Land's' recurrent theme of sterility and the imagery that pervades Hemingway's 'Hills like White Elephants.'[79]

Flora's comparison is especially striking. Hemingway's story connects the destruction of symbolic significance with the negation of sexual fecundity. The male speaker rejects his female lover's attempt to read the distant hills as a symbol of white elephants, and we gradually gather that this refusal of semiotic fertility is of a piece with his insistence that she abort their child. Like 'The Waste Land's' mingling of artistic with sexual sterility, this technique unmistakably reveals the influence of Pound. The convergence of symbolic and sexual barrenness is originally Aristotelian, but Pound insisted on its application in modernist literature. He also enjoyed jesting about it with his literary proteges. In the last letter between the two men (1935), Pound criticizes Hemingway for hunting lions instead of 'the buggars back of the Bank of Paris,' and blames the deficiencies of Hemingway's safari on the avarice of 'some sodomitical usurer.'

Such terminology recalls Hemingway's allusions to Eliot, which focus on the connections between financial, sexual and artistic infertility to a degree which raises the suspicion that they were performed, at least in part, for Pound's benefit. Sometimes the barrenness is merely poetic: Eliot's poems are fine, but 'there are very few of them.'[80] But Hemingway particularly loved to dwell on Eliot's poetic debt to Pound, claiming in 1950 that Eliot 'would not have existed but for dear old Ezra.' In 'Homage to Ezra' (1925) he announces that, while Pound is a 'major' poet, Eliot is merely a 'minor' one. When Robert Manning interviewed Hemingway in 1954, he found him 'not warm toward T.S. Eliot,' preferring to 'praise Ezra Pound,' and even suggesting that Pound should have won Eliot's Nobel Prize.[81] In *A Moveable Feast* Hemingway recalls mocking Eliot for Pound's amusement:

> I mixed things up a little by always referring to Eliot as Major Eliot pretending to confuse him with Major Douglas an economist about whose ideas Ezra was very enthusiastic.[82]

Major C. H. Douglas, leader of the Social Credit movement, was England's most famous opponent of usury. Pound called him 'the first economist to include creative art and writing in an economic scheme.'[83] 'Major' Eliot, international debt-collector for Lloyds' Bank, made a temptingly ironic contrast, and of course the nickname also alludes to Eliot's failure to serve in the war. Hemingway's ostentatious hostility toward 'buggars' and 'usurers' seems more neurotic than rational, and it is possible that it has primal sources in the peculiarities of his psyche. It has been suggested, notably by Harold Loeb, that Hemingway's notorious *machismo* was rooted in his childhood resentment of his mother's attempts to feminize him in dress and manner. He also took extreme offence when she wrote to him that '[a] mother's love seems to me like a bank' and that, having made no 'deposits which keep the account in good standing,' Ernest was now 'overdrawn' and 'there is nothing before you but bankruptcy.'[84] Hemingway's enraged, exaggerated reaction suggests that he found this usurious conception of love, perhaps combined with her early subversion of his natural gender, absolutely intolerable. He referred to his mother as 'that bitch' ever afterwards.

It has frequently been observed that Hemingway's work tends to reflect on the ethical, aesthetic and psychological significance of economics. Jacqueline Vaught Brogan points to the fascination evinced by *The Sun Also Rises* with 'the replacement of ethical values with "monetary" values.'[85] The novel's characters are determined by their attitudes to money, from Count Mippipoplous' offer of cash in exchange for Lady Brett's company, to Mike Campbell's failure to pay for his drinks. Jake Barnes neatly encapsulates this alienation of essential, human qualities into quantitative, financial form: 'I spent a little money and the waiter liked me. He appreciated my valuable qualities' (188). Such transpositions of morality into finance provide the novel's most prominent figural device, and it proves so apposite that it becomes literal. When Lady Brett asks: 'Don't we pay for all the things we do...?' (22) financial reciprocity is indistinguishable from moral retribution. The ethic of exchange temporarily provides Jake Barnes with a hard-boiled, homespun philosophy:

> No idea of retribution or punishment. Just exchange of values. You gave up something and got something else. Or you worked for something. You paid some way for everything that was any good.... Enjoying living was learning to get your money's worth and knowing when you had it. You could get your money's worth. The world was a good place to buy in. It seemed like a fine philosophy. (119)

Hemingway's seminal modernist novel meditates at length on the moral implications of this philosophy. It shows what happens when symbols impose themselves on reality. The chaos within the characters' minds finds its objective correlative in the Spanish fiesta. In Bakhtinian style, the carnival unleashes a temporary trans-valuation of all values, and Hemingway expresses this process in specifically financial terms. As the peasants come into town from their villages:

… it was necessary that they make their shifting in values gradually. They could not start in paying café prices. They got their money's worth in the wine-shops. Money still had a definite value in hours worked and bushels of grain sold. Late in the fiesta it would not matter what they paid, nor where they bought. (122)

The fiesta renders value relative, and the novel is a commentary on the ethical consequences of relativism, both moral and financial. As a journalist in post-war Europe, Hemingway had witnessed the social chaos that sudden variations in financial value could cause. His article 'German Inflation,' which ran in *The Toronto Daily Star* on September 9, 1922 personifies the Deutschmark's collapse in the poignant poverty of an old man:

He went up the street walking very much as white bearded old gentlemen of the old regime walk in all countries, but he had looked very longingly at the apples. I wish I had offered him some. Twelve marks, on that day, amounted to a little under two cents. The old man, whose life's savings were probably, as most of the non-profiteer classes are, invested in German pre-war and war bonds, could not afford a twelve-mark expenditure. He is a type of people whose incomes do not increase with the falling purchasing power of the mark and the krone.[86]

The old man is the 'objective correlative' of the Deutschmark's collapse; his image provides a rhetorical short-cut to a reasonably complex economic opinion. In similar fashion, Hemingway incarnates the 'miracles of exchange' in the 'swinish spectacle' of the French flocking over the border to 'eat themselves sick and gorge on fluffy, cream-filled slices of German cake at five marks the slice' (42).

Anglophone literary modernism developed in the context of a pronounced convergence between the historical trajectories of language and money. Modernist theories of the poetic symbol and modernist attitudes toward financial representation determined each other to an extent that, perhaps, is only becoming clear today. Today we are fully cogniscent of the economy's influence over culture and society. The last few decades have witnessed the simultaneous efflorescence of 'usury' (finance capitalism) and 'sodomy' (concupiscent sexuality), thus lending credence to claims of kinship between them. Today, furthermore, we are keenly aware of the economy's essentially symbolic nature. The postmodern economy is dominated by financial 'derivatives': signs that operate at a much more abstract level of representation than the *fiat* currencies against which Eliot protested. Nobody doubts the performative power of financial derivatives. Their ontological reality is frequently disputed, however, since they refer to nothing tangible even in the financial sense. They are symbols that are, as we might say today, 'hyper-real.' If we wish to arrive at an ethical evaluation of such postmodern phenomena, it will help to study the modernist reaction to their twentieth-century precursors.

NOTES

1. Wallace Stevens, 'Adagia,' in *Opus Posthumus*, ed. Milton Bates (Alfred Knopf, 1989), 191.
2. Alec Marsh, *Money and Modernity: Pound, Williams and the Spirit of Jefferson* (U of Alabama P, 1998), 142.
3. I believe we are justified in assuming Eliot's authorship of these articles, which fell under his remit as head of the bank's Intelligence Department. It is true that, as Lyndall Gordon notes, they are unsigned and therefore 'not listed in the bibliography of Eliot's works.' *T.S. Eliot: An Imperfect Life* (W. W. Norton, 1998), 628. Matt Seybold presumes Eliot was the author (141), although Paul Delaney says that the columns 'have not yet been reliably identified' (218n25). Christopher Ricks' *Poems of T.S. Eliot* cites the inaugural column without equivocation: 'TSE wrote that....' On September 29 1923, Henry Eliot wrote to their mother that 'Tom' was writing an article for Lloyds. The following month Eliot told her that he was working on: 'A review of the money market in France and Spain for the Lloyds Bank Financial Monthly' and 'A digest of Roumanian debt legislation for my Lloyds Bank Extracts from the Foreign Press' (2:254). The publishers of the *Complete Prose* plan to make these columns available through Project Muse on a 'future digital platform' according to Timothy Materer, 'T.S. Eliot: From Undergraduate to Literary Lion,' *Modernism/Modernity* 22.2 (April 2015), 381–387. At present, they are available only by personal appointment at the Lloyds archives in London, where I consulted them in the summers of 2017 and 2018. The curator opined that Eliot was the author of the columns, and that in any case they carried his endorsement and presumably expressed his views.
4. Ian Drummond, *The Gold Standard and the International Monetary System*, 1900–39 (Macmillan, 1987), 11.
5. Cit. Charles P. Kindleberger, *A Financial History of Western Europe* (Routledge, 2006), 85.
6. Cit. Alex Ross, 'Stephane Mallarme, Prophet of Modernism,' *The New Yorker* April 11, 2016.

7. Jean-Joseph Goux, *The Coiners of Language*, trans. Jennifer C. Gage (U of Oklahoma P, 1996), 4. Similarly, Fredric Jameson observes: If modernism is a kind of cancelled realism...then it might be likened to a largely accepted paper money, whose inflationary ups and downs suddenly lead to the introduction of financial and speculative instruments and vehicles.' 'Culture and Finance Capital,' *Critical Inquiry* 24.1 (Autumn 1997), 246–265, 261.

8. Mallarme defines 'literature' by distinction from realist 'description': 'It is not *description* which can unveil the efficacy and beauty of monuments... but rather evocation, *allusion, suggestion....* In literature, allusion is sufficient' ('Crisis in Poetry,' cit. Vassilliky Kolocotroni, Jane Goldman, Olga Taxidou (eds.), *Modernism: An Anthology of Sources and Documents* (U of Chicago P, 1998), 125.

9. Arthur Symons, *The Symbolist Movement in Literature* (E.P. Dutton, 1919), 1.

10. Jacques Derrida, *Of Grammatology*, trans. Gayatri Spivak (Johns Hopkins UP, 1997), 92.

11. James Wilhelm, *The American Roots of Ezra Pound* (Garland Publishing, 1985), 81.

12. Paul Morrison, *The Poetics of Fascism: Ezra Pound, T.S. Eliot, Paul de Man* (Oxford UP, 1996), 9.

13. Ezra Pound, 'What Is Money For?' in Cookson (ed.), 290–303.

14. Stuart Christie, 'Usurious Translation: From Chinese Character to Western Ideology in Pound's Confucian "Terminology",' in *American Modernist Poetry and the Chinese Encounter*, ed. Zhang Yuejun and Stuart Christie (Palgrave Macmillan, 2012), 77–93, 77.

15. Alessandro Lanteri, 'Douglas, Gessell and the Economic Ethics of Ezra Pound,' *History of Economic Ideas* 19.1 (2011), 147–166, 171.

16. Ezra Pound, 'Gold and Work' (1944), in *Selected Prose 1909–1965*, ed. William Cookson (New Directions, 1973) 346–347.

17. See William M. Chace, *The Political Identities of Ezra Pound and T.S. Eliot* (Stanford UP, 1973), 89.

18. Jeffrey Mark, *The Modern Idolatry: Being an Analysis of Usury and the Pathology of Debt* (Chatto and Windus, 1934).

19. Eugene Vance, 'Chaucer's *House of Fame* and the Poetics of Inflation,' *Boundary 2* 7 (Winter 1979), 19.

20. Richard Sieburth, 'In Pound We Trust: The Economy of Poetry/The Poetry of Economics,' *Critical Inquiry* 14.1 (Fall 1987), 146.

21. Sieburth describes the *Cantos* as 'a mosaic of signifiers without signifieds (or, more precisely, of signifiers treated as if they were signifieds). The monies that Pound has here banked on the page function less as tokens of commodities or signs of value than as sheer inscriptions, sheer traces...' (144).

22. Jacques Derrida, 'White Mythology: Metaphor in the Text of Philosophy,' *New Literary History* 6.1 (Autumn, 1974), 5–74.

23. Marc Shell, 'The Wether and the Ewe: Verbal Usury in *The Merchant of Venice*, *The Kenyon Review* 1.4 (Autumn 1979), 65–92, 66.

24. Ezra Pound, *Canto XLV*.

25. Cit. Charles Moran *Money* (New York: D. Appleton & Co., 1863), 185.

26. Ezra Pound, 'Gold and Work,' 345.

27. Frederick Soddy, *Wealth, Virtual Wealth and Debt* (1933), cit. Mark, *The Modern Idolatry*, 85.

28. Arthur Kitson, *Banker's Conspiracy! Which Started the World Crisis* (London: Elliot Stock, 1933), 27. On the various thinkers who influenced Pound's on the gold standard, see Ellen Cardona, *A Historical Study of Ezra Pound's Anti-Semitism* (Ph.D. Dissertation, U of Texas, Dalla, 2014).

29. Willis Overholser, *A Short Review and Analysis of the History of Money in the United States* (Progress Publishing, 1936), 14.

30. Brooks Adams, *The Law of Civilization and Decay: An Essay on History* (Macmillan, 1916), 337, cit. Pound 'Gold and Work', 340.

31. As Robert Casillo observes: 'Where the bad poet multiplies mere words, the usurer increases and values the mere sign of wealth (money) without a corresponding increase in commodities and has not the slightest respect for representational truth, natural growth, or intrinsic value.' 'Troubadour Love and Usury in Ezra Pound's Writings,' *Texas Studies in Literature and Language* 27.2 (Summer 1985), 125–153, 129.

32. Cit. Anthony David Moody, *Ezra Pound, Poet: A Portrait of the Man & His Work* (Oxford UP, 2014), 2:241.

33. On anti-Semitism and Pound's economics, see Victor C. Ferkiss, 'Ezra Pound and American Fascism', *Journal of Politics* 17.2 (1955), 173–197; David Murray, 'Pound-Signs: Money and Representation in Ezra Pound' in *Ezra Pound: Tactics for Reading*, ed. Ian Bell (Barnes and Noble, 1982); Andrew Parker, 'Ezra Pound and the "Economy" of Anti-Semitism,' *boundary 2* 11 (Fall/Winter 1982–1983), 103–128; Peter Nicholls, *Ezra Pound: Politics, Economics and Writing: A Study of the Cantos* (Macmillan, 1984); Jean-Michel Rabate, *Language, Sexuality and Ideology in Ezra Pound's Cantos* (Macmillan, 1986), 142–172; Robert Casillo, *The Geneaology of Demons: Anti-Semitism, Fascism and the Myths of Ezra Pound* (Northwestern UP, 1988); Leon Surette, *Pound in Purgatory: From Economic Radicalism to Anti-Semitism* (U of Illinois P, 1999); David A. Moody, '"EP with Two Pronged Fork of Terror and Cajolery": The Construction of his Anti-Semitism (Up to 1939),' *Paideuma* 29.3 (Winter 2000); Meghnad Desai, *The Route of All Evil. The Political Economy of Ezra Pound* (Faber and Faber, 2006); Michael North, *The Political Aesthetic of Yeats, Eliot and Pound* (Cambridge UP, 2009);

David Barnes, 'Fascist Aesthetics: Ezra Pound's Cultural Negotiations in 1930s Italy,' *Journal of Modern Literature* 34.1 (2010), 19–35; Matthew Feldman, *Ezra Pound's Fascist Propaganda, 1935–45* (Palgrave, 2013); Daniel Swift, *The Bughouse: The Poetry, Politics, and Madness of Ezra Pound* (Farrar, Strauss & Giroux, 2017).

34. On Eliot's anti-Semitism, see Christopher Ricks, *T S. Eliot and Prejudice* (Faber & Faber, 1988); Anthony Julius, *T. S. Eliot, Anti-Semitism, and Literary Form* (Cambridge UP, 1995); Ronald Schuchard, *Eliot's Dark Angel: Intersections of Art and Life* (Oxford UP, 1999). In January 2003, *Modernism/modernity* 10.1 featured a section entitled 'Eliot and Anti-Semitism: The Ongoing Debate,' including Ronald Schuchard's essay 'Burbank with a Baedeker, Eliot with a Cigar' and several responses.

35. See Paul Delany, *Literature, Money and the Market: From Trollope to Amis* (Palgrave, 2002), 162–171.

36. G. Elliott Smith, 'The Glamour of Gold,' *The Criterion* 3.2 (April 1925).

37. *The Letters of T.S. Eliot Vol. II*, eds. Valerie Eliot and Hugh Haughton (London: Faber & Faber, 2009), 1. Further letters from this volume are identified by date.

38. Matt Seybold, 'Astride the Dark Horse: T.S. Eliot and the Lloyds Bank Intelligence Department,' in *T.S. Eliot Studies Annual*, John D. Morgenstern (Liverpool UP, 2017), 131–156, 134.

39. Pound to Quinn, 4 June 1920. Cit. *The Waste Land: A Facsimile*, ed. Valerie Eliot (Harcourt, 1971), xviii.

40. Cit. Robert Crawford, *Young Eliot: From St. Louis to The Waste Land* (New York: Farrar, Strauss and Giroux, 2015), 406. See Ezra Pound, "Credit and the Fine Arts: A Practical Application," *The New Age* 30.22 (30 March 1922).

41. W.H. Auden, 'In Memory of W.B. Yeats,' 36.

42. T.S. Eliot, 'Hamlet and His Problems" in *The Sacred Wood and Major Early Essays* (Dover Publications, 1998), 58. Flemming Olsen summarizes the distinguishing feature of Eliot's 'objective correlative': 'whereas conventional metaphors... only serve to illuminate a given emotion, and have, accordingly, no "independent" existence, Eliot's correlative is something that exists in its own right.' *Eliot's Objective Correlative: Tradition or Individual Talent?* (Sussex Academic P, 2012), 56.

43. Ronald Schleifer, *A Political Economy of Modernism* (Cambridge UP, 2018), 10.

44. Ezra Pound, 'Vorticism' *Fortnightly Review* NS 96 (September 1914), 461–471.

45. James Dowthwaite, *Ezra Pound and 20th-century Theories of Language: Faith with the Word* (Routledge, 2019), 13.

46. Ezra Pound, 'A Few Don'ts by an Imagiste,' *Poetry* (1913).

47. Ezra Pound, 'A Retrospective,' in *The Literary Essays of Ezra Poundi*, ed. T.S. Eliot (New Directions, 1954), 3.
48. Ezra Pound, *ABC of Reading* (Faber & Faber, 1991, org. 1934), 17–18.
49. Emily Rich, '"To Act on One's Definition": Ezra Pound, Carl Schmitt and the Poetics of Sovereignty,' *Intertexts* 20.2 (Fall, 2016), 135–153, 142–143.
50. Ernest Fenollosa and Ezra Pound, *The Chinese Written Character as a Medium for Poetry*, ed. Haun Saussy, Jonathan Stalling, and Lucas Klein (New York: Fordham University Press, 2008).
51. Michael Kindellan and Joshua Kotin, '*The Cantos* and Pedagogy,' *Modernist Cultures* 12.3 (November 2017), 345–363, 345.
52. Cit. Vassiliki Kolocotroni, Jane Goldman and Olga Taxidou (eds.), *Modernism: An Anthology of Sources and Documents* (U of Chicago P, 1998), 110.
53. Jason Harding, 'Introduction' to *T.S. Eliot in Context*, ed. Jason Harding (Cambridge UP, 2011), 3.
54. Christina Stough,'The Skirmish of Pound and Eliot in *The New English Weekly*: A Glimpse at Their Later Literary Relationship,' *Journal of Modern Literature* 10.2 (1983), 231–246, 231.
55. Ezra Pound, 'Mr. T.S. Eliot's Quandries,' *The New English Weekly*, April 26, 1934, 48, cit. Stough, 238.
56. Adam Trexler observes: 'Great symbolic importance was attached to Britain's suspension of the gold standard in 1919: sterling and all the international currencies dependent on it were now unsecured from value. This loss of symbolic value is dramatized in *The Waste Land* by the woes of the Thames daughters and the Rhine daughters, who are charged with guarding the gold that secures the nations of Britain and Germany.' 'Economics,' in Harding (2011), 275–284, 278.
57. Since they have not yet been republished, the easiest way of referring to these columns is to give the date of *Lloyds Bank Monthly* in which they appeared.
58. The idea that Eliot may have been homosexual was first floated by in 1952 by John Peter in 'A New Interpretation of "The Waste Land",' but publication was suppressed after Eliot threatened to sue. The essay was eventually published following his death, in *Essays in Criticism* 14.2 (April 1969), 140–175. For a more recent reading along similar lines see especially Carole Seymour-Jones, *Painted Shadow: The Life of Vivienne Eliot* (Doubleday 2002).
59. Ernest Hemingway, *In Our Time: Stories* (Scribner, 1958), 152.
60. Cit. John Cohassey, *Hemingway and Pound: A Most Unlikely Friendship* (Macfarland, 2014), 30.
61. Ernest Hemingway, *Death in the Afternoon* (Simon and Schuster, 2002), 113.

62. Suzanne Churchill, 'Outing T.S. Eliot,' *Criticism* 47.1 (Winter 2005), 7–30, 10.
63. Jess Cotton, '"Rimbaud in Embryo": Collaborative Representations in T.S. Eliot and Hart Crane,' *Modernist Cultures* 41.1 (2009), 36–52. Cotton's argument builds on Wayne Koestenbaum, *Double Talk: The Erotics of Male Literary Collaboration* (Routledge, 1989), 112–141.
64. David Roessel, '"Mr. Eugenides, the Smyrna Merchant," and Post-War Politics in "The Waste Land",' *Journal of Modern Literature* 16.1 (Summer, 1989), 171–176. See Cassandra Laity and Nancy Gish (eds.), *Gender, Sexuality, and Desire in T. S. Eliot* (Cambridge UP, 2004). Lawrence Rainey notes that '"The Waste Land"… repeatedly conflates financial and sexual economies into an amorphous world of uncontrolled circulations.' *The Annotated Waste Land with Eliot's Contemporary Prose* (Yale UP, 2005), 'Introduction,' 9.
65. Christopher Ricks (ed.), *Poems of T.S. Eliot Vol. 1* (Johns Hopkins UP, 2015).
66. Gabriel Hankins, *Interwar Modernism and the Liberal World Order: Offices, Institutions and Aesthetics After 1919* (Cambridge UP, 2019), 91.
67. Cit. Cardona, 22.
68. Cit. Lea Baechler, A. Walton Litz, and James Longenbach (eds.), *Ezra Pound's Poetry and Prose: Contributions to Periodicals*, Etc. (Garland Publishing, 1991), 6:343. As early as 1957, Victor Ferkiss emphasized that Pound's real target was always 'the money power.' 'Populist Influences on American Fascism,' *Western Political Quarterly* 2.361 (June 1957).
69. Andrew Parker, 'Ezra Pound and the "Economy" of Anti-Semitism,' *boundary 2* (1982), 103–128, 104.
70. Ernest Hemingway, *The Sun Also Rises* (Simon and Schuster, 2002), 9. On anti-Semitism in Hemingway see Gay Wilentz, '(Re)Teaching Hemingway: Anti-Semitism as Thematic Device in *The Sun Also Rises*,' *College English* 52.2 (February 1990), 186–193.
71. See Dan Grossman, 'Hemingway's Schlemiel,' *The Tablet*, June 20, 2018.
72. Harold Loeb, 'The Mysticism of Money,' *Broom* 3 (September 1922): 115–130, 117.
73. Harold Loeb, *Life in a Technocracy: What It Might Be Like* (Syracuse UP 1996, orig. 1933), 195.
74. Cit. Dan Grossman, 'Hemingway's Schlemiel,' *The Tablet*, June 20, 2018.
75. See Alan Brown and Nicholas Joost, 'T.S. Eliot and Ernest Hemingway: A Literary Relationship,' *Papers on Language & Literature* 14.4 (Fall 1978); Joseph Flora, 'Ernest Hemingway and T.S. Eliot: A Tangled Relationship,' *The Hemingway Review* 32.1 (January 2012), 72–87; Nancy Duvall Hargrove, *T. S. Eliot's Parisian Year* (U of Florida P, 2009).
76. Ernest Hemingway to Harvey Breit, July 9, 1950, *Selected Letters 1917–61*, ed. Carlos Baker (Scribner, 1981), 701.

77. H. R. Stoneback, *Reading Hemingway's The Sun Also Rises* (Kent State UP, 2007).
78. Wendolyn Tetlow, *Hemingway's In Our Time: Lyrical Dimensions* (Bucknell UP, 1998), 16.
79. Joseph Flora, *Reading Hemingway's Men Without Women: Glossary and Commentary* (Kent State UP, 2008), 42–53.
80. Cit. Michael Reynolds, *Hemingway: The Paris Years* (W. W. Norton, 1989), 273.
81. Robert Manning, 'Hemingway in Cuba,' *The Atlantic*, August 1965, retrieved September 25, 2018: https://www.theatlantic.com/magazine/archive/1965/08/hemingway-in-cuba/399059/.
82. Ernest Hemingway, *A Moveable Feast* (Scribner, 1992), 106.
83. Ezra Pound, 'Murder by Capital,' *The Criterion*, July 1933.
84. Cit. Kenneth Lynn, *Hemingway* (Harvard UP, 1987), 117.
85. Jacqueline Vaught Brogan, 'Questionable Values/Valuable Questions,' in Teaching Hemingway's *The Sun Also Rises* (2003, ed. Peter L. Hays), 29. See Scott Donaldson, 'Hemingway's Morality of Compensation,' *American Literature* 43.3 (November 1971), 399–420, 401.
86. Ernest Hemingway, 'German Inflation,' in *The Toronto Daily Star*, September 9, 1922, in *By-Line: Ernest Hemingway*, ed. William White (Bantam Books, 1967), 40–43, 41–42.

CHAPTER 8

Against Financial Derivatives: Toward an Ethics of Representation

8.1   What's the Problem?

Over the last 30 or so years, the economy has greatly expanded its influence over the rest of society, while the financial sector has attained a corresponding prominence within the economy. At the same time, speculative derivatives have become the most prominent and influential sector of finance, which means that they are now the driving and steering force behind the global economy and thus arguably the single biggest influence on human life in the twenty-first century. They are immensely powerful. But the remarkable and recent rise to power of financial derivatives has yet to be evaluated in ethical terms. Their influence has certainly been criticized on pragmatic and political grounds: the reign of speculative derivatives appears to make the economy vulnerable to sudden crashes, for example, and the constant process of re-evaluation they demand has deleterious effects on the quality of our individual working lives. More generally, financial derivatives tether production to the dictates of exchange, further demoting labor within the hierarchy of economic interests. However, little attention has been paid to the moral implications of attributing such a degree of autonomous power to financial symbols.

At this stage, we must distinguish between traditional derivatives, which are ancient and speculative, and financial derivatives, which originate in the 1970s and have attained their current degree of dominion

© The Author(s) 2020
D. Hawkes, *The Reign of Anti-logos*, Palgrave
Insights into Apocalypse Economics,
https://doi.org/10.1007/978-3-030-55940-3_8

only in the twenty-first century. Traditional derivatives refer to substantial commodities: to use-values, generally in agriculture. They are typically used for hedging. In a traditional derivative, for example, a farmer might contract to sell his wheat for a certain price if the dollar fell below a particular rate against the rouble at a particular date. In a financial or speculative derivative, however, the commodity from which the derivative is derived is itself a financial symbol. Financial derivatives thus refer not to use-value but to exchange-value. For example, a trader might contract to trade his euros for shekels once they were worth a certain amount of yen.

Financial derivatives can be conceived as hyper-money, as meta-money or as money squared, but the best way to understand them is as *the money of money*. They provide a medium in which different species of money can be compared, including money's value in the future and across the world. Financial derivatives impose equivalence on different kinds of money, just as money imposes equivalence upon different things. Economic historians often neglect the significance of this distinction. Thus Peter Bernstein claims that the seventeenth-century Dutch tulip bubble 'burst as a result of the issuing of options whose essential features were identical to the sophisticated financial instruments in use today.'[1] But the options issued in seventeenth-century Amsterdam were referential, they represented tulips. Today's financial derivatives represent only money, and this is their salient characteristic. The financial derivative embodies the performative power of representation making it, in the words of Fredric Jameson, the 'paradigmatic structure' of postmodernity.[2]

In recent years, the proportion of speculative or financial derivatives to traditional or hedging derivatives has rapidly increased. As Thomas Lagoarde-Segot noted in 2016: 'Over the past three decades, speculative transactions have skyrocketed across a wide spectrum of financial products … the notional value of annual over the counter (OTC) derivative transactions has increased tenfold between 1998 and 2014.'[3] Financial derivatives impose equivalence on different kinds of money, just as money itself imposes equivalence upon different things. They therefore constitute a self-referential turn in financial representation that has often been seen as analogous to the linguistic turn taken by postmodern philosophy. This chapter argues that financial value as expressed in speculative derivatives, and linguistic representation in its postmodern form, are both examples of performativity, as that term has been understood by philosophers like J. L. Austin, Judith Butler and Jean Baudrillard. It draws an analogy with early modern culture's response to the first stages of capitalist finance which, as we saw in previous chapters, elaborated an ethical critique of performative representation through moralistic attacks on magic, idolatry and usury as projections of human labor-power onto efficacious symbols.

The economist Christopher Schinckus follows Baudrillard by defining speculation in derivatives as the manipulation of autonomous exchange-value: 'an exaggeration of the conception of an exchange-value without link with the productive sphere.'[4] He describes the emergence of a 'financial reality where quotations become symbols with less and less connections with the productive sphere,' which both facilitates and is made possible by 'an increase in the speculative activities compared to hedging activities.' The original purpose of derivatives was to hedge against material losses; now, it is to speculate for financial profits, while the emergence of ever-more complicated derivative instruments means that 'finance tends to be more and more dedicated to speculative activities.' This gives a self-referential character to the financial market, as profits are generated from relations among various kinds of financial sign, rather than by reference to the real world of production and consumption:

> The 'financial hypermarket' appears to be what Baudrillard calls a simu-lacrum, i.e., exchange field which does not propose a real exchange but rather a self-referent exchange (without any link with the economic reality) in a continuous logic where there is no more referent. (1080)

Perhaps paradoxically, this process of abstraction has been accompanied by a rise in finance's practical, political power.[5] In recent years, for example, financial experts have told us that should Greece fail to pay its debts on time, this will trigger derivatives known as 'credit default options.' These resemble insurance policies that creditors have taken out against such defaults; triggering them would diminish capital's confidence in Greece's national credit-worthiness, force Greece to supply massive collateral to its creditors and thus lead to rapid national impoverishment. This is the destructive effect of speculative derivatives in action. But nobody has criticized such financial instruments on specifically moral grounds, and without such a critique it will be impossible correctly to understand their nature or accurately to observe their effects.

The world of finance is inherently symbolic, like a language. The Greek word for symbol—*sema*—also means both 'word' and 'coin.' The cognate indicates that both language and money are forms of *nomos*, of custom, as opposed to *phusis* or nature. As David Graeber reminds us: 'When

Aristotle argued that coins are merely social conventions, the term he used was *symbolon*—from which our term "symbol" is derived.'[6] The world of finance constitutes an intricate network of valuable symbols (exchange values), which originally represent substantial commodities (use-values). The world of derivatives forms an extra layer of symbols, which represent or are 'derived' from the symbols of traditional finance. In 2003, Norman McIntosh suggested that, as a result of these developments, 'it is high time that finance and accounting researchers, at least some of us, take the *linguistic turn* adopted in many of the social sciences and humanities in recent decades.'[7]

The objective reality to which economists are supposed to respond has changed with great rapidity in recent years. Over the last three decades, the market in derivatives has grown exponentially, to the point where it is far more valuable than the traditional financial market. The market in 'real' financial commodities such as stocks and bonds (which are themselves only symbols of useful commodities) is over-shadowed by a market in their representations. This development is part of the general shift, throughout the social totality, toward what postmodernist philosophers call 'hyper-reality.' Although it originates in philosophy, this term has been used in economic discussions for at least 20 years. McIntosh lists 'the sundry Black and Scholes-type models used for pricing options, swaps, and derivatives' among the definitive characteristics of a postmodern condition in which '*[h]omo semioticus* has replaced *homo economicus*' (454). As early as 1997, Elton McGoun asked: 'what if "real" finance (finance which refers to the real economy), is in fact "hyper-real" finance (finance which refers to nothing but itself)?'[8] More recently, Randy Martin has observed that:

> More so than the commodity of the nineteenth century, the derivative appears as a magical or fictitious object, an ephemeral, chimerical specter that references a world that has become unmoored from underlying value, that cannot orient itself to what is real, that is obsessed with all that is spectacular and speculative.[9]

Philosophers like Martin, along with economists like Schinckus, have undertaken linguistically based analyses of the economic market. Since, however, these studies usually admit to having been influenced by linguistic determinism—'inspired by post-structuralism' (Schinckus, 2010) in Schinckus's case and by J. L. Austin in Martin's—they tend to take an ethically neutral view of representation's performative power. McIntosh seems correct to note that traditional economic theory has yet to come to grips with the self-referentiality of financial derivative instruments:

> In this hyperreal capital market, there are no underlyings from which the market price of financial instruments, such as derivatives, are derived. What is required to make sense of this strange situation, then, is a paradigm shift of some sort, such as adopting a linguistic perspective. Economic theories and scientific positivism, valuable for making sense of the production order, seem to be out of touch with the changing nature of today's financial world. (455)

McIntosh's call for a 'linguistic turn' in financial theory has been taken up by several subsequent commentators. The impulse behind it can be traced back as far as Deirdre McCloskey's *The Rhetoric of Economics* (1985), which called for economists to pay attention to the semiotic mediation inherent in their own discourse. In French philosophical circles the connection is older still. Early works of postmodernist philosophy such as Jean Baudrillard's *For a Critique of the Political Economy of the Sign* (1972) and Jean-Francois Lyotard's *Libidinal Economies* (1974) explored the nexus between semiotics and economics from the perspective of the former, and recent decades have witnessed the emergence of an entire school of literary theory known as the New Economic Criticism. But perhaps the most extensive recent attempt to interpret derivatives in linguistic terms is Arjun Appadurai's *Banking on Words* (2016). Appadurai points out that:

> ... the derivative is above all a linguistic phenomenon, since it is primarily a referent to something more tangible than itself: it is a proposition or a belief about another object that might itself be similarly derived from yet another similar object. Since the references and associations that compose a derivative chain have no status other than the credibility of their reference to something more tangible than themselves, the derivatives' claim to value is essentially linguistic. Furthermore, its force is primarily performative.... Thus, when an entire market driven by derivatives comes to the edge of collapse, there must be a deep underlying flaw in the linguistic world that derivatives presuppose.[10]

It seems to me however that rather than 'a referent to something more tangible than itself,' a derivative is actually another sign, and that its performative power derives precisely from its semiotic nature. The development of financial derivatives is the economic equivalent of the linguistic process described by Derrida, whereby Saussure's 'signifier' ceases to designate any 'signified' and generates meaning (or value) out of its relations to other signifiers, not by reference to any extralinguistic reality. By treating them as referents rather than signs, moreover, Appadurai neglects the potent ethical objections that performative signs have always attracted. Financial derivatives are the postmodern versions of magical icons or idols: alienated representations of 'the works of men's hands.' Exciting and innovative as his book certainly is, Appadurai finally fails to raise his criticism of derivatives from the pragmatic to the ethical level.

When it has been evaluated in ethical terms by philosophers, postmodern hyper-reality has usually been hailed as liberating humanity from the tedious constrictions of essentialism. But if we understand the emergence of financial derivatives as part of this more general movement, the ethical status of postmodernity in general may be brought into question. An ethical critique of derivatives would logically extend to the postmodern condition as a whole. Such a critique is thus different from either a solely pragmatic or an entirely political critique. Derivatives have often been denounced for their destructive practical effects. In 2002 Warren Buffett described them as 'time bombs,' warning that:

> The derivatives genie is now well out of the bottle, and these instruments will almost certainly multiply in variety and number until some event makes their toxicity clear... In my view, derivatives are financial weapons of mass destruction, carrying dangers that, while now latent, are potentially lethal.[11]

Derivatives have also been attacked on political grounds, frequently in terms reminiscent of class war. According to Charles H. Ferguson, for example, 'over the last thirty years, the United States has been taken over by an amoral financial oligarchy,'[12] which has seized and consolidated power by the deployment of derivative financial instruments. There are undoubtedly serious political drawbacks to the economic power of derivatives. Derivatives impose a profound instability on labor, as they do on every aspect of production and exchange. The price volatility which they exploit and thereby amplify makes large-scale economic planning impossible. They are often used to evade regulation, thus further enriching speculators at the state's expense. It seems to me however that far from exacerbating any class war, the power of derivatives suggests that capitalism's essential, definitive contradiction does not involve social classes at all, but is rather the polarity between human life and the objectified representation of human life that we once called 'money.' In the form of derivative financial instruments, human labor-power confronts its opposite and adversary in an unprecedentedly direct manner. This chapter attempts to interpret derivatives in such a way as to make possible an 'ethics of representation.' Before we can attempt such a critique, however, we must understand the nature of financial derivation, and in order to do that we must study its history.

8.2 The Money of Money

The symbolic economy of the twenty-first century is an intensification of trends discernible in the most germinal form of exchange. In the opening pages of *Capital*, Marx traces the roots of financial value to the simple exchange of one object for another. In such an exchange, one object must be conceived as the other's value, its significance—we might say its *meaning*. In order to swap a pig for a cow, human beings must learn to see the value, the meaning, of the cow in the physical body of the pig. The pig must be conceived as representing the cow. All exchange is thus predicated on representation. For large-scale exchange to be possible, argues Marx, representation must become autonomous. It must be extracted from the physical body of the object and embodied in the form of a common denominator, in which the value—the significance—of anything can be expressed. This common denominator is what we call 'money.' Money is commensuration incarnate; it imposes an artificial equivalence on things that are essentially different. The epochal, quantum leap taken by financial derivatives consists in the fact that they fulfil this commensurative role with regard to money itself.

For two millennia, financial value, the image that we impose on nature through exchange, was conceived as a kind of spirit which inhabited the physical body of precious metal. The 'bullionist' thinkers of early modern Europe simply equated value with gold. But the genie of value was liberated from matter by the influx of American (and African) gold to Europe, followed by the inflations and debasements of the sixteenth century, which conclusively established that value and gold were separable and thus different things. By the seventeenth century, London's goldsmiths were issuing bank-notes that were obviously worthless in themselves and thus could only be valuable in a symbolic sense. At first, paper money was conceived as a referential symbol. Each note supposedly referred to a specific quantity of specie. And until President Nixon abandoned the gold standard in 1971, the idea that all the money in the world was theoretically redeemable by material gold remained officially intact. Nixon's decision has led commentators like Joel Kurtzman to claim that money has 'died,'[13] and value has certainly departed from its physical incarnation. Yet financial value did not achieve total discorporation until the later twentieth century, when credit cards and electronic banking finally and irrefutably confirmed that value exists only in the human mind and that the money that represents value is a sign.[14]

At this stage, value finally floated free of its physical incarnation, as massive price volatility in exchange and interest rates ensued. This volatility made speculation in financial instruments immensely profitable, thus impelling traders to develop ever-more elaborate forms of transaction. Whereas the traditional market in derivatives had been based around tangible, usually agricultural goods, the derivatives market of the late-twentieth and early twenty-first-centuries spawned a brood of purely financial, symbolic commodities. Meanwhile, the rapid growth of computing capacity made it possible to design, price and market multifarious, complicated packages of swaps and options in order to hedge and speculate with super-human speed and efficiency. Deregulation's dramatic relaxation of government oversight removed most actual and potential obstacles to derivatives' domination of the financial sector.[15] They provided an extra gear, an additional source of symbolic exchange-value, through which the financial sector consolidated its pre-eminence within the 'economy.' This process also coincides, historically and conceptually, with the rise of the 'economy' to cultural and political hegemony over society as a whole. The use of taxpayer money to bail out the banks in 2008 was only the most blatant confirmation that the interests of finance are paramount in government policy, to the extent that finance has effectively become a part of government—and far from the least important part.

Several recent commentators have argued that this 'economic imperialism,' through which the 'economy' imposes its influence on what were previously conceived as discrete sectors of society, means that financial derivatives are the most important and influential phenomenon of our time. Matt Davies argues that '[f]inancialization could be said to be the effect of finance on social relations.'[16] Randy Martin suggests that derivatives express a general logic running through twenty-first-century culture:

> ... daily life seems to have undergone a process of financialization, where what once belonged to bankers' boardrooms now seems to have escaped and colonized the rest of the world.... If derivatives at their root have to do with some kind of overflow, with the disassembly of some whole into parts and the bundling together of those attributes into something that moves away from or independently of its source, then finance may turn out to be less the originator of this social logic than a particularly prominent expression of derivative principles at work.[17]

The history of money is a process of abstraction, and the rise of financial derivatives is the latest stage in that process. In financial terminology, 'derivative instruments' are distinguished from the more traditional 'cash instruments,' such as securities, loans, and deposits. Whereas the value of cash instruments is based directly on the exchange of useful commodities, the value of financial derivatives is determined by some 'underlying' factor such as interest rates or currency exchanges. Imagine a casino in which the main floor is overlooked by a row of corporate boxes, as in a sports stadium. In these boxes, high rollers lay bets on the bets laid by the gamblers below them on the main floor. There is literally no limit, either to the sums that may be wagered or to the Byzantine complexity of the bets themselves. One might wager, for example, that the rate of loss incurred by red-headed women aged under 50 on the roulette table will be under 5% more than the rate of winnings enjoyed by bisexual men on the 2-dollar fruit machines every other Thursday, between yesterday and Easter 2025. Such a bet would be equivalent of a speculative derivative.

The postmodern era in economics is heralded by our knowledge that, as McGoun puts it: 'money acquires its exchange-value because it is a symbol for the use-value of the things it can buy and not because it is a symbol for the use-value of some reserve commodity underlying it' (99). The salient characteristic of today's speculative derivatives is that they represent only different forms of money. The deregulation that inaugurated the reign of financial derivatives was a revolution comparable in scope and effect to the invention of paper money. In the words of McIntosh:

> ... financial capital markets are ungrounded. That is to say, they are free-floating and unconnected to the real economy of production and consumption of goods and services ... the financial market is a hyperreal economy that floats almost unconnected to the real material economy....
> (456)

Derivatives fully exploit the symbolic nature of money. Language is a medium in which things and concepts are represented in symbolic form, and money plays this role with regard to commodities. As we saw in Chapter 1, Derrida describes the relation of writing to speech as 'a sign of a sign,'[18] while announcing the epistemological (and implicitly the ethical) priority of signification's secondary degree. As the money of money, as financial symbols that are derived from other financial symbols, derivatives constitute a meta-symbolic dimension appropriate to the age of hyper-reality. Derivatives can be used to manage risk (to 'hedge' bets), or to speculate for profits. In the kind of derivative known as an 'option,' for example, the buyer purchases the right to buy or sell a particular commodity from the seller for a particular price at a particular date. That option has value, and can itself be traded as a commodity. This gives financial derivatives a degree of leverage so great as to deserve its own name: it is known as 'gearing.' The effect of gearing is vastly to exaggerate changes in prices, thus increasing the profits to be made from the process of exchange. It increases the practical power of representation, by allowing investors to control vast financial resources through ownership only of a symbolic fraction.

Financial derivatives are simultaneously a medium of exchange for various forms of money and tradeable commodities in their own right. Thus they violate one of the most the ancient objections to usury: they make a medium of exchange into an object of exchange. In the English Renaissance, usury was frequently criticized on those grounds, because it commodified money. In 1580 for example, the anonymous *The Ruinate Fall of Pope Usurie* condemns as a usurer anyone who:

> Useth the gain of his stock, turned from wares into money, supposing suche dealing to be as lawful to haue the increase of his money as of wares, considering not the difference that is between wares and money.
> (3)

The 'difference... between wares and money' is that money is a symbolic medium for the exchange of wares, and for centuries it was considered morally imperative to remain conscious of this distinction. Today, in insouciant violation of that principle, financial derivatives turn the convoluted instruments of usury itself into commodities. The type of derivative known as a 'swap' offers an instance of general principle of financial derivation. The first swap took place between the World Bank and IBM in 1981. By 2011, swaps were the most common financial instrument in the world, with a combined value of $350 trillion. A swap is an agreement to exchange different forms of cash flow—interest rates or currencies—over a certain period of time. The value of a swap is based on the exchange of different forms of exchange-value, in the same way that financial value itself is based on the exchange of different use-values. For example, the counterparties might contract to exchange the cash flow from tobacco stocks for the cash flow from government bonds if the dollar falls below €3, or to exchange the revenue derived from sub-prime mortgages in Alabama for the income produced by certificates of deposit issued in Iceland as soon as the British government cuts interest rates by more than 1%.

Such examples present derivatives in their most basic and simple form. In practice, the packaging and marketing of derivatives involve a baroque complexity, as combinations of bets and hedges are tailored to fit the rapidly, constantly changing requirements of investors. Those who construct these edifices are known as 'financial engineers,' but 'designers' or even 'artists' would seem more appropriate terms, were it not for their inappropriately creative connotations. For the shapes taken by derivatives are not formed by any human being, although human minds are used to mold them, nor do their gyrations follow any human logic. They are designed by computers, and their behavior is determined solely by the demands of money. The market in derivatives lies beyond human capacities.

In fact, the speculative derivative market only became conceivable with the advent of the computer. Quite suddenly, financiers were able to run logarithms, conduct analyses, make predictions and invent financial instruments of far greater complexity, and with incomparably greater speed, than had been possible using the human mind alone. Market analysis became literally superhuman, and the effect was vastly to increase volatility, with all the attendant practical dangers for the real world.

The public was thus confirmed in its impression that financial instruments are developing independently of any human will, that money is following its own, internal, unknowable logic and pursuing interests that diverge more and more sharply from those of human beings whose alienated labor-power it originally represents. It was the reckless marketing of derivatives—securities ultimately derived from sub-prime American mortgages—that drove the world to the brink of financial collapse in 2008. The geographical, temporal and conceptual distance of such metaphysical financial instruments from the insecure home mortgages which they ultimately represented was the main cause of the disaster.

Fernand Braudel famously argued that financialization is a necessary stage in the evolution of capital. Once a polity has accumulated a sufficient store of capital by trade in substantial commodities, the economy turns in upon itself, and people begin trading in money. As competition intensifies and investment in commodities becomes risky, accumulators naturally develop a taste for liquidity. The consequent financialization gives capital a new flexibility and also a new kind of power. Physical productive capacity and trade in physical commodities are subject to natural limitations: there are only so many things in the world. But this is not true of finance which, being entirely symbolic (a critic might say 'imaginary'), can theoretically continue to reproduce indefinitely. Building on Braudel's research, Giovanni Arrighi describes financial capital as a mobile power, shifting among states from Genoa to Holland, then to England and the USA. As he recalled in 2009:

> ...I called the onset of financialization the signal crisis of a regime of accumulation, and pointed out that over time—usually it was around half a century—the terminal crisis would follow. For previous hegemons, it was possible to identify both the signal crisis and then the terminal crisis. For the United States, I ventured the hypothesis that the 1970s was the signal crisis; the terminal crisis had not yet come—but it would.[19]

Departing from Braudel, Arrighi saw financialization as a cyclical process with a built-in limit. When that limit was reached, a 'terminal crisis' ensued, and it seemed to Arrighi, like many others, that such a crisis must be imminent for the USA. However, Arrighi (who died in 2009) did not specifically address the phenomenon of speculative derivatives. The recent, exponential expansion of financial derivatives means that the kind of physical relocation of capital he describes is no longer necessary. Instead of a terminal crisis followed by a new start somewhere else, twenty-first-century finance capital becomes self-referential. It can thus generate apparently new value out of itself, free from the constraint of reference to physical commodities, and thus also unconstrained by location in any particular polity. In the words of Matt Davies:

> ... as values and their exchange are increasingly reduced to or mediated through financial instruments or derivatives of financial instruments, finance itself is financialized and financial motives, financial markets, financial actors, and financial institutions come to refer increasing to themselves.[20]

The self-referential nature of the derivatives market has thus far enabled the financial system to avoid a terminal crisis, since there is no longer any need for the physical relocation of capital described by Arrighi and Braudel. It seems that financialization is not an end but a beginning. In the words of Edward LiPuma and Benjamin Lee:

> Present-day financial derivatives might better be conceptualized as a primary stage in a new economic trajectory whose ultimate direction and implications will depend on how the global community, particularly the metropolitan nation-states, responds to their effects.[21]

To the extent that the economy becomes financial, it also becomes psychological. The futures, options and swaps of twenty-first-century capitalism have no material existence: they exist only in the mind. This means that they can be studied through their effects on the mind—in fact, that is arguably how they should be studied. The approach currently taken by professional economists assumes that the arcane symbols of high finance enjoy an objective, independent existence. But that is not true. Like any other kind of symbolic figuration, they have no force or meaning outside the *psyche*. Economic debates are finally about how we think.

When a subjective experience such as 'credit' or 'confidence' is translated into a financial instrument, it is reified: transformed into a thing. In similar fashion, any wage laborer must learn to conceive of his time, which is his life, as a thing that he owns and can exchange for money. The advent of derivatives projects this process of reification deep within the mind, where it breeds monsters which re-emerge, projected into the world as objective, external powers expressed in figurative terms. When they are financialized, turned into currency, originally subjective experiences such as hope, fear, love and hate are alienated, projected externally, and represented in symbolic form. Their value can then be subjected to an objective rather than a subjective means of assessment; it can be expressed in quantitative, numerical terms. Through the commodification of risk, the postmodern market-place (which is not a place or even a concept but rather a language) subjects even Fortuna to financialization. Having reviewed something of the history and nature of financial derivatives, we are now in a position to consider their ethical status.

8.3   MONEY AS REPRESENTATION

An ethical critique of derivatives must start from the recognition that the function of money is symbolic. Its primal purpose is to represent things that are not physically present. Financial value, like linguistic meaning, is mediated through a system of symbols. In such systems, money and words attain analogous signifying properties, forming what Jean-Joseph Goux calls 'the structural homology between money and language.'[22] This means that finance can be subjected to the same kinds of analysis, and judged by the same ethical criteria, as other semiotic systems. The history of representation develops as a totality, so that our conception of language changes along with our use of money. In the early twentieth century, Ferdinand de Saussure, the founder of linguistic structuralism, drew attention to the analogy between finance and language in a chapter entitled 'Linguistic Value':

> These two features are necessary for the existence of any value. To determine the value of a five-franc coin, for instance, what must be known is: (1) that the coin can be exchanged for a certain quantity of something different, e.g., bread, and (2) that its value can be compared with another value in the same system, e.g., that of a one franc coin, or of a coin belonging to another system (e.g., a dollar). Similarly, a word can be substituted for something dissimilar: an idea. At the same time it can be compared to something of like nature: another word. Its value is therefore not determined merely by that concept or meaning for which it is a token. It must also be assessed against comparable values, by contrast with other works.[23]

Saussure distinguishes here between referential and relational significance, and he claims that this distinction applies in both linguistics and economics. Both spheres contain two kinds of value. In language, the meaning of words can be produced either by their reference to concepts or by their position within the linguistic structure. In finance, the value of money can be produced either by its reference to a substantial use-value or by its position within the monetary system. Financial signs refer to use-values in the same way that verbal signs refer to concepts. This is a referential significance, for things and concepts are referents outside the system of signs. In addition to this referential significance, however, both verbal and financial signs attain a relational meaning, which is derived from their relation to other signs within the wider semiotic structure. This self-referential significance is formally analogous to the financial value of derivatives. Such parallels between economic and linguistic representation were observed by Talcott Parsons:

> Just as the word 'dog' can neither bark nor bite, yet 'signifies' the animal that can, so a dollar has no intrinsic utility, yet signifies commodities that do, in the special sense that it can in certain circumstances be substituted for them, and can evoke control of relations with them in the special kind of process of social interaction we call economic exchange.[24]

The relation between the word 'dog' and either the concept of 'dog' or the furry barking animal is a referential significance, for things and concepts are referents outside the system of signs. In contrast, the word's relational meaning is derived from its relation to other signs within the wider semiotic structure—the word 'dog' attains its meaning by virtue of its formal difference from 'doc' or 'dag.' This mode of meaning is self-referential, because it is produced from the structure of language itself. This self-referential significance is formally analogous to the financial value of derivatives. In formal as in chronological terms, then, derivatives are the postmodern form of finance. Their semiotic effect relates to traditional stocks and bonds in the same way as postmodernism relates to modernism, as post-structuralism relates to structuralism, or indeed as hyper-reality relates to reality.

The analogy is clearly visible in the relation of post-structuralist linguistics to structuralism. The structuralist Saussure divided the linguistic sign into two parts: the signifier (e.g., the word 'cow') and the signified (e.g., the concept of a cow). Although meaning is generated out of language in this model, it remains referential in the sense that the signifier refers to the signified. By the 1960s, however, post-structuralists like Derrida were denying the distinction between word and concept, claiming that concepts were themselves linguistic constructs. Instead of the signifier referring to a signified, Derrida viewed language as an endless chain of signifiers, each one pointing to the next, but none of them referring to any extralinguistic sphere of ideas. This was the death of ancient distinctions between appearance and essence, matter and form, and body and soul that have informed philosophy for two and a half millennia. It was also the end of 'logocentrism,' the logos being Derrida's term for the ultimate source and guarantor of referential meaning: the 'transcendental signified.' In the work of Derrida, and thus of postmodernists in general, logos is discredited and swept away by the force of semiotic différance. In analogous fashion, financial value was driven from its telos in material gold by the value-generating power of symbols. The economic manifestation of différance is the financial derivative. As McIntosh puts it:

> ...in many cases, neither accounting signs nor financial market signs appear to be grounded in any external reality. Instead, accounting signs model market signs, which in turn model accounting signs. In this hyperreal financial economy of simulation, the difference between signs and their referents implodes. (457)

In financial derivatives, as in post-structuralist linguistics, signs cease to be referential, they no longer refer to concepts or objects beyond themselves. Instead, financial signs become performative—they contain their value within themselves, and they thereby achieve a practical, effective potency. Exchange-value separates the value of an object from its body, giving this value an autonomous, performative agency. But as Dick Bryan and Michael Rafferty point out, derivatives are capable of separating and evaluating the performance of exchange-value from exchange-value itself:

> By framing an exposure to the *performance* of an underlying asset as itself tradable, things which have not hitherto been priced relative to each other are now presented in a form where critical dimensions of their relative values can be measured.[25]

Elsewhere, Bryan and Rafferty explain that derivatives give 'ownership of the "performance" of a corporation, but without any ownership of the corporation itself.'[26] The term 'performative' is sometimes used by financial theorists in a different sense from my own. For instance, Thomas

Lagoarde-Segot uses 'performative' to mean the effect that academic finance has on financial markets: 'academic finance... bears several similarities with the performative idiom: knowledge in finance is not purely representative, but also has the ability of bringing into existence or modifying various types of realities.' This is not what I mean by the term 'performative' here; my reference is to the sense of the term used by Austin and, later, by theorists like Judith Butler. In their work 'performative' refers to signs that achieve an objective effect in the real world. In *How to Do Things with Words* (1962), Austin distinguished between 'constantive' statements (like 'the fox is brown'), which refer to an extralinguistic referent, and 'performative' statements (like 'open sesame') that refer to nothing beyond themselves, but rather perform the action they describe. Performative 'speech-acts,' as Austin called them, are powerful. They can bring about a marriage, impose a curse, or name a ship.

The financialization of capitalism involves the acquisition of this kind of performative power by financial signs. With the stuttering yet inexorable legitimization of usury, money attained the power to reproduce. That is the definitive characteristic of life, and with it money took on the action and volition of a living creature. The ability to reproduce gave money a superhuman, unnatural mobility and efficacy. In the late twentieth and early twenty-first centuries, the power of money grew exponentially, to entirely unprecedented levels that were made possible by its self-referential independence of any material basis.[27] Thus we arrive at the condition described by McGoun, following Baudrillard, as hyper-reality:

> Decisions affecting production and employment are made on the basis of stock price, and not on the basis of production and employment. It is not the 'real' economy that shapes 'reality', but activity in the financial economy. The financial economy is thereby more 'real' than the real economy itself; it is a hyperreal economy. (108)

The emergence of speculative derivatives was the ultimate logical consequence of financial representation's autonomous reproduction. The system of options, futures and swaps now forms a mechanism through which each individual stage of production, exchange and consumption can be evaluated without the constraints of space or time. Converted into the form of derivatives, any stage or part of capital can be measured against any other. Financial derivatives thus constitute the autonomy of representation in its financial form. In the words of Bryan and Rafferty: 'Derivatives permit a separation of the asset itself from volatility in that asset's price.'[28] They can be conceived as performative representation in the economic sphere. As Bryan and Rafferty put it, financial derivatives 'involve a form of capital with ownership of the "performance" of a corporation, but without any ownership of the corporation itself.' The market in derivatives thus makes a commodity of value, creating value out of value, just as post-structuralist semiotic meaning is generated from the system of signification.

The self-referential nature of speculative evaluation was clearly stated by J. M. Keynes in *The General Theory of Employment, Interest and Money* (1936). In his speech accepting the 2013 Nobel Prize, Robert Shiller summarized Keynes' famous 'beauty contest theory':

> Each reader was invited to submit from a page with one hundred photos of pretty faces a list of the six that he or she thought prettiest. The winner would be the one whose list most closely corresponded to the most popular faces among all the lists of six that readers sent in. Of course, to win this contest a rational person would not pick the faces that personally seem prettiest. Instead one should pick the six faces that one thinks others will think prettiest. Even better, one should pick the faces one thinks that others think that others think prettiest, or one should pick the faces one thinks that others think that others think that others think prettiest.... That is how speculative markets function, Keynes said.[29]

Financial derivatives are the logical culmination of the tendency described by Keynes. They are signs representing other signs, whose significance (or value) therefore emerges out of the system of representation, rather than by reference to any external or 'real' world. The system of derivative pricing is known as 'mark-to-market.' McIntosh describes its inherent tendency to self-referentiality:

> Players in the market...use reported earnings signs to judge if the company's current stock price differs from its fundamental or intrinsic value, that is to say, from the market value of its 'underlyings'. So, the accounting sign of the financial instrument is based on the market price of the instrument, while simultaneously that market price is based on the accounting signs. The stock market prices then become the underlyings supporting the derivative prices, which become part of the company's reported earnings. Accounting for financial instruments is a paradox of self-reference. (456)

Because the value of a derivatives contract is to be paid in the future, the counterparties often fantasize about what might happen in the intervening period, a tendency known as 'mark-to-myth.' This enables both counterparties to report impressive but clearly fictional profits. By this stage though, the fictional has effectively become indistinguishable from the real. Once again, speculative derivatives are symptomatic of postmodern capital in general. David Harvey describes the emergence of 'fictitious' capital: 'When banks lend to other banks or when the Central Bank lends to the commercial banks who lend to land speculators looking to appropriate rents, then fictitious capital looks more and more like an infinite regression of fictions built upon fictions.'[30] This does not mean that 'fictitious' capital does not exist, or that it refers to nothing at all. This kind of capital is 'fictional' in the sense that its value derives from reference to other forms of capital.

This develops into a serious practical problem in the case of derivatives. By packaging a debt attractively, marketing it skillfully, and dividing it into pieces, banks are able to disguise the fact of the debt's referentiality, and thus to underplay the amount of risk it carries. It appeared to those who bought Collaterized Debt Obligations, the ostensibly autonomous financial instruments under the guise of which sub-prime mortgages were often traded, that their value was independent of any referent in the real world. The purchasers were rapidly disabused of this illusion when real people defaulted on their payments, thus emptying these symbolic financial instruments of value. By means of a post-structuralist chain of representation without final reference known as a 'securitization food chain,'[31] predatory mortgage loans can be sold on to investment banks, which repackage them into structured investments in finance, which are purchased by hedge funds, pension funds and other big investors. The conceptual distance between the financial signs and the 'real' estate they originally represent is so great as to be unfeasible, and arguably unethical—and both qualities arise out of their departure from referentiality.

By applying money's commensurative effects to the medium of commensuration, derivatives logically raise the question of referentiality. Is it even logically possible for a sign to become efficacious, or for a financial instrument to derive its value from its relation to other such instruments? There is perhaps a logical case against financial derivatives to add to the pragmatic and political objections noted above. As yet, however, none of these criticisms has been addressed to the ethical nature of financial derivatives. An ethical criticism would have to move beyond their effects to attack their essence. The postmodern mind seems almost inadequate to the task, and postmodern thinkers have generally been content to hail hyper-reality for the ludic pleasures it allegedly entails. To attain a proper perspective on derivatives, to discern what they actually are, we must therefore adopt a strategy that is anathema to today's professional economists. We must look to history; we must have recourse to the wisdom of the past.

In cultures that encounter performative financial signs for the first time, we will find stern and rational warnings against usury, magic and idolatry, many of which seem applicable to our own predicament. Anthropologists tell us that African and South American cultures often react to the monetization of local economies with witch hunts and campaigns against sorcery.[32] People responded similarly to the dawn of capitalism in the early modern Europe, where it was frequently remarked that usury, magic, and idolatry were all forms of a single ethical transgression: the fetishization of representation as performative. Furthermore, this attribution of subjective power to signs was understood to flow from a single, underlying error: the confusion between subject and object. Human beings must not, according to all traditional ethics, treat people as if they were things, or treat things as if they were people. Magic, idolatry, and usury all do both. An economy based on financial derivatives *demonstrably* does both. That is of course the source of its power. Might it also be its fatal flaw?

8.4   DON QUIXOTE AND DERIVATIVES

J. L. Austin coyly confessed his desire to 'play old Harry' with the metaphysical pieties of the Western tradition, and certainly the exploitation of performative signs has been variously anathematized as idolatry, sophistry, magic, usury, and as licensing all kinds of psychological fetishism. Austin chose not to explore the wider implications of the priority he afforded the performative, but subsequent theorists have made up for his reticence. In Derrida's famous deconstruction of Austin in 'Signature Event Context,' and in his subsequent dispute with J. R. Searle published as *Glyph* and *Limited, Inc.*, Derrida portrayed constative utterances as parasitic on performatives. All statements, he claimed, are performative, though only some are constative. Austin himself had glimpsed the possibility of this interpretation of his work: 'When we issue any utterance whatsoever, are we not "doing something?"' For Derrida, language was fundamentally performative rather than referential in nature. In fact, all human experience was 'constructed' out of systems of representation. Even subjectivity itself was inescapably mediated through various representational discourses, of which the financial and the linguistic were homologous examples, and on which Derrida bestowed the general term 'writing.'

Derrida thus built on Austin to construct an ethics of performativity, broadly adapted from Nietzsche's provocative aphorisms of a century before. As we saw earlier, Nietzsche claimed that is 'no doer behind the deed—the deed is everything.' The human self, in this view, could not be separated from its manifestations. Identity was a function of performance, and Nietzsche extended this anti-essentialism to every field he surveyed. In fact, Nietzsche viewed truth itself as a purely linguistic construct: 'a mobile army of metaphors.' Derrida's deconstructions of Austin and Saussure seemed to provide Nietzsche's polemical intuitions with a solid basis in the philosophy of language. For Derrida, significance was produced by the autonomous force of 'writing,' whose central characteristic was 'iterability,' the capacity to retain its meaning when repeated in the author's absence. As Judith Butler observes, this is also a definitive characteristic of performative speech-acts: 'As utterances, they work to the extent that they are given in the form of a ritual, that is, repeated in time, and, hence, maintain a sphere of operation that is not restricted to the moment of the utterance itself.'[33] The financial theorist Elie Ayache stresses that this quality of 'iterability' is shared by the financial signs of the derivatives market, which he therefore classifies as a type of 'writing.' Ayache bases his theory of value on Derrida's concept, arguing that the value of derivatives is produced by their 'writing' alone: 'It is the pure, material writing of contingency. It is pure difference. Writing is difference, as Derrida would say.'[34]

A futures contract, forward, option or swap relies on the same instrument having a different value in an altered context. In other words it depends on 'iterability,' and for this reason Ayache takes Jorge-Luis Borges' story 'Pierre Menard, Author of the *Quixote*' as his illustrative model. In Borges' fable, a twentieth-century French author reproduces sections of Cervantes' novel word-for-word, thus revealing a wholly new, and vastly richer, set of meanings within the unchanged text. Ayache argues that profit from derivatives trading emerges out of a similar elevation of value above reference. The meaning of Menard's text is imposed upon it from the outside, it is completely dependent on its context. In similar fashion, the derivatives market is dependent on techniques for measuring value—for measuring measurement itself—because value, rather than commodities, is what it trades in. Until recently, the most popular method for valuing derivatives was the Black-Scholes model. Ayache criticizes the Black-Scholes model on the grounds that it fails to consider the self-referential nature of derivatives. Black-Scholes calculates the price of derivatives on the basis of the perceived probability of various 'states of the world.' According to Ayache, however, the derivatives market operates at the level of purely internal 'contingency,' and pays no regard to any external state of affairs, such as might be measured by traditional concepts like probability.

Ayache thus departs conclusively from the conventional understanding of derivatives. In the realist or traditional view, as summarized by Appadurai:

> ... the derivative is above all a linguistic phenomenon, since it is primarily a referent to something more tangible than itself: it is a proposition or a belief about another object that might itself be similarly derived from yet another similar object. Since the references and associations that compose a derivative chain have no status other than the credibility of their reference to something more tangible than themselves, the derivatives' claim to value is essentially linguistic.[35]

Ayache certainly agrees that the value of a derivative is 'essentially linguistic,' but he disputes the referential model of value described by Appadurai. As we have seen, derivatives play the same role in Ayache's economics as that played by 'writing' in Derrida's semiotics. Derrida argues that identity and meaning emerge out of the difference between signs, so that *differance* itself becomes the fundamental, constitutive category in the construction of meaning and identity. In similar fashion, Ayache conceives of derivatives as the primary financial instrument, not as secondary or supplemental. In fact, then, *derivatives are not derivative*. Ayache declares that 'derivative' is a misnomer since, like *differance*, derivatives are a primary and not a secondary phenomenon. He denies that they derive their value from their underlying referent:

...we should no longer think of derivatives as derivatives because if you call them derivatives... we have something called the underlying upon which the derivatives are written, and the underlying according to the metaphysics of possibility and probability is going to find itself in several possible states of the world, to which we will assign several probabilities, and each of the states upon which the derivative depends is derivative from each of those states – the derivative is a function of those states, hence " deriving" from those states. However, the major driver here is the underlying itself, which we partition into states, etc. So, in the end, the derivatives are not absolute because they depend on the underlying.[36]

Ayache takes up the postmodern hostility to 'metaphors of depth': for him even financial value—the symbol to which the symbols of derivatives refer—is an essentialist fantasy. Only *price*, the surface expression of value—value's symbol—is real. The notion that the price of something might not express its true value is impossible for Ayache. Every price is the *justum pretium*. Thus does the postmodern 'logic of the supplement,' in which the 'Other' is constitutive of and prior to the 'Self,' run from linguistics and philosophy, through finance, and finally into every corner of the mind and every cranny of experience, revealing previously unsuspected homologies between various spheres of experience, and loudly demanding a revision of the morality that once resulted from their artificial separation.

In philosophy, this movement of mind is currently exemplified by Quentin Messailoux, Ray Brassier, and other 'speculative realist' thinkers. They take the position that contingency (the limitations placed on human thought by our historical and cultural location) is not an accidental, inconvenient, or undesirable barrier to true knowledge, but the ultimate ground of knowledge itself. Contingency is primary. Kant was wrong to conceive of our ignorance of *noumena* as an absence or lack; it is rather the basic ground of all experience. This new form of nihilism moves beyond Nietzsche's exultation at the death of *logos*, to arrive at a sunny, suburban relativism. Brassier describes himself as a follower of Nietzsche, but with an important caveat: 'unlike Nietzsche, I do not think nihilism culminates in the claim that there is no truth. Nietzsche conflated truth with meaning....'[37] Because he conflated truth with meaning, Nietzsche experienced the death of *logos* as a grand, tragic event. For Brassier, in contrast, meaninglessness is truth, and all that remains is to scratch our heads at the folly of previous generations who believed otherwise. A similar claim is made by Messalioux, who portrays Kant's insight that human beings can have no knowledge of the 'thing-in-itself' as establishing 'absolute contingency' as the positive basis on which all human knowledge is constructed.

In this manner, the deconstructionist claim that *differance* is prior to significance extends its influence throughout postmodern thought. We have already seen how many philosophers have hailed the rise of performative representation as politically and personally liberating. Western universities are full of ardent advocates of performativity, which is viewed as enabling a revolt against the oppressive constrictions of essentialist identity. The idea that the rise of performativity in identity politics is replicated in the rise of financial derivatives is not often expressed by the radicals of the twenty-first century. In my opinion, however, this connection is the proverbial elephant in the drawing room of contemporary political philosophy. Once we understand that performative theories of personal identity are conceptually implicated in, as well as historically simultaneous with, the logic of derivative-based finance capitalism, the entire field of identity politics, and its relations to the politics of the 'economy,' will have to be substantially re-conceived.

The growth in the autonomy of representation would appear to be exponential. Financial value has grown ever-more powerful, and ever-more independent of any external referent, with ever-increasing velocity, since it was first liberated as an efficacious force by the relaxations of the usury laws in the sixteenth century. It is only natural that our ability to criticize that power has diminished with almost equal speed. Certainly, the professional economists of our own day seem incapable of elaborating an ethical critique of derivative finance, and insofar as philosophers have taken a moralistic approach to the independence of signs from referents, they have generally applauded it as politically and personally emancipatory. That is partly because they have neglected to consider the homology between the economic and the semiotic versions of performative representation. But is also facilitated by a willful exclusion of historical perspective, and I will therefore conclude this essay with a brief and provisional attempt to locate the rise of efficacious representation in its historical context.

The independence of signs from their referents is not an ontological but an historical fact. It is salutary to remember just how egregious a violation of traditional ethics it involves. The attribution of agency to symbols has traditionally been the definition of ritual magic. The great European 'witch-craze,' which killed around one hundred thousand people over the sixteenth and seventeenth centuries, was a hysterical reaction to the unprecedented rise to power of autonomous representation. This was also the era of Reformation iconoclasm, an extended campaign against the power of liturgical idols, which involved a concerted effort to instruct the population in the dangers of idolatry: the mistaking of the sign for the referent. Radical Protestants frequently linked witchcraft with 'popery.' As John Gaule wrote in 1646: 'not only their Popes, Priests, Fryers, Nuns (many of them) have been notorious Witches: but their praestigious miracles, & superstitious rites little better then kindes of Witch-crafts.'[38] Iconoclasts and witch-hunters could cite several Biblical passages to confirm the essential unity of their aniconic campaigns. In 2 Kings 23–24 for instance, Josiah purges Jerusalem of 'workers with familiar spirits, and the wizards, and the images, and the idols.' This period also saw opponents of usury pointing out that it too involved the autonomous reproduction of financial signs, and noting the homologies between usury and other modes of fetishized representation such as magic and idolatry.

In each of the popular and intellectual campaigns against usury, magic, and idolatry, the people of early modern Europe rose up in indignation at the prospect of being ruled by signs. If we are to develop an ethical critique of derivative finance, the postmodern world needs to re-learn what the pre-modern world understood: magical totems, liturgical idols, and self-generating money are different species of performative sign. Each of them can be, and often has been, subjected to ethical criticism, on the grounds that they encourage and express the postlapsarian human tendency to fetishism. The moral problem with fetishism, or idolatry, is that it involves worshipping graven images, signs that are the products of human labor. The Psalmist prognosticates that the consequence of idolatry is psychological objectification: 'Those who make them are like unto them, so is every one that trusteth in them' (115.8, 135.18). In secularized form, this claim was repeated by philosophers from Plato to Marx. The postmodern displacement of *logos* by *eidolon* is only the latest manifestation of this recurrent self-assertion of representation.

Performative speech-acts abolish human intention as a factor in the formation of significance. The couple is objectively married once the priest declares them so, even if he subjectively intends them to remain single. The meaning of Menard's *Quixote* escapes the intention of Cervantes, as of Menard himself (and indeed, as Ayahce's reading shows, of Borges). The witch-hunters of the seventeenth century said the same about the talismans of ritual magic: they operate efficaciously apart from, and even in spite of, the intention of the magician. In the metaphysical discourse of their age, they traced the source of magical efficacy to 'Satan,' the declared enemy of the human soul. We do not need to resort to such anachronistic terminology to see that the power of financial derivatives is fundamentally antihuman. That seems clear on pragmatic grounds alone. The most interesting question, however, is whether the ethical critique of independently efficacious representation should be extended to the semiotic, cultural, and psychological spheres. Is there a logical link between the self-referential signifiers of postmodernist philosophy and the self-referential signs of twenty-first-century finance? If we find the rule of finance to be morally reprehensible, should we not extend that criticism to performative representation as a whole?

8.5   Toward an Ethics of Representation

The economization of life, the financialization of the economy, and the increasingly abstract and self-referential nature of finance itself are the most prominent means by which autonomous representation has come to rule the world. But these supposedly 'economic' developments are paralleled by homologous processes that span the totality of human experience. The newly independent power of representation is reflected in the rise of semiotics as an intellectual discipline, in the emergence of linguistic determinism and philosophies such as deconstruction and neo-pragmatism, in the proliferation of technological media, in the growth of branding as a means to profit, in the sudden appearance of an entire virtual world online, in the reduction of political debate to spin and perception, in the worship of empirical science, the spread of pornography, the consolidation of a degraded, instinctive materialism as the default popular worldview, and the widespread cultural focus on superficial appearance to the exclusion of non-apparent essence.

The independence of signs from their referents is paralleled by the rise to economic power of market exchange, and it is salutary to remember how egregious a violation of traditional ethics it involves. The bestowal of autonomous efficacy on a sign, the attribution of subjective agency to symbols, has traditionally been the definition of magic. Although Silvia Federici correctly describes the 'witch-craze' as a necessary ideological counterpart to the process of economic primitive accumulation[39]; it was also an hysterical reaction to the rise of autonomous representation in general. The Renaissance produced a glorious flowering of the arts, but it was also an age when mobs invaded churches to smash icons that they perceived as oppressive. It was also the period when the autonomy of money took a quantum leap, as theoretical and practical restrictions on usury were lifted. Having attained the power of independent reproduction, money quickly acquires its own needs and interests, to which it eagerly sacrifices the needs and interests of human beings. Magical totems, liturgical idols, and self-generating money are different species of performative signs. Thus, in *Capitalist Sorcery: Breaking the Spell*, Philippe Pignarre and Isabelle Stengers urge:

> ... we must turn towards knowledges that we have disqualified. There has, for a long time, been a name for something that manages to produce a coincidence between enslavement, the putting into service, and subjection, the production of those who do freely what they are meant to do. It is something whose frightening power and the need to cultivate appropriate means of protection against is known by the most diverse of peoples, except us moderns. Its name is sorcery.[40]

The moral problem with fetishism, or idolatry, is that it involves worshipping graven images: 'the works of men's hands.' In a sense, all images are graven, for an object becomes an image in the same way as an icon becomes an idol: by human psychological labor, within the mind. Fetishism is a subjective not an objective process. As Victorian missionaries were well aware, to recognize it is therefore to abolish it. In order to transcend it, we need to recognize our own fetishism as the projection of our own minds. Marx gave the name 'commodity fetishism' to modern idolatry, but the domination of financial derivatives has removed the need for the adjectival qualifier. Not only do financial derivatives commodify purely abstract concepts like risk (fortune), they commodify the means of commodification itself. Thus they are revealed as fetishism incarnate, or rather, disincarnate. Derivatives give symbolic form, and thus practical power, to psychological fetishism.

So one moral criticism of derivatives might focus on liturgical fetishism or idolatry. To idolize something is to impose a subjective, psychological power upon an object. This is what commodity fetishism does; it subjectifies the object. It also objectifies the subject. An economy based on wage labor commodifies human labor-power, which is co-terminus with human life considered in the abstract: it objectifies the subject. By virtue of their hyper-symbolic, meta-metaphorical nature and the exponentially increased practical power bestowed on them by their ultra-figurative status, financial derivatives embody (or rather disembody) the psychological confounding of subject and object. They are entirely subjective phenomena (they exist only in the mind) that have attained objective power (they determine events in the real world), and unlike traditional forms of money, they openly announce themselves as such. In the financial derivative, fetishized labor finds its ultimate graven image.

The autonomy that financial signs have achieved from their referents has produced malign ethical and practical effects that are now becoming clearly visible. In rhetorical terms, we might say, a derivative is an illegitimate use of the figure of exchange: what rhetoric calls *ennallage*. More specifically, a derivative is a morally deleterious trope of exchange, a catachresis masquerading as a conceit. All financial instruments are signs that have acquired efficacious, performative power, but the degree of abstraction achieved by derivatives, as well as the degree of separation between sign and referent or, put another way, the infelicity of the metaphor, renders their practical effects disastrous, and their moral consequences reprehensible. What is a derivative, finally, but an abuse of representation, which forces signs into an autonomous position and a reproductive role that they do not naturally possess?

Another, closely related critique of derivatives concerns their confusion of nature and custom, *phusis* and *nomos*. The ability to add significance to experience, to impose culture, reason, meaning, and will on nature, is what separates humanity from nature, from beasts. The archetypal imposition of human culture on nature is not language, as has often been supposed, but exchange. The human capacity to conceive of qualitatively different objects as equivalent for the purpose of exchange is prelinguistic, both historically and logically: in fact it arguably makes language possible. The basic ability to see something as what it is not, to represent nature as custom, is presupposed by the most elementary exchange of, as it might be, a pig for a cow. This is the root of all representation, which facilitates the human subject's escape from the primordial swamps of objective nature. In nature, a pig is a pig and a cow is a cow. But human beings, and only human beings, can turn a pig into a cow via the medium of representation.

There are thus, for human beings, two worlds, realms or spheres of experience: custom and nature. At the beginning of money's rise to power, people axiomatically identified it with custom, which Aristotle calls the 'second nature.' This 'second nature' can easily be mistaken for the original. At the dawn of money's modern independence, during the sixteenth and seventeenth centuries, ethical criticism portrayed the market-place as a vast machine dedicated to the confounding of custom and nature. Thus Martin Luther calls money *verbum diabli*, 'the word of the devil, through which he creates everything in the world, just as God creates through the true Word.'[41] Thus in John Milton's *Paradise Lost* (1667), Mammon uses Hell's gold to construct a demonic parody of God's natural creation, 'in emulation opposite to heaven' (2.298). Today by contrast, as nature itself begins to mutate under the influence of custom, the world created by money is fast becoming the only world we can know in a physical as well as a psychological sense. We no longer perceive the objective environment but only its symbol. We inhabit a symbolic environment derived from reality, not reality itself, and this domain is ruled by performative images, efficacious signs, that have no existence outside the human mind. In this hyper-real world, such non-existent things achieve tyrannical power over the human beings whose minds they inhabit. What they do not and cannot do, however, is exist. We can. We do.

NOTES

1. Peter L. Bernstein, *Against the Gods: The Remarkable Story of Risk* (Wiley, 1998), 4.
2. Fredric Jameson, 'The Aesthetics of Singularity,' *New Left Review* 92 (April–May 2015).
3. Thomas Lagoarde-Segot, 'Financialization: Towards a New Research Agenda,' *International Review of Financial Analysis* 51(C) (2016), 113–123, 115.
4. Christopher Schinckus, 'The Financial Simulacrum,' *Journal of Socio-Economics* 73.3 (2008), 1076–1089.
5. For insightful recent accounts of the transition from a production-based economy built on 'real' capital to the usurious economy of today, see E. Michael Jones, *Barren Metal: A History of Capitalism as the Conflict between Labor and Usury* (South Bend, IN: Fidelity Press, 2014) and Richard Westra, *Unleashing Usury: How Finance Opened the Door for Capitalism Then Swallowed It Whole* (Atlanta, GA: Clarity Press, 2016).
6. David Graeber, *Debt: The First 5,000 Years* (Melville House, 2011), 28.
7. Norman McIntosh, 'From Rationality to Hyperreality: Paradigm Poker,' *International Review of Financial Analysis* 12.4 (2003), 453–465, 455.

8. Elton McGoun, 'Hyperreal Finance,' *Critical Perspectives on Accounting* 8.1–2 (1997), 97–122, 99.

9. Randy Martin, *Knowledge LTD: Towards a Social Knowledge of the Derivative* (Temple UP, 2015), 5.

10. Arjun Appadurai, *Banking on Words: The Failure of Language in the Age of Derivative Finance* (U of Chicago P, 2016), 4.

11. Warren Buffet CEO, *Berkshire-Hathaway Annual Report*, 2002.

12. Charles Ferguson, *Predator Nation: Corporate Criminals, Political Corruption and the Hijacking of America* (New York, 2013), 3.

13. Joel Kurtzman, *The Death of Money* (New York: Simon and Schuster, 1993).

14. Though as David Graeber reminds us, 'there's nothing new about virtual money. Actually, this was the original form of money. Credit system, tabs, even expense accounts, all existed long before cash.' David Graeber, *Debt: The First 5,000 Years* (Melville House, 2011), 18. Steve Fleetwood also makes a fair point: 'It is, I feel, incumbent on those who argue money is not a commodity but a signifier, sign or symbol, to explain why 20 kg of tea and 10 kg of coffee are systematically (that is, non-accidentally) worth x units of symbolic money and not y units).' 'A Marxist Theory of Commodity Money Revisited,' in *What Is Money?*, ed. John Smithin (Routledge, 2000), 192n20. The answer, surely, is that money is a *performative* symbol, a sign that has attained objective reality.

15. As LaPuma and Lee remind us: 'the secretary of the Treasury in the late 1990s, Robert Rubin, his successor Paul O'Neill, and the present vice-president Dick Cheney, all commanded companies that architects of, and principals in, derivatives trading' (199n2).

16. Matt Davies, 'The Aesthetics of the Financial Crisis: Work, Culture, and Politics,' *Alternatives: Global, Local, Political* 37.4 (2012), 317–330.

17. Randy Martin, *Knowledge LTD: Towards a Social Logic of the Derivative* (Temple UP, 2015), 7.

18. Jacques Derrida, 'Linguistics and Grammatology,' in *Of Grammatology*, trans. Gayatri Spivak (Johns Hopkins UP, 1998).

19. Giovanni Arrighi, 'Winding Paths of Capital,' *New Left Review* 56 (2009), 61–94.

20. Matt Davis, 'The Aesthetics of the Financial Crisis: Work, Culture and Politics,' *Alternatives: Global, Local, Political* 37.4 (November 2012), 317–330, 320.

21. Edward LiPuma and Benjamin Lee, *Financial Derivatives and the Globalization of Risk* (Duke UP, 2004), 18.

22. Jean-Joseph Goux, *The Coiners of Language*, trans. Jennifer Curtiss Gage (U of Oklahoma P, 1984), 4.

23. Ferdinand de Saussure, *Course in General Linguistics* (Bloomsbury, 2013), 135.

24. Talcott Parsons, *On Institutions and Social Evolution* (U of Chicago P, 1982), 224.
25. Dick Bryan and Michael Rafferty, 'Why We Need to Understand Derivatives in Relation to Money: A Reply to Tony Norfield,' *Historical Materialism* 20.3 (2012), 97–109, 104–105.
26. Dick Bryan and Mike Rafferty, *Capitalism with Derivatives: A Political Economy of Financial Derivatives, Capital and Class* (Palgrave, 2006), 69.
27. Elton McGoun distinguishes between the 'symbolic value' of money and its 'sign' value: 'defining a symbol as "standing in place of something" and a sign as "having cultural meaning" should sufficiently differentiate the two admittedly somewhat confusing terms' (104). By the 'sign' value of money, McGoun means the social implications of wealth as described in Thorstein Veblen's *Theory of the Leisure Class* (1917). Here I am concerned only with what McGoun calls money's 'symbolic' value.
28. Bryan and Rafferty (2006), 11.
29. R.J. Shiller, 'Prize Lecture: Speculative Asset Prices' (2013), retrieved from https://www.nobelprize.org/uploads/2018/06/shiller-lecture.pdf (October 5, 2019).
30. David Harvey, *The Enigma of Capital and the Crises of Capitalism* (Oxford UP, 2010), 15.
31. Ferguson (2013), 40.
32. See Michael Taussig, *The Devil and Commodity Fetishism in South America* (U of North Carolina P, 1980) and Jean and John Comaroff (eds.), *Modernity and Its Malcontents: Ritual and Power in Post-colonial Africa* (U of Chicago P, 1993).
33. Judith Butler, *Excitable Speech: A Politics of the Performative* (New York: Routledge, 1997), 3
34. Elie Ayache, *The Blank Swan: The End of Probability* (John Wiley & Sons, 2010), xix.
35. Arjun Appadurai, *Banking on Words; The Failure of Language in the Age of Derivative Finance* (U of Chicago P, 2016), 4.
36. 'The Blank Swan: Dan Tudball Talks to Elie Ayache,' *Wilmott*, April 2007, 43.
37. Ray Brassier, interview with *Kronos* (2011), retrieved April 1, 2020: http://www.kronos.org.pl/index.php?23151,896.
38. John Gaule, *Select Cases of Conscience Touching Witches and Witchcraft* (London, 1646), in *English Witchcraft 1560–1736*, vol. 3, ed. Malcolm Gaskill (Pickering & Chatto, 2003), 124–125.
39. Sylvia Federici, *Caliban and the Witch: The Body and Primitive Accumulation* (Autonomedia, 2004).
40. Phillipe Pignarre and Isabelle Stengers, *Breaking the Spell: Capitalist Sorcery*, trans. Andrew Goffey (Palgrave Macmillan, 2011), 182.
41. Cit. Marc Shell, *Art and Money* (U of Chicago P, 1995), 191n2.

CHAPTER 9

The Future-Sign: Representation in the Anglophone Yoruba Novel

9.1 Afro-Postmodernism

Karl Marx dealt a fatal blow to the Western sense of superiority when he described the attribution of independent agency to symbolic exchange-value as 'commodity fetishism.' The Portuguese word *fetice* was originally used to describe West African animism, and Marx called attention to an uncomfortable truth when he reminded Europeans that the modern capitalist economy rests on the same psychological processes as supposedly primitive witchcraft. In a speech delivered to the World Bank in 1998, Africa's most famous novelist Chinua Achebe committed a similar *faux pas* when he pointed out the kinship between his own art of fictional narrative and the theories elaborated by the professional economists in the audience. Achebe recalled being struck by an epiphany at a meeting of the Organization for Economic Development ten years previously:

> It suddenly became clear to me why I had been invited, what I was doing there in that strange assembly. I signaled my desire to speak and was given the floor. I told them what I had just recognized. I said that what was going on before me was a fiction workshop, no more and no less! Here you are, spinning your fine theories to be tried out in your imaginary laboratories. You are developing new drugs and feeding them to a bunch of laboratory guinea pigs and hoping for the best. I have news for you. Africa is not fiction. Africa is people, real people.[1]

D. Hawkes, *The Reign of Anti-logos*, Palgrave Insights into Apocalypse Economics, https://doi.org/10.1007/978-3-030-55940-3_9

Achebe criticized academic economics as a species of fiction masquerading as objective science. From credit default swaps to compound interest and exchange-value itself, the concepts studied by professional economists are no more ontologically authentic than the fantasies of the story-teller. Finance is symbolic, like language. Its efficacy is real enough, but it takes place within the human mind. Financial causality works through a system of signs that make people think and behave in certain ways, which is to say that it is magical. Achebe's point recalled the argument, made in the discipline of economics by Dierdre McCloskey's *The Rhetoric of Economics* (1985) and since advanced in literary studies by practitioners of the New Economic Criticism, that economics is a fundamentally semiotic discourse. But the most striking feature of Achebe's speech is his ethical insistence on the ontological distinction between fiction and reality. He suggests that to collapse this distinction would be ethically malign, because it would involve the objectification of human beings. The independence of the human subject is, for him, irreducibly real, and he defends the distinction between representation and reality for that reason.

Achebe's moral proposition flies in the face of postmodern culture, and especially of postmodernist ethics. Postmodernist thinkers conceive of performative representation as politically liberating, and of logocentrism and essentialism as politically oppressive. They will naturally contest the dichotomy between fiction and reality, along with the polarity between *nomos* and *phusis*. They will view the human subject as material, because they conceive it as constructed by systems of representation. This view accords conveniently with the ideologically dominant materialism of evolutionary psychology and sociobiology, which reduce autonomous subjectivity to the mechanical operations of the brain. For Achebe, in contrast, the autonomous human subject is the last bastion of authentic reality, a redoubt beyond the reach of representation, whether linguistic or financial. His speech treats the categories 'real' and 'people' as coterminus. To the Western delegates in his audience, who think of it in solely economic terms, 'Africa' is unreal, an abstraction, a thing. But for Achebe this reified condition is fictional. In reality, 'Africa is people.'

Achebe explores this point at greater length in his own fiction which, like the Anglophone African novel in general, provides a medium well-adapted to a detailed discussion of modernity's impact on subjectivity. The Anglophone African novel was shaped, as a genre, by the same imperative that evidently inspired Achebe's speech: the need to reflect on the subjective consequences of neo-imperialist capitalism. These include the weakening of binary oppositions in general, and of the polarity between reality and fiction in particular. Three centuries previously, the Western novel also emerged as a venue for debating the subjective effects of capitalism. As a medium that elevated the expression of interior subjectivity above adherence to pre-existing formal requirements, the novel was well-suited to that purpose. As Georg Lukacs famously argued in his seminal *The Theory of the Novel* (1916), this turn to interiority was a reaction to the departure of *logos* from human experience:

> The novel is the epic of a world that has been abandoned by God. The novel hero's psychology is demonic; the objectivity of the novel is the mature man's knowledge that meaning can never quite penetrate reality, but that, without meaning, reality would disintegrate into the nothingness of inessentiality.[2]

In Lukacs' Hegel ian terminology, capitalism's 'alienation' of subjective activity in the symbolic form of exchange-value meant that the *logos* or 'totality' was no longer 'immanent' in human experience, which consequently could only find 'meaning' by contemplating itself. The inability to perceive *logos* is definitive of a 'demonic' *psyche*, which is deprived of access to 'meaning,' prevented from perceiving experience as a system of signs with ulterior reference, and so turns in upon itself. In the novel, the kind of quest and adventures that epic literature depicts in objective, external form take place at the interior level. As Lukacs puts it: 'the content of the novel is the story of the soul that goes to find itself, that seeks adventures in order to be proved and tested by them, and, by proving itself, to find its own essence' (89). This quest is a matter of form, not of content: the most mundane of plots would facilitate the same kind of self-reflexive consciousness to which the novel form gives expression.

Although Lukacs does not say so directly, the archetypal novel according to this definition would be James Joyce's *Ulysees*, which concentrates the supernatural, symbolic landscape of Homer's *Odyssey* into the mundane, quotidian encounters of Leopold Bloom. The novel is formed out of the decline of allegory (which conceives of phenomena as signs that refer to abstract referents) into realism (which locates significance at the surface, in appearance). This aesthetic process is historically contemporary with the earliest forms of Western capitalism. It is already evident, for example, in the mutation of the Vice figure from the medieval morality plays into the credible human form of Shakespeare's Falstaff. The novel's focus on interior, subjective experience made it an ideal form in which to reflect on the psychological changes wrought by the introduction of wage labor, commodity exchange, and usury. In John Bunyan's *The Pilgrim's Progress* (1678), arguably the earliest English novel, allegorical images like Vanity Fair are located in a recognizable landscape, and their effects on the subjective conditions of the characters are portrayed as eminently real.

British missionaries loved *The Pilgrim's Progress*, and Bunyan's influence on the Anglophone African novel cannot be over-stated. Amos Tutuola in particular utilizes strikingly similar techniques, but Bunyan casts a long shadow over the African novel to this day. Like his allegorical landscapes, the African novel has, throughout its relatively short history, provided a medium through which to consider the psychological effects of rapid integration into an exchange-based, financialized economy. It was not until the 1950s that African novelists began to be published in English. By that time, Africans had learned to adapt the ideologies and aesthetics of the colonial powers to their own purposes. They integrated the Western novel into traditional, oral narrative forms, just as the syncretic religions of Africa and the African diaspora assimilated monotheism into polytheistic and animist belief-systems. This juxtaposition of diverse traditions challenged any single culture's claims to absolute, transcendent standards. It also relativized tradition, encouraging Africans to approach their own assumptions about narrative, subjectivity, and the role of representation through an imported, alien cultural form.

Some critics identify two phases in the history of the African novel: a politically committed, optimistic period up to, and immediately after independence, followed by a turn toward magical realism and fantasy in the disillusioned years after 1980. African critics often voice reservations about this recent vogue for the supernatural. In 2002, Wole Ogundele complained that African writers were abandoning 'history' for 'myth,' thus depleting their work of social, political, or economic relevance:

> In the last decade or so, the postcolonial African novels that have had the most impact have been those employing marvelous or fantastic realism.... This new genre has not only been explained in terms of cultural hybridity, but has also been traced back to African oral-mythic narratives. These causal explanations are fine, but they do not fully relate the novels to the primary concerns of the main genre(s) of postcolonial African novels that were produced, roughly, between 1958 and the early 1980s. The concerns

may be summarized simply as culture and nationhood. The one implies myth, folklore, etc.; the other, history and politics. But just as culture has intertwined with the politics of nationalism, so have myth, folklore etc. intermingled with history. The outcome of this cross- and intermingling has been the displacement of history by myth in the postcolonial African novel in English.[3]

Ogundele retains a post-Marxist distinction between historical base and mythical superstructure, and he regards the former as more authentic than the latter. This model seemed appropriate to the era of production-based capitalism. In an era dominated by autonomous finance, however, the difference between myth and history, like the distinction between reality and representation, may be harder to discern. Financial phenomena are mythical, in the sense that they are imaginary, but today they are also the motor that drives history. The increased prevalence of myth, magic, and the supernatural in the twenty-first-century African novel can be seen as a response to—or rather a part of—contemporary historical circumstances, not an escape from them. This is what leads Anthony Appiah to differentiate between the treatment of the supernatural in African writers like Ben Okri and the 'magical realism' of Latin America. Appiah identifies a specifically African genre of 'spiritual realism,' in which 'the world of spirits is not metaphorical or imaginary, rather, it is more real than the world of everyday.'[4]

I will limit this discussion mainly to the Yoruba novel in English. Similar developments are evident throughout sub-Saharan Africa, but Yoruba culture seems especially well-adapted to examining the ethics of representation, and a large proportion of well-known African novelists are Yoruba, including Fugunwa, Tutuola, and Soyinka. Although not Yoruba himself, Ben Okri is a fellow Nigerian, and all Nigeria ns were forced to come to terms with the radical disruption of customary values that resulted from the discovery of oil in the late 1950s, and the consequent monetization of the national economy. Okri's work frequently alludes to the Yoruba tradition and, as Sarah Fulford observes: 'Although Okri isn't Yoruba n, he can be seen to be adopting aspects of Yoruba n aesthetics.'[5] Ato Quayson also comments perceptively on 'the filiation of Ben Okri to the writing of Tutuola and Soyinka.'[6] The Yoruba novel is concerned above all with the problem of what Francis Nyamnjoh calls 'undomesticated agency.' This term refers to a kind of power that has become independent of any obvious agent, that seems to roam freely through the world of causality, instigating random and frequently malign events and experiences. Undomesticated agency resides in the 'forest' or the 'bush,' whether literal or figurative. It can manifest itself as money or magic—as any kind of performative symbol—and its effect is to sever the connections between individual and community. As Nyamnjoh suggests, undomesticated agency violates the collectivist 'conviction that no agency is rewarding for the collectivity, or even, ultimately, for the individual if undomesticated. Undomesticated agency is greed, and success that comes by greed can only be achieved by sacrificing others or their interests.'[7]

This interest in imperceptible, uncontrollable agency is well-suited to understanding post-colonialism. The end of colonial rule brought little improvement to the lives of most Africans, because overt, political imperialism was replaced by a more insidious, economic form of oppression. The twenty-first-century mode of domination known as 'post-colonialism' or 'neo-imperialism' certainly has recourse to physical force when necessary. For the most part, however, the monopoly of violence enjoyed by the colonial nation-state has been replaced by the abstract power of international capital. The nominally independent nations of Africa are ruled not by force but by usury. Insofar as force (or the threat of force) is used, it is generally in the service of debt collection, or to enforce the structural adjustment programs mandated by the World Bank or the IMF to ensure repayments. As Thomas Sankara, President of Burkino Faso, told the Organization of African Unity in 1987, the debt is 'a cleverly organized reconquest of Africa' designed to 'turn each of us into a financial slave.' His conclusion was unambiguous: 'the debt is another form of neocolonialism, one in which the colonialists have transformed themselves into technical assistants. Actually, it would be more accurate to say technical assassins.'[8] Sankara knew whereof he spoke: he was himself assassinated three months later.

The discourse and practice of witchcraft have dramatically grown in prominence throughout Africa since the end of the colonial era. This is partly because colonial regimes refused to prosecute witches for witchcraft, on the manifestly spurious grounds that it does not exist. What the colonial state really meant by this was that witchcraft is inefficacious, that it does not work, but that position is less than tenable in a hyper-real postmodern environment ruled by the ghostly symbols of finance. The rapid resurgence of magic since independence suggests that, as in early modern Europe, magical concepts provide a means of coming to terms with the new, invisible and symbolic forms taken by power in the postcolonial era. This helps to account for the predominance of magic in the African novel. But notwithstanding the protests of critics like Ogundele, the African novel has always invoked the supernatural as a means of coming to terms with neo-imperialism. Even the first generation of Anglophone African novelists, which included Chinua Achebe, Wole Soyinka, and Ngugi Wa' Thiong' O, used traditional mythology and Christianity to evoke the invisible power of neo-imperialist capital. I have discussed elsewhere how Ngugi's *Devil on the Cross* (1980) indicates the spiritual implications of international finance by describing a 'Devil's Feast' held by 'Satan, the King of Hell' masquerading under the guise of the 'Organization of International Thieves and Robbers.'[9]

It is true that novels like Dambudzo Marechera's *Black Sunlight* (1980) and Ben Okri's *The Famished Road* (1981) utilize the fantastic in a manner that evokes the magical realism of Gabriel Garcia Marquez. But their interweaving of money and magic is also realistic in the sense that it accurately reflects everyday experience. Jean and John Comaroff have described the 'occult economies' of twenty-first-century Africa, in which 'the exuberant spread of innovative occult practices and money magic, pyramid schemes, and prosperity gospels; the enchantments, that is, of a decidedly neoliberal economy whose ever-more inscrutable speculations seem to call up fresh specters in their wake.'[10] Peter Geschiere agrees that 'modernity in Africa brings a reinforcement of witchcraft rather than a weakening of it, as in the West,'[11] while Margaret Drewal observes how in West Africa 'rapid social change stimulates a traditionalizing process in which rituals and ritual symbols proliferate.'[12] From the perspective of people newly subjected to its influence, the usurious global economy of postmodernity seems to run entirely on magical principles. The forces it releases are invisible, and they manifest themselves in arcane, symbolic systems legible only to initiates. As Henrietta Moore and Todd Sanders put it: 'Stories, of zombies, cannibalism and headhunting are imaginative, moral frameworks for making sense of wage labor, consumption, migration, productive regimes, structural adjustment programs, development policies and the functioning of markets.'[13]

The aesthetic techniques evoked by the 'occult economy' are associated with 'postmodernism' in the West, and critics today often refer to an 'African postmodernism.'[14] In fact, Anglophone African literature was 'modernist' from the outset. As Quayson points out, the very title of Achebe's seminal work *Things Fall Apart* (1958) 'gestures towards a Modernist sensibility' by its allusion to W.B. Yeats.[15] Unlike their Western counterparts, however, African novelists never had a realist tradition to depart from. Such formal techniques as descriptive naturalism, a plausible plot-line, or the omniscient narrator had never sunk deep roots in their cultures. Just as Bertolt Brecht found proletarian audiences the most amenable to his 'alienation effect' because they had never grown accustomed to realistic theater, so African novelists adopt the narrative techniques associated with modernism as the natural aesthetic expression of the *Zeitgeist*. As Peter Kalliney explains, a major reason why Faber and Faber decided to publish the work of Amos Tutuola, the first African novelist to write in English, was 'his freedom from the conventions of European fiction.'[16]

9.2   Amos Tutuola's *The Palm-Wine Drinkard*

Tutuola's debut *The Palm-Wine Drinkard* was published in 1952. It met with much acclaim in the West, where it was impelled to fame by Dylan Thomas' enthusiastic review in *The Observer*. Thomas called the novel 'bewitching,' and its immersion in the occult world of witchcraft was an important source of its appeal in Britain. It was also the cause of considerable embarrassment among African intellectuals, who viewed Tutuola as indulging Western preconceptions about African primitivism.[17] It is true that Tutuola's work is of special interest because its untutored, immediate style allows it to reflect the impact of modernity on the mind in a particularly vivid manner. His lack of formal education and imperfect mastery of English grammar give his stories a demotic quality that Western critics regarded as authentically popular and Africans scorned as clownish. The first generation of postcolonial scholars, whose over-riding concern was to repudiate Western condescension, tended to agree with V.S. Naipul's 1958 review in *The New Statesman*: 'Tutuola's English is that of the West African schoolboy, an imperfectly acquired second language. In what other age could bad grammar have been a literary asset?'[18]

   Of course, bad grammar is not considered an obstacle to literary merit in the postmodern West, and even African opinions of Tutuola's work had changed dramatically by the early twenty-first century. His style–which eschews linear plot, lucid prose, conventional grammar and a coherent narrator in favor of wild shape-shifting, dramatic oscillation between levels of reality, supernatural causality, and vivid but obfuscatory language— has been profoundly influential on the African novel. In 1996 Femi Osofisan warily compared the work of the new generation to 'Tutuola in delirium.'[19] Scholars like Thomas Jay Lynn and Franics Nyamnjoh have recently re-evaluated Tutuola's apparently naïve, fractured, and fragmentary prose as a precursor of postmodernism, and his work is now widely acknowledged as an eloquent response to neo-imperialism, as well as an intuitive adaptation of Yoruba tradition to twentieth-century concerns.

Tutuola's confident, assertive attitude toward traditional mythology was echoed by Chinua Achebe's 1968 translation of D. O. Fugunwa's *Forest of a Thousand Daemons*. Originally written in Yoruba in 1938, Fugunwa's fantastic novel renders traditional folk-tales in a style that strikes the Western reader as recognizably modernist. It was the most important indigenous influence on Tutuola, who draws heavily on the same oral tradition. In the works of both writers, a hero invariably finds him or herself stranded in an alien, supernatural environment. The grotesque world of the 'forest' or 'bush' through which the narrators wander is central to Yoruba folklore. Like the 'wood' through which the narrator strays at the start of Dante's *Divine Comedy*, it is simultaneously literal and figural, subjective, and objective. The inter-penetration of subject and object is also reminiscent of *The Pilgrim's Progress*—another novelistic response to the emergence of an exchange-based economy that describes an objective environment and a subjective consciousness profoundly imbricated with supernatural logic and magical causality.

The Pilgrim's Progress was translated into Yoruba in the eighteenth century, and it established a model for subsequent fictional narratives. Fugunwa's *Forest of a Thousand Daemons* particularly evokes Bunyan's Vanity Fair, and anticipates Tutuola, in its connection of market exchange with the supernatural. The narrator, 'Akara-ogun, Compound-of-Spells' visits the 'Forest of Irunmale':

> I had not slept very long when I awakened, and indeed it was the cries of ghommids coming to trade at the night market that woke me...As the ghommids arrived they sat round the tree; they were all of a great variety, like the clothing of alagemo—some walked on their heads, others hopped frogwise, one had neither arms nor legs; his appearance was like a rubbery tub. Last of all came the king's crier and he began his summons thus: 'Lord of Forests! Lord of Forests! you are the merchant prince of ghommids; I say you are the merchant prince of ghommids; there is no trader to equal you.[20]

Fugunwa's description is reminiscent of both Yoruba folklore and such Western works as Christina Rossetti's 'Goblin Market' in its conception of the market-place as an unnatural environment. The imposition of symbolic exchange-value upon substantial use-value is viewed with suspicion in almost every culture, but the connection of witchcraft with commerce seems particularly pronounced in African literature. The African novel emerged as a genre during the era of decolonialization, in which imperialism ceased to be political and became financial, and African novelists continue to conceive of the supernatural in financial terms to the present day. Chris Abani's *Graceland* (2004) utilizes the traditional notion that 'markets were supposed to be the crossroads of the living and the dead,'[21] while the narrator of Ben Okri's *The Famished Road* (1991) recalls 'the first time I realized it wasn't just humans who came to the marketplaces of the world. Spirits and other beings come there too. They buy and sell, browse and investigate.'[22]

The market economy is conspicuous by its absence from the opening pages of Tutuola's *The Palm-Wine Drinkard*. The novel begins by evoking a recent past of happy, unreflective, instant gratification. The narrator links this vanished, idyllic condition to his society's exclusion from the system of finance:

> I was a palm-wine drinkard since I was a boy of ten years of age. I had no other work more than to drink palm-wine in my life. In those days we did not know other money, except COWRIES, so that everything was very cheap, and my father was the richest man in our town.[23]

The narrator is perfectly satisfied to drink palm-wine all day, and suffers no social or parental disapprobation in consequence, because the only money his society uses is the cowrie shell. Cowries were the common currency of pre-colonial West Africa, and they continued to be widely used well into the twentieth century. Unlike the metaphysical, reproductive money of the West, cowrie shells were purely referential: they were used solely to facilitate barter. They were material, not abstract, and this meant that they were not autonomous, they did not breed or reproduce independently. They were not performative in their financial capacity, though they were often used as potent tokens in magical rituals. The absence of reproductive money removes the possibility of accumulating wealth, and therefore deprives the Drinkard of the incentive to work. It is not that the whole society is idle—the Drinkard's brothers are 'hard work-ers'—but the narrative voice through we experience the story is innocent of any work ethic. His father indulges him by engaging 'an expert palm-wine tapster' to provide for his needs, and the tapster's labor precisely matches the Drinakrd's consumption. Just as the Drinkard 'had no other work more than to drink palm-wine in my life' (181), so the tapster 'had no other work more than to tap palm-wine every day' (181).

This Edenic existence is abruptly halted by the accidental death of the tapster, which throws into relief uncomfortable questions about the relation of labor to value. It is important to note at this stage that the slave trade hovers in the background of the entire Yoruba novel tradi-tion. It is an ever-present influence, even when it is not named directly.[24] In *The Palm-Wine Drinkard*, for example, a harmonious, non-monetary economy in which production and consumption are perfectly balanced is abruptly disrupted when labor is suddenly removed from the process of production. The rapid diminution of labor-power due to the slave trade did indeed cause massive economic disruption throughout West Africa. In the absence of the tapster, there is no more palm wine. Destructive chaos immediately ensues. Deprived of his sustenance, the Drinkard embarks on a quest to find his dead tapster in 'Deadstown.' He is plunged into an otherworldly, supernatural realm in which he is forced to work for a living, and in which value—especially the value of labor–is alien, relative and negotiable.

Tutuola claimed to have heard the novel's adventures in the stories told by Yoruba elders, and critics like Bernth Lindfors insist that many of the novel's *motifs* 'can be documented as traditional among the Yoruba.'[25] Yet *The Palm-Wine Drinkard* seems also to reflect the influence of English missionaries. The profound impact of Bunyan is obvious, but it is also possible to detect echoes of Daniel Defoe's seminal celebra-tions of retail trade, especially *The Complete English Tradesman* (1726), and even his of picaresque depiction of the vagaries of the market-place in *Moll Flanders* (1722). Like Bunyan and Defoe, Tutuola conveys the psychological effects of commodification primarily through the device of personification. The story of the 'curious creature in the market-place' is canonical in Yoruba folklore, but Tutuola adapts it into a commen-tary on the deceptive spectacles of exchange-value. An innocent young lady visits the market-place, where she encounters a 'beautiful gentleman' who is simultaneously a 'curious creature.' His primary characteristic is his commodification:

> He was a beautiful 'complete' gentleman, he dressed with the finest and
> most costly clothes, all the parts of his body were completed, he was a tall
> man but stout. As this gentleman came to the market on that day, if he
> had been an article or animal for sale, he would be sold at least for £2000
> (two thousand pounds). (201)

This being has two apparently contradictory identities. He is a 'beautiful
"complete" gentleman,' but this identity is inseparable from his artificial
exchange-value as a commodity, so that he is also a 'curious creature.'
Entranced, the lady follows the 'beautiful gentleman' around the market-
place and eventually into an 'endless forest.' This is the realm of magic and
the supernatural. But the supernatural is not associated with any pristine
African culture—to the contrary, it is the consequence of commodification, and it represents the illusory power of symbolic exchange-value. Like
Helen of Troy, the lady suffers a quasi-sexual seduction that leads her
into an alien land. The fascinating 'curious creature' is soon revealed to
be 'beautiful' in appearance only. His beauty turns out not to belong to
him essentially; it is merely 'hired' as a commodity:

> As they were travelling along in this endless forest then the complete
> gentleman in the market that the lady was following, began to return the
> hired parts of his body to the owners and he was paying them the rentage
> money. When he reached where he hired the left foot, he pulled it out,
> he gave it to the owner and paid him, and they kept going; when they
> reached the place where he hired the right foot, he pulled it out and gave
> it to the owner and paid for the rentage. Now both feet had returned to
> the owners, so he began to crawl along on the ground, by that time, that
> lady wanted to go back to her town or her father, but the terrible and
> curious creature or the complete gentleman did not allow her to return
> or go back to her town or her father again and the complete gentleman
> said thus: 'I had told you not to follow me before we branched into this
> endless forest which belongs to only terrible and curious creatures, but
> when I became a half-bodied incomplete gentleman you wanted to go
> back, now that cannot be done, you have failed.' (202)

The supernatural power of symbolic value creates 'terrible and curious
creatures.' It also separates the lady from her kinship and tribal affinities.
The imposition of figurative exchange-value on substantial use-value leads
consciousness into the realm of the supernatural, where illusions are indistinguishable from reality. The 'complete gentleman' eventually returns all

the 'beautiful' features of his body as 'rentage,' until he is 'reduced' to nothing more than a 'Skull.' This is entirely compatible with Christian allegory: the flesh is a mere 'lending' which we must return at death. But Tutuola syncretizes such Christian allusions with references to traditional Yoruba culture. The Skull imprisons the lady by hanging a cowrie shell around her neck. The cowrie emits a 'terrible noise' if she tries to escape. Since the cowrie shell is the traditional currency of West Africa, and is also frequently employed in magic rituals, the lady is effectively imprisoned by the magic of money. As S. M. Tobias points out:

> Through this tale Tutuola hints at the way in which colonial and, subsequently, postcolonial socioeconomic systems serve to chain their African victims to money and other seemingly positive trappings while simultaneously trying to remove their ability to voice resistance.[26]

The Skull lives among other Skulls in a village, where they store cowrie shells in an immense pit, leading the narrator to observe: 'I believed that the cowries in that pit were their power' (209). It is not immediately clear whether the cowries actually *are* powerful, or if it is just that the narrator 'believed' in their power, but the difference is otiose. The cowries are efficacious signs, which enable the Skulls to usurp human agency. As Tutuola explains in *The Feather Woman of the Jungle*, cowries also functioned as a type of writing:

> Long, long ago, before the Yoruba people had ever dreamed of the white people and as there was no book knowledge, the Egba people had the means of communication by means of symbols which we used as letters and some of them are as follows—If two cowries were tied together faced each other, meant, 'I want to see you.' But if a long feather was added in return, it meant 'be expecting me.' If two cowries were tied back to back, meant 'I shun you away.' If another cowrie was added in return, it it meant 'I kick you off....'[27]

Tutuola frequently employs cowries as magical tokens in his other works. In *Simbi and the Satyr of the Dark Jungle*, the title character's experience of 'poverty and punishment' begins when she appeals to a magical penny. The penny leads her to a soothsayer, who conducts an Ifa divination using sixteen cowrie shells, which 'were going to explain to the soothsayer in the code words of what Simbi wanted to know.'[28] The Ifa divination of the Yoruba works by casting cowrie shells or palm nuts on 'the tray of his

Ifa, the god of oracle' (11), to form *odu* or graphemes, through which the deities or *orisha* communicate with the visible world. The *babalawa* or diviner interprets the signs to tell the future, and recites an appropriate allegorical narrative. Yet Ifa bestows determining power on the system of *odu* representation itself, rather than on the divining priest. As Adeleke Adeeko puts it, Ifa divination works by the 'association of consistently named, visibly embodied signs with prognostic narrations.'[29] The diviner's stories illustrate the problems and solutions indicated by the signs. Although, as Adeeko explains: 'The sign revealed and the illustrative stories told must bear some allegorical semblance to the problems the client wants to solve,' the grapheme contains its significance within itself: 'the referent of the Ifá story is the inscription and not the event of the story' (23).

Tutuola presents his stories about life in the bush as just such an allegorical answer to the problems of slavery, usury, and oppression. The threat of suddenly being captured and transported to work as a slave in another world was an aspect of African modernity that seemed best understood using magical concepts. Money is the conduit through which human beings are reified–turned into something they naturally are not–so money of any kind is perceived as magical. The Drinkard's predicament among the Skulls is typical of Tutuola's vision, in which human beings are repeatedly imprisoned, enslaved, and exploited by grotesque, alien creatures who move fluidly between allegory, fantasy, and realism. Soon after her encounter with the soothsayer, Simbi is kidnapped by a slave trader named Dogo, a 'native of a town called the "Sinners' town," the town in which only sinners and worshippers of gods were living' (15). Polytheistic idolatry is thus connected to slavery, as Simbi embarks on the usual voyage of a Tutuola protagonist through various scenes of captivity, servitude, and witchcraft. These are often fantastic and supernatural, but they can also be historically realistic, as when we are informed that: 'Dogo had no other work more than to be traveling on every path and kidnapping other people's children and then selling them as slaves for the foreigners' (15). Although these 'foreigners' were real enough, they occupy the same sphere of realty within the novel as the most outlandish creatures of fantasy. The fantastic idea of commodifying human beings is commonplace in this nightmarish environment. As Dogo straightforwardly informs Simbi: 'I am taking you to where I am going to sell you and then to spend the money that I sell you for all my needs' (17). The process of Simbi's commodification is described in horrifying detail:

The auctioneer first put Simbi on the weighing scale just to know her exact weight which would enable him to know the real price that he would impose upon her. Having quite sure of her real weight, he wore several oversized garments for her. Each of the garments was sewn with about twenty yards of cloth. After that, he put on her head an oversized hat which swallowed her head so that she was terrible to see at that moment. All these dresses made Simbi bigger than her usual size. After, he put a sofa at the centre of the ground. Simbi sat on it and he compelled her also to swell out every part of her body with pride so that she might be seemed to every intended buyer that she was pleased for selling her. Then a number of the appraisers seated on two benches at a little distance from her. After this arrangement, the touting man of the auctioneer came with a big bell and he stood at the front of her. (22–23)

One version or another of this scenario is found in almost all of Tutuola's fiction. The central character is invariably uprooted from his or her native village and family, usually by financial exigency, and suddenly cast into an environment peopled by autonomous images, where they are repeatedly sold and enslaved. Sometimes they enter this 'bush' or forest' voluntarily, but even then they are impelled by pecuniary concerns. The basic action of a Tutuola story is adumbrated briefly in the plot of *Feather Woman of the Jungle*. The old chief whose stories make up the narrative recalls how he was driven to seek his fortune in the realms of the Jungle Witch when his father grew too old to work the farm and had to 'buy our food, clothes and the rest of our needs in credits. But one day, when he failed to pay some of his debts, his creditor treated him very shamefully.'[30] The Witch offers the family the means to make money, but she also threatens them by drawing their attention to a row of images and telling them 'that every one of the images was a person but with her power she had changed him into the form of image for he had trespassed her jungle. She explained furthermore that we too could change into that of images if we disobeyed her' (24). The money economy has the power to transform people into 'images,' and so does the nightmarish 'jungle' of Tutuola's imagination.

As Francis Nyamnjoh has pointed out, the 'jungle,' 'bush,' or 'forest' in which the chief, Simbi, the Drinkard, and Tutuola's other protagonists find themselves is always teeming with hybrid prostheses. Almost every character the heroes encounter is significantly disabled due to the absence of one or more body part. This forces them to rely on metaphysical agency:

... agency is never absolute but domesticated. Domesticated agency is quite evident in Tutuola's writings. Individuals are characterised by ontological incompleteness (e.g., almost everyone is bodily inadequate in some way). Therefore, their agency is mediated by the relationships and artefacts (jujus, charms, spells, etc.) they are able to harness so as to achieve efficacy and potency.[31]

Tutuola has no difficulty 'domesticating' or incorporating the relatively novel power of money into a traditional world-view. He finds the concepts and causality of traditional magic appropriate as a means of interpreting the impalpable, implacable forces of global finance. The sudden, incongruous commodification of some properly spiritual or psychological quality is another recurrent *motif*. For example, the Drinkard must purge certain elements of his *psyche* before entering a 'white tree,' and he uses commodification as the means to do so:

> Now by that time and before we entered inside the white tree, we had 'sold our death' to somebody at the door for the sum of £70: 18: 6d and 'lent our fear' to somebody at the door as well on interest of £3: 10: Od per month, so we did not care about death and we did not fear again. (27)

The creation of symbolic exchange-value through commodification is a transaction instantly recognizable to participants in the system of magical power, ritual and salesmanship that the Drinkard calls 'juju.'[32] As a self-described 'juju man,' the Drinkard finds it easy to flourish by using money and, in a series of sub-plots and stories within the story, he cleverly exploits the intersection of money and magic to his advantage. Like Bunyan's Mr. Badman or Defoe's Moll Flanders, he constantly shifts his identity, adapting himself to the demands of an economy in which he must sell his labor-power. He magically commodifies himself by taking the form of a canoe, engaging in precise calculations that translate his practical actions into financial terms:

> ... the juju changed me to a big canoe. Then my wife went inside the canoe with the paddle and paddling it, she used the canoe as "ferry" to carry passengers across the river, the fare for adults was 3d (three pence) and half fare for children. In the evening time, then I changed to a man as before and when we checked the money that my wife had collected for that day, it was £7: 5:3d. After that we went back to the town, we bought all our needs. (39)

In Tortuola's work, then, magic is modern. The supernatural is a condition into which the world has recently and unfortunately fallen. The introduction of rule by symbolic value is conceived as entrance into an 'endless forest' populated by magical creatures and driven by an abstract, invisible causality. The Drinkard is frequently enslaved, and his labor exploited, by unnatural and even imaginary powers, and his senses are constantly deceived by artificial 'images.' Having purchased entrance to the 'white tree,' he finds himself in a realm of symbols, both financial and visual. Tutuola captures the impact of such ubiquitous imagery on subjective self-perception, as the narrator himself becomes an image:

> The hall was decorated with about one million pounds (£) and there were many images and our own too were in the centre of the hall. But our own images that we saw there resembled us too much and were also white colour, but we were very surprised to meet our images there, perhaps somebody who was focusing us as a photographer at the first time before the hands drew us inside the white tree had made them, we could not say. (41)

The Palm-Wine Drinkard describes the dissolution of an idyllic, prelapsarian existence as a consequence of a crisis in labor. The tapster's labor is invisible to the Drinkard until his sudden death, after which the necessities of life can be acquired only through mastery of a complicated system of images and symbols. This system is simultaneously magical and financial–in fact, the difference between magic and finance evaporates in the light of their common properties as performative representation. Tutuola presents a world without stable essences, ruled by powerful images, in which appearance and reality are indistinguishable. Towards the novel's end, the Drinkard turns his wife into a wooden doll, in an attempt to save her from being devoured by a 'hungry-creature.' But the demon is not fooled:

> ... he looked at it for more than ten minutes and asked me again was this not my wife? I replied that it was not my wife etc. but it only resembled her, then he gave it to me back and I was going as usual, but he was still following me and crying "hungry" as well. When he had travelled with me again to about two miles, he asked for it for the third time and I gave it to him, but as he held it he looked at it more than an hour and said that this was my wife and he swallowed it unexpectedly. As he swallowed the

wooden-doll, it meant he swallowed my wife, gun, cutlass, egg and load and nothing remained with me again, except my juju. (287)

The hungry-creature's ravenous belief in the reality of the image thus proves self-fulfilling. Swallowing the woman's image has the same effect as swallowing the woman herself. This is the basic principle of sympathetic magic: reality disappears into representation, and representation is the realm of 'juju.'

9.3   SLAVE WARS: TUTUOLA'S *MY LIFE IN THE BUSH OF GHOSTS*

Tutuola deploys fantasy to explore the symbolic mechanisms of financial value. The absence of an African realist tradition facilitates this method, allowing him easily to personify phenomena that the Western mind understands as exclusively economic. He gives the sparsest possible form to the humanoid entities that populate his stories, and many characters are little more than financial phenomena draped in threadbare subjectivity, or subject-positions carved out of economic concepts. Thus in *The Palm-Wine Drinkard* the alienation of future labor-power in the form of a loan is embodied in a figure called 'the Invisible Pawn':

> He said that he wanted to borrow some amount and he would be working for me in return as a "pawn" or as permanent hired labourer. But when he said this, I asked how much did he want to borrow? He said that he wanted to borrow two thousand cowries (COWRIES), which was equivalent to six-pence (6d) in British money. Then I asked from my wife whether I should lend him the amount, but my wife said that the man would be a— "WONDERFUL HARD WORKER, BUT HE WOULD BE A WONDERFUL ROBBER IN FUTURE." (265)

The Pawn lives 'inside a bush which nobody could trace'—the domain of symbols that also figures as the 'endless forest,' and which forms the context of Tutuola's subsequent novel, *My Life in the Bush of Ghosts* (1954). This book is set during:

> … the slave wars which were very common in every town and village and particularly in famous markets and on main roads of big towns at any time in the day or night. These slave-wars were causing dead luck to both old and young of those days, because if one is captured, he or she would be

sold into slavery for foreigners who would carry him or her to unknown destinations to be killed for the buyer's god or to be working for him. (17–18)

No critic to my knowledge had noticed the narrator's remark that he spent precisely twenty-four years in the 'bush.' That is the same amount of time purchased by Dr. Faustus from Mephistopheles in Christopher Marlowe's play and the subsequent Faust tradition. Life in the 'bush of ghosts' is thus equated with Faust's years spent wallowing in sensual pleasure, illusory money, and magical spectacle. Like the Drinkard's Odyssey through the 'endless forest' the narrator's entrance into the 'bush of ghosts' is presented as a fall from grace. He is accidentally separated from his brother during a war, presumably a 'slave war,' and plunges into the 'bush of ghosts.' Like the Drinkard, he enters a hallucinatory cycle of captivity and exploitation that ineluctably evokes the monstrous nature of the historical slave trade. As Thomas Jay Lynn observes, '[t]he story raises the question of whether the practice of slavery is fully human. In certain respects the author presents slavery as an antihuman aberration....'[33] The book's final sentence—'This is what hatred did'—emphasizes that the entire sequence of surreal events that befall the narrator is perverse, unnatural, and was originally set in motion by warfare.

From the beginning, the narrator understands the semiotic character of his new environment. Tutuola establishes a pattern of adapting Biblical tropes to his own ends: 'I entered into the bush under this fruit tree. This fruit tree was a "SIGN" for me and it was on that day I called it — THE "FUTURE SIGN".'[34] This sign announces the bush as the realm of symbols. By placing the bush under the sign of the fruit tree, however, Tutuola also invokes Scriptural imagery. The narrator associates his entrance into the realm of the symbolic with banishment from Eden. He also associates the bush with the future, and with repudiation of the past. The 'slave wars' have violently separated him from his family, and from a past life that he recalls with nostalgia throughout his nightmarish journey. The first hallucinatory environment he enters is a house inhabited by three spirits: a 'golden-ghost,' a 'silverish-ghost' and a 'copperish-ghost.' These spirits evoke the coined forms of financial value, and each of them shines its light on the human protagonist in an attempt to enslave him. The 'three old ghosts' fight over him until he is captured by a tribe

of different, 'smelling-ghosts.' Just as the Drinkard magically commodified himself as a canoe, the smelling-ghosts 'see' the narrator as various
beasts of burden, and their perception becomes real:

> ... when the rest of the smelling-ghosts noticed that I was useful for such
> purpose then the whole of them were hiring me from my boss to carry
> loads to long distances and returning again in the evening with heavier
> loads. But as I could not satisfy all of them at a time so they shared me,
> half of them would use me from morning till night, then the rest would
> use me from the night till morning. (40)

Before long, neighboring ghost-towns also announce their desire 'to
see me as a horse.' The narrator's status as a commodity is a matter
of perception, and it can be altered like magic. His Protean status is
mirrored by the environment, which is constantly changing its shape and
attitude. This Bunyan esque landscape contains several allegorical representations of economic phenomena. The characters enter a 'valley' that is
simultaneously a zero-sum vision of the market-place:

> Not knowing that the meaning of the name of this valley which is — "Lost
> or Gain Valley" means as we put all our clothes down at this first edge
> before crossing it, it is so for those who are travelling towards us from the
> opposite direction who should put down all the clothes off their bodies at
> the second edge as well before they could climb it and after climbing it
> then they will take any clothes that they meet there and wear them instead
> of their own which they leave before climbed it. Perhaps the clothes that
> they might meet there might cost more than their own, so it is their gain
> and if the one that they meet there are not worth their own it is also their
> loss.... (131)

Tutuola presents twentieth-century technology as indistinguishable from
magic, and the narrator easily integrates technological images into the
supernatural landscape. He broadcasts his lament to 'over a million
"homeless-ghosts"... who were listening to my cry as a radio,' and the
plot's climactic encounter features a 'television-handed ghostess' who
demands that the narrator lick the filthy sores from the palm of her hand:

> But when she told me to look at her palm and opened it nearly to touch
> my face, it was exactly as a television, I saw my town, mother, brother
> and all my playmates.... But as I was hearing on this television when my

mother was discussing about me with one of her friends with a sorrowful
voice at that time that — "She was told by a fortune teller that I am still
alive in a bush." (165)

Here the narrator is confronted by an imperative to render an image efficacious. The magical television shows an image of his mother using magic
to discover that he is alive, and he determines to make the image real.
Giving thanks to *logos* ('God is good'), he discovers a medicinal plant
whose leaves can heal the ghostess without his having to lick her sores.
He is thus able to return from the realm of images to reality: 'she opened
her palm as usual, she told me to look at it, but to my surprise, I simply
found myself under the fruit tree which is near my home town (the
Future-Sign)' (166). Any expectation of a happy ending is immediately
forestalled, however, when the narrator is seized by slave-traders, and the
cycle begins once again. Although he suffers through numerous enslave-
ments by fantasic creatures while in the bush, the narrator emphasizes that
it was real, historical human beings who captured him after his emergence:
'[t]hey were slave-traders because the slave trade was then still existing'
(167). The story now enters a newly realistic phase, and the narrator is
bought and sold by people, as opposed to monsters from the bush. His
captor explains that his only value is as a commodity:

> When he was taking me to this market for several market days without
> seeing anybody to buy me, then he said — "If I take you to the market
> once more and if nobody buys you on that market day as well so if I am
> returning from the market to the town I will kill you on the way and
> throw away your body into the bush, because you are entirely useless for
> any purpose...." (171)

Eventually, he is purchased by a rich man who intends to sacrifice him
to his gods. In the meantime, his new master treats him with special
cruelty because he cannot work and, as the narrator reminds us, 'every
slave buyer recognised slaves as non-living creatures' (173). The cycle of
illusion and mistaken identity finally ends when, in an echo of the Biblical
story of Joseph, the narrator recognizes that his cruel master is actually
his long-lost brother. Finally free from the bush, he is re-united with his
kin. Throughout the narrator has appealed to the monotheistic God at
moments of crisis, and by framing the narrative within a Biblical story he

suggests that *logos* offers the antidote to the bush's world of oppression and unreason. It is a conclusion common to many Yoruba novelists.

The link between financial and supernatural forms of oppression remains prominent in Tutuola's later work, especially *Ajaiyi and His Inherited Poverty* (1967) and its various sequels. The fact that Tutuola returns to this tale more than once indicates its central significance in his imagination. The story tells of 'the hunchback family,' whose affliction appears to symbolize their poverty, just as the burden carried by Bunyan's 'man in rags' represents his sin. Their background is described in a subsequently published short story entitled 'The Village Witch Doctor,' where we learn that their ancestor had buried his inherited wealth in 'a faraway bush,' from which his best friend, a 'witch doctor,' had stolen it, plunging the family into inescapable poverty. The witch doctor also destroyed his friend's sense of kinship affinity by blaming the crime on his dead father. The young Ajaiyi is assured by the same witch doctor that he will become a 'Money man' if he performs certain expensive sacrifices to his father, for which he needs money, which in turn forces him to 'pawn' his labor out to three separate usurers. Tutuola thus presents witchcraft as deeply entwined with economic exploitation, and the connection is emphasized further in the story's longer, novel version.

In the full-length tale of *Ajaiyi and His Inherited Poverty*, the children of the family notice that the harder their parents work the greater their poverty becomes. The father's culpably naïve response shows that he does not identify the problem as the man-made burden of usury. Instead he conceives of his debt as a natural creature: 'Well, maybe as we are working very hard in the farm it is so our poverty is growing up like a tree.'[35] When his father dies, the funeral expenses drive the narrator himself into debt, and he is eventually forced to pawn himself to 'a wealthy slave-buyer who was also a very strong idol worshipper' (12). As in *Simbi*, idolatry and usury are inseparable, indeed identical. Ajaiyi's monstrous persecutors merge easily into economic oppressors: as he puts it, 'we become the recluses of our creditors' (88). The plot involves a vehement rejection of magic as fraudulent, albeit dangerously powerful. At first Ajaiyi is convinced that his poverty can be explained, and also cured, by magic. After consulting various hostile and dangerous supernatural authorities, he learns that earthly wealth must be sought from the Devil himself. However he wisely refuses any Faustian bargain, and his adventures culminate when he unmasks the evil witch doctor, confiscates his ill-gotten gains and—concluding that 'money is the father of all evils and the creator of all insincerities of the world' (102)—donates his riches to found a series of Christian churches. Once again, *logos* is the antidote to magic.

9.4   Reading in the Work of Ben Okri

Tutuola's fiction is pervaded by the sense that human beings are hapless, passive playthings of evil, super-human powers. Many non-Yoruba African writers convey the same message, and the monsters their heroes must battle are no less arbitrary or formidable when they take a realistic form. In Fatou Diome's *The Belly of the Atlantic* (2006) the young Senegalese football prospect Moussa finds himself abandoned on the streets of Paris, forced to work to pay off his debt to the recruiter who paid for his passage. His personal debt becomes a microcosm of Senegal's national debt, and an 'indebted subjectivity' is imposed on nation and individual alike, as both are persuaded that ethical culpability lies with the debtor rather than the lender.[36] Other African novelists respond to financial neo-liberalism by assimilating magical causality, tropes, and *motifs* into modernity. A character in Achebe's *Anthills of the Savannah* (1987) jokes about his proximity to the dictator: 'How many times now have I managed to read the Big Shot's mind better than all the courtiers? Who knows, I may soon be suspected of witchcraft....'[37] The informed reader will be aware that this is no joke, and that witchcraft accusations are commonplace in postmodern African politics. They are certainly no more outlandish than the economic theories with which Achebe's American journalist bombards the President:

> ... she began reading His Excellency and his subjects a lecture on the need for the country to maintain its present (quite unpopular, needless to say) levels of foreign debt servicing currently running at slightly more than fifty-one percent of total national export earnings. Why? As a *quid pro quo* for increased American aid in surplus grains for our drought provinces! (78)

The book's main characters are a group of disillusioned intellectuals who are disgusted by the hold such magical thinking has attained over their head of state. The dictator is revealed as a puppet of neo-imperialism by his obsequious enthusiasm for usury. After pouring scorn on Fidel

Castro's advice that postcolonial nations should repudiate their debts, the American continues:

> What we must remember is that banks are not houses of charity. They're there to lend money at a fair and reasonable profit. If you deny them their margin of profit by borrowing and not paying back they will soon have to shut down their operations and we shall all go back to saving our money in grandmother's piggy-banks.' 'Or inside old mattresses,' added His Excellency whose deferential attitude to this piece of impertinence had given me a greater shock than anything I could think of in recent times. Deference and a countenance of martyred justification. He seemed to be saying to the girl, 'Go on; tell them. I have gone hoarse shouting the very same message to no avail.' (79)

The fearsome dictator's docility to voodoo economics indicates that the deterioration of the state into tyranny has been achieved by the black magic of financial capitalism. This connection is made explicit in Dambudzo Marechera's *Black Sunlight* (1980): 'Was there a difference between the chief on his skull-carpentered throne and the general who even now had grappled all power to himself in our new and twentieth-century image?'[38] Contemporary African novelists remain concerned with the ethical status of hyper-real finance, and Sarah Lincoln has recently shown how Ben Okri's deployment of magical realist techniques reflects 'the typically modern process by which financial value comes detached from its material base and becomes dependent instead on public opinion, sentiment and superficial perception.'[39] Lincoln persuasively suggests:

> … that we read Okri's magical realist vision as an attempt to bear witness to the oil economy's radical disruption of the bond holding signifier to signified, representation to reality, and the signs of value to its substance…. (250)

Okri's short story 'The Stars of the New Curfew' (1989) gives an instructive account of the intersection between magic and commerce in postcolonial Nigeria.[40] The protagonist Arthur is unable to find work fit 'for one of my qualification' and is forced to take a job as a salesman of patent medicine.[41] The word 'medicine' has extensive connotations in Nigeria, and it is often used to refer to magic. Arthur is effectively peddling magic and, in his guilt, he begins to suffer nightmares. He eventually becomes a 'salesman of nightmares,' hawking an intoxicant branded 'POWER DRUG' (98). A bus driver purchases his product and promptly crashes his vehicle, killing seven, and the narrator flees to his home town, which lives under the tyranny of two 'disgustingly rich' families. These rivals for power hold a competition to literally bury the town in money. Okri's description of the scene makes it clear that the magical self-reproduction of money has displaced other forms of spirituality as the object of popular idolatry:

> … I passed a group of fishermen who had come to the event with nets. They had come to catch money. In a moment of hallucinated illumination it struck me that all those present—the market-women from the creeks of dark rivers, the clerks from remote bureaucracies deep in the delta villages—had one thing in common. We needed modern miracles. We were, all of us, hungry. We had all abandoned our private lives, our business lives, our leisure, our pain, because we wanted to witness miracles. And the miracle we had come to witness, which seemed to comprise the other side ritual drums and dread, was that of the multiplying currency. We had come to be fed by the great magicians of money, masters of our age. (104)

The people humiliate themselves by fighting for the bills, and for coins dropped from a helicopter. Chaos ensues when rain falls, washing away the false inscriptions on the bills and revealing them as counterfeit. Resigned to the fact that the 'big men' use money to 'create our reality,' Arthur returns to his former job and, in a nod to Tutuola, becomes a palm-wine drinker, in an effort to erase what he now sees as the living nightmare of an existence in which what counts as 'reality' is 'manufactured' by financial power.

Okri's later work, *The Freedom Artist* (2019) describes a conflict between two models of representation. The book's heroic characters are distinguished from the rest by their incessant *reading* of their environment. They insist that everything has significance, being 'obsessed with signs and words.'[42] When Karnak passes a bookshop '[h]e took this for a sign, and went in' (96). Asked who the people walking alongside her are, Ruslana replies 'I don't know, but they're a sign.' These people's literacy isolates them, however, for the story takes place in a post-truth dystopia where words have been replaced by depthless images. Ruslana's wise father explains the situation:

> The world is full of signs.... Some of the signs are sent to help you find
> your way. Most people pay no attention to the signs because they have
> not been taught to see them. They are taught that there is nothing to see.
> They are kept blind. But pay attention. (228)

The society Okri depicts is divided between a small minority who can
read the signs, and an oblivious herd which does not understand referentiality, and therefore believes that the signs are real. This ignorant majority
eagerly devours stories about fake celebrities served up for their entertainment by a nebulous but tyrannical authority known as 'the Hierarchy.'
Books have disappeared, and bookshops contain only holograms, '[t]he
economy was managed by a handful of superbankers' (21) and reality
itself is constructed by the Hierarchy. The distinction between economics
and aesthetics has evaporated: as one 'gray-haired gentleman' remarks,
'the artist is the new banker' (79). This gentleman converses with a man
he considers the greatest artist of the age, who declares that the 'really
great artist creates a new value' as opposed to a 'work.' In fact works
of art 'are merely justifications, objective correlatives, coins to make an
idea concrete' (90). His exposition of this 'new value' is worth quoting
at length:

> The question is this: what is the most important value of our times? What is
> the most important symbol? I'll tell you. It's simple. It's all around. Cities
> are made of it, civilizations are sustained by it, religions need it, pyramids
> are erected with it. Long have we looked right through it while it shapes
> our lives. Artists have created all manner of things, but never has an artist
> created this value, with this symbol. For the first time in human history, an
> artist has sculpted at last with this magic value, painted with it, drawn with
> it, and used it as the primal force in his art, the chief idiom of his work.
> Great bankers have created vast edifices of power with it. Merchants have
> funded whole eras of art with its power. Kings and popes have used it. But
> I am the first and the only one so far to have created this value entirely in
> itself. I am the first artist of money.... (91)

As we saw in Chapter 8, after the deregulation of the 1990s, and
especially after the repeal in 1999 of the Glass-Steagall Act separating
investment from retail banking, the symbolic forms taken by financial
value have grown increasingly complicated and inventive. Economists
have long spoken of 'financial engineering,' but the arcane symbolism
of swaps, futures, and default options through which the economy

now conducts its business is closer to aesthetics than to engineering. The difference between economics and aesthetics disappears when the economy is symbolic. Okri is not the first novelist to have remarked on this process: Will Self's *My Idea of Fun* (1993) features a 'money critic' who evaluates the artistic merits of various financial instruments. Okri departs from his predecessors, however, in the strongly ethical approach he takes to the issue of financial representation. The artist who advocates the aesthetics of money is given plenty of rope to hang himself in his lengthy speech. He shifts his emphasis from the aesthetic appeal of financial signs to their performative power:

> Money is the most important force of our times. The person who masters money masters society. The artist who masters money masters the future. No longer is there religion. There is only the art of money, its temples, its altars, its apotheoses, its mountain peaks, its dreams.... Money is the new imagination. The genie of our age, from the magic lamp of our times, is money. It is the only reliable open sesame. To mint money is primitive; to incarnate money is genius. Why has no-one thought of it before? Money sends our thoughts around the world. Money is the new *Mona Lisa*, its smile more mysterious and seductive. People are interested in my works not because they see art, but because they see money. I have compelled money and art to get into bed with each other. It is the new alchemy. Turning lead into gold—that is too laborious and quant. But turning anything I look at into money, now that is the new alchemy. Midas had to touch things to turn them into gold. I merely have to think of them and they are changed.... (91–92)

The artist understands that the purely symbolic nature of today's money gives it magical power. Today's financiers have achieved what the alchemists of the past could not: they have created value out of nothing. As Achebe informed the World Bank, such value is essentially fictional. It exists only in what Okri's artist calls the 'new imagination.' Nor is there any reason why this magical power should limit itself to the 'economic' sphere. On the contrary, the symbolic nature of money reveals its kinship with other systems of representation. The mutations of representation's financial form are paralleled by developments in aesthetics. The rise of the performative sign within the 'economy' is inseparable from the burgeoning of performativity throughout the totality of experience. As Okri's artist concludes:

I am yet to discover what the limits of money are. I see none. With money
I have compelled destiny, altered fate, and coerced providence. With money
I have erected a value more lasting than bronze and my immortality is more
certain than the mountains. Beyond money where can you go? There is
nothing beyond. Money is the last frontier of the imagination. It is the
last object in art. Artists of the future have nowhere to go. There will be
no new beginnings. I am the end of art. (92)

The final sentence establishes the artist's ethical bankruptcy. Art merges
into money, along with everything else. Okri is a master of allusion, and
the echoes of Shelley's 'Ozymandias' in the artist's megalomaniacal rant
suggest that, at least in the long term, his ambitions are doomed. The
novel ends with a heroic revolution led by the forces of literacy against
the tyranny of the performative sign. Like Achebe, Okri's main ethical
objection to the nonreferential status of representation is that it destroys
the autonomous human subject. The performative sign is antithetical to
the soul. Ruslana's father repeatedly asks her 'Are you only your body?'
(226) and she admits that, in spite of the social pressure to deny it, she
cannot help acknowledging that she feels: 'Something in me that is aware,
that watches, that listens' (227). Meanwhile, an underground political
opposition evokes the ancient idea that the soul is imprisoned in the body
by launching a graffiti campaign asking 'WHO IS THE PRISONER?'
(19).

As the novel progresses, *The Freedom Artist*'s characters are gradually
gripped by an uneasy sense that appearance is not, after all, co-terminus
with reality. They reach this conclusion via the recognition of the soul.
Gazing into a mirror, Amalantis suddenly becomes aware that she is not
identical with her body: '*Who is behind the mask that everyone thinks is
me?* she wondered. This question was the beginning of her troubles' (28).
The acknowledgment of the soul brings 'troubles' because it does not fit
into existing social arrangements. Okri describes a disjunction between
the soul and society, suggesting that the postmodern condition is simply
incompatible with autonomous subjectivity. As Tutuola also suggested
in his allusion to the famous twenty-four years, Okri's work indicates
that the legend of Dr. Faustus is the definitive myth of modernity.[43] He
departs from the pessimism of the Faust myth, however, in *The Freedom
Artist*, where the soul is liberated by the letter, and reading proves literally redemptive. When the story begins, people have ceased to read. Books
have disappeared, and the act of interpretation is officially discouraged:

Every word became only what the word meant. A tree was a tree, nothing more. Poetry died. People couldn't think symbolically. They turned against myth. Realism became the only truth. The written word became poorer than conversation. (106)

In Okri's dystopia, there is no meaning beneath the surface, no essence underlying appearance. When this logic is applied to human beings, this means that there is no soul–no 'prisoner' within the body, as Okri puts it—and it is this prospect that eventually drives the novel's heroes to revolt. They raise their rebellion under the standard of *logos*, and they triumph by deploying the power of logocentric, referential representation against the idolatry of the performative sign. The book's last few chapters depict a war between these two systems of significance. The uprising begins after the Savior-figure Mirababa worships at the tomb of 'the great father-bard' who lies dead with a book in one hand and a sword in the other. Mirababa thus discovers 'the conjuring power of the word' (185), with which he does battle against the empty signs of the Hierarchy. He deploys logocentric language as a weapon against performativity. Victory is certain once he discovers that logocentric language can also be efficacious, because it works on the soul. Okri's description of language's power emphasizes its interiority. The magic of language works in the 'mind,' the 'inner places,' the 'heart':

Phrases became icons in his mind. The words disappeared and became magic wands and changed the inner places in him.... From the magic alphabets of which all things were made, great wisdom leaped out of the book and clung to his heart. He learned of syllables that could alter reality. He learned of incantations that could render things invisible. (188–189)

The equally heroic Ruslana experiences similar symptoms, and Okri describes them using the familiar tropes of logocentric theology. She has a vision of 'a face that turned into a single word which she did not understand' (220). But her father promises that 'it will reveal things to you,' and she finds it true. Okri's language approaches an explicitly Christian terminology as Ruslana learns to refer the phenomena of experience to the 'word,' and thus to read their meanings:

The word grew in her till she found herself understanding things she had not learned.... She understood that the world was not what it seemed....

> She found that she could look at symbols and they would speak to her. They would teach her things. (224)

Okri hints at the redemptive power of *logos* when Ruslana dreams of a 'magician' who demands she give him her word: 'Because I have everything I need to attain immortal life except that word' (229). But redemption eventually takes a more earthly, political form as Ruslana and Karnak lead the people in the destruction of 'the dark tower,' ultimately followed by 'the prison.' These images are simultaneously a realistic reference to mass incarceration, a figure for the forces of metaphysical evil, and a literary allusion to Robert Browning's poem 'Childe Rolande to the Dark Tower Came.' Okri crowds his text with such allusions to the literary canon, thus replicating in his audience the novel's division into those who can read and those who are blind. These allusions grow more numerous as the novel approaches its climax. The heroes first destroy the 'dark tower,' which alludes to Browning. Yet Browning's title is itself a literary allusion, to the words of a song in Shakespeare's *King Lear*. One allusion leads on to another, and Okri repeats the technique as he describes the liberation of the prisoners: 'They came out of the prison like ghosts. There were so many. No one knew that so many had been lost in the dark' (328). Literate readers will catch the reference to T. S. Eliot's 'The Waste Land': 'I had not thought death had undone so many.'[44] Eliot is, of course, alluding in turn to Dante's *Inferno*, so Okri once again sets in motion a train of reference to the literary canon that divides his readership into the initiated and the ignorant.

It may seem ironic, even contradictory, that a postcolonial writer should communicate his ethics, as well as his aesthetics, by pointed allusion to the canonical works of Western literature. But Okri alludes just as heavily to African tradition, which he finds readily adaptable to postmodern circumstances. What he really values, as *The Freedom Artist* makes clear, is not any particular canon, but rather the general ability to *interpret*, to 'read' in the widest sense. The idolatrous nightmare-world he evokes in the novel is impervious to interpretation. The 'Hierarchy' has made the act of reading socially unacceptable and effectively impossible. Like all of the novelists discussed in this chapter, Okri finds this ethically unacceptable because the end of referential reading means the death of the human soul. The soul is a referent, not a sign. If signs have no referents, the question Ruslana is asked by her father must be answered in the affirmative: we are indeed only our bodies. Okri suggests that this answer is currently being foisted on humanity by the same power that seeks to render all signs performative. The power that denies significance to signs also denies the existence of the soul. The oldest and best name for that power is *anti-logos*.

NOTES

1. Chinua Achebe, 'Africa Is People,' in *The Education of a British-protected Child* (New York: Alfred Knopf, 2009), 155–164, 157.
2. Georg Lukács, *The Theory of the Novel: A Historico-Philosophical Essay on the Forms of Great Epic Literature*, trans. Anna Bostock (The MIT Press), 1971, 88.
3. Wole Ogundele, 'Devices of Evasion: The Mythic Versus the Historical Imagination in the Postcolonial African Novel,' *Research in African Literatures* 33:3 (Autumn 2002), 125–139.
4. Anthony Kwame Appiah, 'Spiritual Realism,' *The Nation* (August 1992), 146–148, 147.
5. Sarah Fulford, 'Ben Okri, the Aesthetic and the Problem with Theory,' *Comparative Literature Studies* 46:2 (2009), 233–260, 239.
6. Ato Quayson, *Strategic Transformations in Nigerian Writing* (Indiana UP, 1997), 9.
7. Francis B. Nyamnjoh, 'Delusions of Development and the Enrichment of Witchcraft Discourse in Cameroon,' in , *Magical Interpretations, Material Realities: Modernity, Witchcraft and the Occult in Postcolonial Africa*, Henrietta L. Moore and Todd Sanders (Routledge, 2001), 42.
8. Cit. Kevin Shillington, *A History of Africa* (Macmillan, 2019), 485.
9. David Hawkes, *The Faust Myth: Religion and the Rise of Representation* (Palgrave Macmillan, 2007).
10. Jean and John Comaroff, 'Millenial Capitalism: First Thoughts on a Second Coming,' *Public Culture* 12:2 (April 2000).
11. Peter Geschiere, *Witchcraft, Intimacy and Trust: Africa in Comparison* (U of Chicago P, 2013) xii.
12. Margaret Drewal, 'Ritual Performance in African Today,' *TDR* 32.2 (Summer 1988), 25–30, 25.
13. 'Introduction' to Moore and Sanders (ed.) (2001, 15).
14. See M.J. Lamola, 'African Postmodernism: Its Moment, Nature and Content,' *International Journal of African Renaissance Studies* 12.2 (July 2017), 110–123.
15. Ato Quayson, 'Modernism and Postmodernism in African Literature,' in *The Cambridge History of African and Caribbean Literature*, ed. F. Abiola Irele and Simon Gikandi (2000).
16. Peter Kalliney, *Commonwealth of Letters: British Literary Culture and the Emergence of Postcolonial Aesthetics* (Oxford UP, 2013), 155.

17. See Francis Nyamnjoh, *Drinking from the Cosmic Gourd: How Amos Tutuola Can Change Our Minds* (Langaa: Bamenda, Cameroon, 2017), 11–12.

18. V.S. Naipul, review of Amos Tutuola's *The Brave African Huntress, The New Statesman* (1958), cited in Nyamnjoh (2017, 12).

19. Femi Osofisan, 'Warriors of a Failed Utopia?' *African Studies Bulletin* 61 (1996), 11–36.

20. D.O. Fugunwa, *Forest of a Thousand Daemons: A Hunter's Saga*, trans. Wole Soyinka (City Lights Books, 1982), 12.

21. Chris Abani, *Graceland* (Picador, 2004), 9.

22. Ben Okri, *The Famished Road* (Vintage, 2003), 19.

23. Amos Tutuola, *The Palm-Wine Drinkard and My Life in the Bush of Ghosts* (New York: Grove Press, 1984), 180.

24. See Laura Murphy, 'Into the Bush of Ghosts: Specters of the Slave Trade in West African Fiction,' *Research in African Literatures* 38:4 (Winter 2007), 141–152.

25. Bernth Lindfors, 'Amos Tutuola: Debts and Assets,' *Cahiers d'Études Africaines* 10.38 (1970), 306–334, 317.

26. S.M. Tobias, 'Amos Tutuola and the Colonial Carnival,' *Research in African Literatures* 30.2 (1999), 66–74, 72.

27. Amos Tutuola, *Feather Woman of the Jungle* (City Lights, 1988), 2.

28. Amos Tutuola, *Simbi and the Satyr of the Dark Jungle* (City Lights, 1988), 11.

29. Adeleke Adeeko, *Arts of Being Yoruba: Divination, Allegory, Tragedy, Proverb, Panegyric* (Indiana UP, 2017).

30. Amos Tutuola, *Feather Woman of the Jungle* (Faber and Faber, 2015), 5.

31. Francis Nyamnjoh, *Drinking from the Cosmic Gourd: How Amos Tutuola Can Change Our Minds* (Cameroon: Langaa RPCIG, 2017), 159–160.

32. Tutuola's personal attitude to money may also have contained elements of superstition. Before any of his books were published, the unknown Tutuola sent to a London publisher a manuscript entitled *The Wild Hunter in the Bush of Ghosts*. It was not published until 1982 but, as the title suggests, it contains numerous pre-figurations of his later work. Its pre-occupation with the aesthetic effects of commodification is even more pronounced, however. In what appears to be an early Nigerian phishing scheme, the eponymous narrator offers to pass on messages to any dead person the reader may wish to contact on receipt of five shillings. The money is to be sent to: 'The "Wild Hunter" c/o Amos Tutuola, 35 Vaughan Street, Ebutie-Metta (Lagos), Nigeria.'

33. Thomas Jay Lynn, '"Redemption Song": Slavery's Disruption in Amos Tutuola's *My Life in the Bush of Ghosts*,' *English Studies in Africa* 59.2 (2016), 54–63.

34. Amos Tutuola, *The Palm-Wine Drinkard and My Life in the Bush of Ghosts* (Grove Press: New York, 1984), 21.
35. Amos Tutuola, *Ajaiyi and His Inherited Poverty* (Faber and Faber, 2015), 3.
36. See Aleksandra Perisic, 'Toward the Promised Land: Immigration and Debt in Fatou Diome's *The Belly of the Atlantic*,' *Research in African Literatures* 50.1 (Spring 2019), 80–94.
37. Chinua Achebe, *Anthills of the Savannah* (William Heinemann Limited, 1987), 46.
38. Dambudzo Marechera, *Black Sunlight* (William Heinemann Limited, 1980), 13.
39. Sarah Lincoln, '"Petro-Magic Realism": Ben Okri's Inflationary Modernism' in *The Oxford Handbook of Global Modernisms*, Mark Wollaeger and Matt Eatough (Oxford UP, 2012) 249–266, 249.
40. As Sarah Lincoln explains, Okri's *Stars of the New Curfew* shows how, following the collapse of world oil prices in the early 1980s, 'the resulting psychic and material conditions manifested as a crisis of representation' (250).
41. Ben Okri, *Stars of the New Curfew* (London: Penguin Books, 1990), 83.
42. Ben Okri, *The Freedom Artist* (New York: Akashic Books, 2019), 209.
43. See David Hawkes, *The Faust Myth* (Palgrave Macmillan, 2007).
44. T.S. Eliot, 'The Waste Land' (63), in *The Waste Land and Other Poems* (Broadview Press, 2011).

INDEX